Sandy, !
for the music!

[handwritten signature]
Sept 21 1990

Fire in the RAIN...
Singer in the STORM

FIRE
IN THE RAIN...
SINGER
IN THE STORM

An Autobiography
Holly Near
with Derk Richardson

WILLIAM MORROW AND COMPANY, INC. NEW YORK

Grateful acknowledgment is made for permission to quote lyrics from:

"All of Me"
Seymour Simons and Gerald Marks
Copyright © 1959 (revised) by Marlong Music Corp.
All rights reserved. Used by permission.

"Waterfall"
Words and music by Cris Williamson
Copyright © 1975 by Bird Ankles Music
All rights reserved. Used by permission.

"Twelve Gates to the City"
New words by Lee Hays, Fred Hellerman, Erik Darling, and Ronnie Gilbert
Copyright © 1959 (renewed) by Sanga Music Inc.
All rights reserved. Used by permission.

Recognizing the importance of preserving what has been written, it is the policy of William Morrow and Company, Inc., and its imprints and affiliates to have the books it publishes printed on acid-free paper, and we exert our best efforts to that end.

Library of Congress Cataloging-in-Publication Data

Near, Holly,
    Fire in the rain . . . singer in the storm : an autobiography / Holly Near, with Derk Richardson.
        p.   cm.
    ISBN 0-688-08733-7
    1. Near, Holly.   2. Singers—United States—Biography.
I. Richardson, Derk.   II. Title.
ML420.N375A3   1990
782.42164'092—dc20
    [B]   90-5784
                                                                         CIP

Printed in the United States of America

First Edition

1   2   3   4   5   6   7   8   9   10

BOOK DESIGN BY LISA STOKES

This, my first book, is dedicated

To my family, to my partners,
and
To all who sing in the storm

Acknowledgments

MY SINCERE THANKS TO DERK RICHARDSON, MUSIC CRITIC AND PO-
litical thinker, for diving into this project with me and maintaining a
humble and flexible position throughout, offering essential and con-
sistent help to me as I wrote this book.

My lifelong appreciation to Anne Near for always being my first
editor and finest critic.

Love to my partners, Jo-Lynn Worley (who is also my manager)
and Joanie Shoemaker (who is also executive director of Redwood
Cultural Work). Their constant and ever-unfolding friendship is with
me always.

My deepest thanks to Jo-Lynne and Joanie, and to Mollie Katzen,
Carl Shames, Amy Horowitz, Torie Osborn, Melissa Howden, Susan
Freundlich, Marianne Schneller, Penny Rosenwasser, Jan Jue, and
Frank Stricker for reading all or parts of the book and offering their
valuable experience and opinions.

Thanks also to John Bucchino, pianist and constant companion on
the road, who literally watched me write this book on planes and in
backstage dressing rooms.

Thanks to Jerry Rubino, Irene Young, Owens Hill, Stephen Powers, Sheila Kuehl, and Cynthia Frenz for helping with the photographs;
to Judi Clark for saving me from computer nightmares; to Virginia Giordano, Adrienne Torf, and Ladyslipper for last-minute help; to the staff
at William Morrow; to Redwood Staff and friends; and to the people
who have worked with me and my music for so many years—the concert
promoters, the record distributors, the media, the community organizers, and the audience.

Thanks to Marion Rosenberg, my theatrical agent, who intro-

Acknowledgments

duced me to Joy Harris, who became my literary agent, who introduced me to Doug Stumpf, who invited me to William Morrow and
became my editor and who challenged me line for line, at the same
time consistently respecting the integrity of the content.

I want to thank all those who are mentioned in the book. It would
have been impossible to write this book without the inclusion of others.
Still, I am aware there are some who may have preferred their privacy.

I am also aware that we live in a world where our real lives are not
always acceptable. I have made my choices but I do not want to make
them for others. So, with complete understanding and without judgment, I have changed a few names to protect the threatened. However,
my most heartfelt thanks go to all of you who are ''out.'' Your courage
touches me so.

And finally I want to thank the reader, for with the exception of
myself, it is for you I wrote this book.

Contents

PROLOGUE: FIRE IN THE RAIN

I SIT HERE, IN A STATE OF WONDER THAT I DECIDED TO WRITE A BOOK. The stories are traveling from my brain to yours. What will happen to them in the space between us?

When I first considered doing a book, I was not thinking of myself as the writer. Rather, I would talk into a tape recorder and someone else would write it. But along the way it became clear that I would have to write . . . and write . . . and write. More important, I was going to have to come to terms with my life.

And as I approach the last pages, I find I don't know when a book should end. My studio apartment is full of roses, the wall covered with greeting cards, as I celebrate my fortieth year. I have never been this peaceful before. Writing the book helped me arrive at this state of contentment and, as Bernice Johnson Reagon writes in one of her lesser-known love songs, "I am well pleased."

All my life I have gone out on a limb, but I have turned the limb into a bridge, and there is cool, clear water flowing under. The world is a challenging lover, and I, helplessly in love. Time has passed through me and become a song. I have always counted on such a song to never let me be complacent with the truth. She grins at me and says, "What if this is also true?" and draws my attention to the mighty desert, which I had not even noticed for having focused on the sea. The new song has a note so low that I must be exceptionally relaxed to sing it, and a note so high that I must be in rare, passionate form to glide to it effortlessly. And as I walk onstage from the peaceful darkness of the wings, into the challenge of the light, I see the ghosts of the singers who have stood on this stage before me. I hear myself whisper to them, "Don't let the singer down!"

Prologue: Fire in the Rain

Long-ago years ago, I stood with my family on the front porch listening to Potter Valley's new fire engine cry through the rainy night, heading for the Mitchells' barn, which was all ablaze. I could see the flames miles away, wild and irreverent, and it made me wonder . . . if water puts out fire, why is there a fire in the rain?

1
HAPPY NEW YEAR

I PACED AROUND MY SMALL ROOM. THERE WASN'T MUCH ON TELEVI-sion. New Year's Eve is pretty much a bust unless you are foolish enough to get in your car and gamble with statistics. The room was cozy, every corner carefully layered with thirty-four years' worth of stuff.

I had full use of the house, even though I paid only $150 a month for my room. Tess was a good friend and landlord, as well as Redwood Records' accountant. She shared her wood stove and Rosebud the cat with me during the few days a month I returned from the road. In the early mornings we drank hot strong coffee, and talked about sex, South Africa, and the politics of baseball.

I let the stove's fire lick at one more piece of wood so the house would be warm for Tess when she got home, then went to bed even though it was only eleven-thirty. "Well, it's the New Year some-where," I said to myself. 1984. Goddamn George Orwell. What a setup. I would be thirty-five in 1984. This was the year I was supposed to die.

I had a vision years ago concerning my death. It hadn't scared me, it just was. Now I was tired. I was ready. I had done a lot in thirty-five years. Enough is enough.

I enjoyed the feel of the flannel sheets, a present from England. Then I fell into a deep, lonely sleep.

The next morning I rose early and watched the dawn of the first day. I meant to think forward, in the tradition of the New Year, but my mind kept flying back to the past, not in order, not like a résumé for a job application, but like a swirl—memories out of order.

I sat on my favorite rock and mimicked the Columbia Records

15

A&R man in the leather chair. "Well, you have a fine voice, little lady, but you're singing pretty grown-up songs for a ten-year-old. Do you know any children's songs, like 'Does the Spearmint Lose Its Flavor on the Bedpost Overnight?' or . . ."

I didn't think that was a good suggestion. I tried to think of a song he might like and sang "It's Only a Paper Moon."

Connie, my voice teacher, had set up the audition in Hollywood through her previous student, Johnny Mathis. She believed in my talent. I leaned on the rock the way Connie leaned on the piano, and tried to imitate her smooth nightclub voice. "You have great potential, Holly, to be anything you want to be—an actress, a singer, a dancer. I don't want to force you to do anything you don't want to do. I want to help you make your dreams come true. You can be a huge star. I can help you do that." Trying to imagine "stardom," I stood up on the rock and began to croon, "ALL OF ME, why not take all of me? can't you see, I'm no good without you. . . . "

My mother and father told me: "You don't have to do anything you don't want to do, pumpkin. We love you just the way you are, and if you just want to stay in Potter Valley and play on jungle gyms, and be in PTA talent shows, and play tetherball, that's fine with us. If you decide you want to go to Hollywood, well, we'll try to help you do that, too. We love you either way."

This was tough. I moved off the rock and started to wander down the hill to the dirt road that led back to the farmhouse, trying to imagine life without going to the trampoline center with Cindy and Scott Leask. I wondered if they had trampolines in Hollywood.

My body began to dance like a rag doll, loose and going off in every direction: I want to sing, I want to be a star, I want to be normal and go skating with Cindy. I want to be a stewardess. I want to be an ambassador.

Sure, I know "Does the Spearmint Lose Its Flavor?" I think it's a dumb song. What's wrong with the songs I sing?

I had sat, feeling tiny in the big office chair, thinking very hard, my feet barely touching the floor. I looked at the man in the leather chair and with my most sincere voice I said, "I'm not as young as you think."

Mom dropped me off in front of Connie's bright-red house, where she had her studio. Connie had been a well-known club singer and voice teacher around San Francisco during World War II. But when the man she loved took a job in Ukiah, she abandoned her career to be with him. She taught piano, accordion, organ, guitar, and voice. Johnny Mathis, who had studied with her in San Francisco, was famous now. She was looking for a new pride and joy.

Connie was a round, soft woman with tiny hands, very white skin, and bleached blond—or sometimes red—hair. For many hours a day, she sat in the window next to the grand piano, sometimes concentrating on her students' scales and practice tunes, sometimes gazing out at her tulip garden. Connie had a few favorite students who always made her turn from the tulips and focus intensely on the lesson at hand.

I was one of those. She had "discovered" me at a talent show put on by the Veterans of Foreign Wars. Timothy, my older sister, was going to do a dance to "Hernando's Hideaway." I wanted to dance too, although I didn't understand the concept of choreography yet. I thought I could just put on a record and dance and that would be okay. Mom enjoyed spontaneity in all of her children, but was afraid I would be offended if the adults laughed, so she suggested I sing a song instead. I was only seven at the time, but singing was already a way of life for me. I learned "Oh What a Beautiful Mornin' " from *Oklahoma!*, a cappella. Connie approached me and Mom and offered to accompany me on piano the night of the show. Mom turned to me. It was my decision. I thought this sounded like lots of fun.

Mom always let me decide. She never wanted to be a stage mother. When calls would come in from people in the community, asking me to sing at a tea or a convention, they would ask to speak to my mother, but when Mom got on the phone, she would say to them, "Well, you will have to ask Holly." Once I had made the decision to do the event, she and Dad would both be right there to help, but not until then.

I came in second place in the talent show, but my real prize was Connie. I had found a teacher. Now, two years later, I ran up the walkway and into the studio, knowing something was up. I had a direct line to my dad, who was on the board of directors of the county fair. The board had met with Connie last Wednesday night and approved her proposal for a three-day talent show, which she would produce at the Redwood Empire Fair. Johnny Mathis had agreed to be the official judge who would read the applause meter. My concern was that I had

17

nothing to sing. But before the hour was up, Connie and I had devised a plan. It wasn't an easy plan. It would require some help, some figuring out. It would require Anne and Russell.

"Dad, I want to fly."

"Don't we all, darlin'," he replied, without dismissing the dream. Russell never laughed at dreams. He just let them sit.

"No, I mean *really*, Dad. For Connie's talent show at the fair. See, we have this great idea. I'll be Peter Pan. And I'll fly onstage, back and forth a few times. Then I'll land, I'll sing 'I've Gotta Crow,' and fly off. It will be spectacular and I'm sure to win first prize."

"How do you plan to do that, pumpkin?" he said.

"Well, I thought maybe you and Mom could help me. It's not that hard to do, is it, Dad? Mary Martin did it on Broadway."

Russell knew there were always a couple of different ways to fix a fence. One voice was saying, "Oh, honey, just sing a sweet little folk song with your ukulele, you'll do great." Another voice was saying, "Every kid deserves to be Peter Pan, isn't that what revolution is for?" He could already see how it might work. He would get John Wipf, his friend the dairyman down the road, and Merle Cooke, the logger who lived in the little house across the way, to help him. They would think he was crazy for even asking, for saying yes. Neither of them had kids, and they thought the Nears were eccentric.

"Well, Hol, I don't know if your old man is smart enough to figure out how to fly a bale of hay without dropping it on a turkey—but maybe if we think lovely thoughts . . ." I was ecstatic. I knew he could do it if he put his mind to it. He also revealed something that I always loved: He knew the words to Peter Pan; he had been listening to me practice, even if he'd seemed deeply engrossed in the evening paper. I would think lovely thoughts. I was thinking them right now. In fact, I didn't think thoughts could get much lovelier than this. Life had its ups and downs, but it never got much better than the *thought* of getting to fly.

Flying was complicated. It took hours in the hot summer sun waiting for the men to get it right so that I could take off from the wings, be pulled stage right and stage left while acting as if I were moving under my own power, and then land gracefully without a thump, without the cable falling on my head (which happened in practice). I was feeling some panic: Maybe it would all go wrong, maybe I wouldn't win, maybe it had cost Dad and Mom too much money for the cable. Mom had gone to San Francisco to rent a harness,

18

and had made a beautiful green costume. I wondered if it was natural to feel so excited. And was the excitement worth feeling so depressed and scared and alone? Had Mary Martin gone through all this just to be Peter Pan?

I didn't win first place—little seven-year-old Ernie Shelton, a tap dancer in a space suit, did. It stunned me. I was so disappointed. But he was my friend, and in the end I had to make it feel okay. I decided that if I never ever competed again, I would never have to lose.

I tried to think about the good parts. I had flown and I had gotten to do a wonderful duet with my sister Timothy. We wore matching outfits Mom had made from the green-and-white material we had picked out in town. Johnny Mathis signed my baritone uke. All in all, that was pretty terrific! And, unknowingly, I had signed up to be a dream-maker, to be a Peter Pan, to help others think lovely thoughts, to believe in a better life than we are sometimes handed.

Mom took us to San Francisco at least once a year to see ''the city''—the winter holidays were a favorite time, the air so cold and windy, the colored lights blinking, the escalators crowded with people who didn't look anything like us. This year I was especially excited. I was going to make a record to send Grandma for Christmas. Mom found the name of a studio in the phone book, and as we climbed the narrow stairs, I could have just as well been entering outer space.

''How can they put my voice right onto the record, Mom?'' This would be my first direct-to-disc performance. The engineer put a box on the floor for me to stand on so I could reach the mike, and I sang ''Hi Lili Hi Lo'' out full, clearing my throat between verses two and three, which I somehow didn't realize would get on the record.

Mom and Timothy gathered around the record machine to listen to the playback. I watched them enthusiastically listening to—''her.'' No longer was the attention on me. I had made a record, but I wasn't at all sure it had been a good idea!

I saw her coming from across the room, focused and determined. I wasn't afraid. This was my second year singing at the Talmage State Hospital in Ukiah, California. At first I had been a little nervous about singing for ''crazy people,'' but mostly curious. This year I was older. I was ten and I knew I would be met at the reception office by Elena Bell, the program director, and taken from ward to ward to sing my songs.

I looked across the drab gray room at people dressed in drab gray smocks. Only a few sat in the arranged chairs; the others moved from chair to refreshments to window to chair. But she was coming straight on, straight on to the music, her hand stretched out, her body leaning forward toward the strings of my guitar. She wanted to touch the music as it touched her. Caressing the strings, she cut off the sound so that only the rhythm of my pick could be heard. I kept singing. Others began to complain that the music had stopped for them. They demanded that she take her hand away and sit down. A nurse came over to guide her back to a seat. I kept watching her as she disappeared into a dream, slouched over in her chair. ". . . shake me I rattle, squeeze me I cry. As I stood there before her I could hear her cry. Shake me I rattle, squeeze me I cry, please take me home and love me."

My host nodded to me that it was time to go to the next ward. But I couldn't end on that note. I looked over at Mom, who often came with me when I went to sing. She sent me a quiet smile. I signaled to my host, just one more. I started in on an upbeat song, an arrangement blending Mahalia Jackson and Weavers versions. ". . . three gates to the north and three in the south, there's three in the east and three in the west, there's twelve gates to the city, Hallelujah!"

Twenty-five years later I was in Managua, Nicaragua. We sat outdoors on a dirt-floor patio in the wet heat. Residents, staff, and guests mingled on this day. The whole country was celebrating Cincuenta Años, the fiftieth anniversary of Sandino, 1984.

The hospital was small and poor, but extremely clean and calm. Some of the residents were victims of war injuries, some were just having a hard time in life. Two chairs had been set up on the steps for me and guitarist Jim Scott. I looked over at my mother, who had made this journey with me to Nicaragua. She looked so beautiful. Jim and I began to play and sing. Some of the residents sat in the arranged chairs and some wandered.

Then I saw her coming, focused and determined, coming to the music, her hand stretched out. She touched my mouth to touch the sound as the sound had touched her. Again, a nurse gently guided her back to a seat. I caught my mother's eye. We had been here together before.

I had just gotten back from a vacation in Mexico. My partner and I had gone with the hope that a little rest and play could nurse our ailing relationship back to health. But instead, I completely demolished it. I needed to think clearly. My folks usually could help me get my feet on

20

the ground. I headed for Hopland, a small town in the Mendocino wine country, where they now lived.

Dad wasn't feeling well. He had been sparring with cancer and an aneurysm for some time. I curled up by his rocking chair and we chatted—about the world, about love, about sex, about the taste of homegrown tomatoes picked hot off the vine on a summer night. He went to bed early. Mom and I sat up a while more, watching the fire, listening to music.

Mom woke me from a deep sleep. "Hol, it's Russell. We have to go to the hospital." I rose and dressed in about two minutes. We helped him into the pickup truck and Mom sat in the middle, holding him as he slumped over in excruciating pain. I drove, quietly humming a melody in hopes it would soothe and calm us all. Later I realized it was a sappy song by Mexican pop star José José that I had heard in Mexico.

The hospital lights were extremely bright compared to the dark night we had traveled through to get into town. The nurses had cared for Russell before. I wondered if they knew this would be the last time. I knew it. Russell lay on the gurney, looked up at me, squeezed my hand tight from the pain, and asked, "Is this it, Hol?" I felt no need to lie to him. "I think so, Dad." I held his hand, wishing the lights in the room weren't so bright. "Can I get something for this pain? The doctor said he wouldn't let me feel the pain." Russell had been given an option by his doctor several months before, whether to operate on the aneurysm or let come what may. It was his decision. I imagine he took a long walk up the hill and decided he didn't want to be kept alive artificially, nor did he want to be an invalid. So he opted for going out when the time came, but he made the doctor promise he wouldn't feel pain. Russell had felt pain all his life from polio and back trouble. He deserved to go out pain-free.

I explained that the nurses were working on it, told him to hang in there. I wanted to ask him if he was scared, but at the same time I wanted to respect his privacy. I just stood quietly next to him, breathing in and out of the pain with him. Mom was filling out papers and soon arrived by his side. When Dad was in a room, and had gotten the shot he so longed for, I went to call my brother Fred, and sisters Laurel and Tim. Fred and Laurel would probably make it in time. I didn't know if Tim would. She was in New York.

I walked down the hall to see how Mom was doing. We had walked these halls before. They seemed surreal tonight. When we were growing up, Mom and Dad had talked freely about death. It was never denied or

21

feared. Dad had been quite specific that he wanted to be cremated. He wanted us all to go back to the farm, eat, drink, dance, sing, have a party—the kind he would have liked to have been a part of.

Mom sat with Dad, watching the pain ease from his face as the morphine began to take over. She seemed to be okay.

Dad came out of the drugs a few times, asked for water, spoke to Mom a little, then felt the pain and wanted more morphine. We had promised not to race him to surgery, not to try to save him. It was a hard promise for me to keep. Laurel and Fred arrived, and as if he knew, Russell woke to see most of his family before him. We told him Tim was on her way. Russell looked at us all for a long moment, and then the pain began again. We found the nurse, who gave him an injection. That would be the last time Russell surfaced. The long vigil began.

The hospital wasn't crowded, so they let us have the room. We moved in for the duration. Timothy finally arrived and we were all together for the last time. I decided to go outside for a few minutes to get a little air. I'd been in the hospital room for about twenty-eight hours. Mom, understandably, didn't want to leave.

When I returned, Dad had gone. It had been a struggle. At the end, he was moaning for shots every ten minutes. I felt he was ready to go but his heart wouldn't stop beating. Mom assured him it was okay to go. We had stood around his bed and said, "It is okay, we are going to be just fine. You can go whenever you're ready." Tim and Laurel said his spirit left the room on wings and moved their arms upward into the air making a whooshing sound, as if they were letting go of a messenger pigeon. Mom stood by his bed and repeated her vows to him: ". . . for richer, for poorer, in sickness and in health, until death do us part." Yes, they had gone the full distance. We left Mom with him alone in the room for a while. Then she packed his things.

I called the mortuary to come and pick up his body. They asked me to leave or drop off any clothes we wanted him to be dressed in. For the cremation? No, he would think that was a total waste of good clothes. Just take his body. I didn't say it was *just* his body; and his soul would not enter the fire. Mom looked small and lost. I wondered if we had given her enough time here, or if it was best to go back to the farm. As we went out of the hospital, she saw Russell's body being put in the back of the hearse. She cried out after him. She had curled up with this man for nearly forty years. Everyone made it into the cars and headed for the farm. I went to the mortuary to sign papers and answer the necessary questions—like, "Do you want the ashes in an urn or a paper bag?"

We honored Russell's request; we ate, danced, drank, wept, laughed, and told stories about him. I missed him so. How would I go on if I couldn't call him from the road and ask him questions like, "Dad, what's the world coming to?" I'd learned about the Vietnam War with him, about feminism and lesbianism. I'd sung in the church choir with him, and gotten the giggles over lyrics like, "And rest my weary head on your blessed breast." Years before, when it was still unspeakable, I'd told him that I was pregnant and that I was going to have an abortion. I'd marched on Washington with him. I'd been his Peter Pan. He had helped me to fly. How could I fly now without him holding one end of the cable?

Except for tonight, as I write this chapter, I have stopped missing him. He seems very far away and I do not call him back. Best to let him rest.

I developed a habit of remembering the pretty picture, the cute, talented, dearly loved, healthy, happy child living in paradise. Only when I hit "the pit" was paradise jolted.

I remember the pit as far back as memory goes. When I fell into the pit, I was unable to proceed or retreat, stuck like a scared wild animal that has fallen into a hunter's trap.

I was an exceptional child in a small farm town, trying to be just like all the other kids, always afraid of being found out. "Holly thinks she's smart! Holly thinks she's smart!" I used to tell the kids I was going to the dentist even though I was really going to sing at an afternoon tea. Sympathy felt better than envy.

I liked Linda Clark. She had Down's syndrome. When I was finished with my lessons, the teacher would send me outside with Linda to help her learn the letters and numbers. I enjoyed the additional responsibility. At the same time, what is a child who wants the moon going to do with the guilt she already feels for having lived in paradise?

I didn't know I was white until I met Joe and Herbert. They were Indian children, and they were brown. I thought they were beautiful. Their grandmother, Edna Guerrera, was a craftswoman and known in the valley for her work as a Pomo historian and collector of indigenous art.

The next time I knew I was white was when I heard black singers and couldn't do what they did. The only difference I could see between me and them was our color. Later, I understood there was culture and religion, there was struggle and survival, there was Africa, there was church. They may have been related to my forefathers but I was not related to their foremothers. Women have a huge river to cross.

When I was in high school I watched the civil rights movement on TV, wide-eyed, stunned, disbelieving, terrified, discomforted, and changed. Closer to home, the high school choir presented *Annie Get Your Gun* as the annual musical. I got excited that the show provided parts for the Indian kids. My heart breaks now when I think of the parts: caricatures of great healers, riders, and hunters, dressed up for comic relief in a "Wild West" show. Still, I was thrilled to be able to spend the afternoon rehearsals with them, since so often they were excluded or chose to separate themselves from school activities.

My friend Barbara, who was in the show, sometimes sent fire out of her eyes to me. The white girls and the Indian girls had fights after city-league volleyball games that would end in hair-pulling and pierced earrings being ripped out. I never saw these fights. Barbara did. She would come to school the next day angry, and refuse to talk to me because I was a white girl. Sometimes Barbara would speak to me through another student. Standing right next to me, she would say to someone else, "Tell Holly that I am mad at her." The go-between would repeat what I had just heard. Barbara made it very clear to me that she was no longer speaking to me, but the door wasn't closed. She was testing me to see if I could stand the fire.

The school bus took kids north and east. It went through the poor white neighborhood called Okie Flats, past the Indian reservation. I got dropped off along Highway 20, where my mom waited to drive me home to Potter Valley. Sometimes the bus was fun; sometimes it was full of tired, quiet kids who had four jobs—studying, managing the household, working for money, and growing up.

One of my friends was a Southern belle who had moved to the North when her dad got a job in Ukiah. I told her I would marry a black man if I was in love with him. She asked how I could be such an expert on the subject when I hardly knew any black people. It was true; the only black person I knew of in Ukiah was the assistant to the manager at the movie theater. But I insisted that we were all brothers on this earth, and that color didn't matter. This is what progressive whites had taught their children at the time.

I had gone to summer music-and-art camp when I was eleven. It was called Perry-Mansfield, after the two women who owned and ran the school that brought the arts to children in the mountains of Steamboat Springs, Colorado. In the little cabin that ten- to twelve-year-old girls shared, I met Jews and Blacks, Mormons and Catholics, and a girl who is probably a lesbian now. Pearl, our counselor, helped us discuss our differences, our holidays, our ideas. Miss Perry and Miss Mansfield thought Pearl was teaching dance and music—there was that, too.

In the late 1970s, Black people started to come to the Ukiah area because of Reverend Jim Jones, who had a church out in Redwood Valley. Black people had a hard time finding housing. My best friend's parents said they wouldn't mind selling to a Black, but they felt they owed it to their neighbors not to. I had a terrible argument about it with them. It was hard to visit after that. Dad, who had gotten into real estate when we left the farm, was approached by Jim Jones for members of his congregation. Dad finally bought a house and rented it to a Black family. I was proud of him. It didn't solve anything but made a point. They brought him home-baked goods to thank him. We went to the church a few times, but there was something discomforting about it. We couldn't quite put a finger on it, but we had a strange feeling. Was it our racism, or our atheism, or something else we couldn't identify?

In 1967, while I was at UCLA, I went to a Nina Simone concert. I was one of the few white people there. I had never before had *that* experience. She amazed me with her power, her anger. I felt the fire from her eyes. I thought of my friend Barbara.

"How do you do it?" asked my strongest supporters, organizers, and fans. They were referring to my schedule. I was touring most of the time (about 150 events a year); writing songs; producing and recording albums; co-running a record company; writing articles for journals; doing interviews for newspapers, TV, radio, and magazines; participating in local, national, and international political work; doing workshops, lectures, and master classes; maintaining some semblance of contact with my family; working on coalition projects; and trying to hold up under the title of "role model." Some ventured to ask if I was all right. This usually annoyed me, and I would respond defiantly, "Yes, of course I am. I'm fine." I believed in and enjoyed hard work and was not afraid of challenges. I didn't know I'd slipped over the line. When everything is about to fall apart, it is too threatening to notice the chaos or listen when others try to point it out.

*   *   *

A critic starts off his review of my concert, ''I hate political music.'' Would the editor send a critic who starts off saying ''I hate opera'' to review Leontyne Price? Oh, give me patience.

It was cold in Nova Scotia. My touring pals had gone out into the April snow to play. I stayed in bed and tried to disappear into the huge comforter. My back was in severe spasm, I could hardly walk, but I kept getting up onstage to sing every night! My mind hurt too. I had opened myself up to so many different experiences, and I couldn't seem to keep all the pieces together anymore. I reached into my bag and found a piece of paper and a pen and wrote to my partners at Redwood Records.

''Dear Joanie and Jo-Lynne, I'm coming to the end of my rope. I'm giving up. I'm dying.'' I knew the vision I had received long ago of my death had been right.

1984. Happy New Year.

2
WATER COME DOWN

Water is like magic, it makes a child feel small
The brave and true for centuries
Have followed when it called
Water rushing by a child who has never seen the sea
Makes me think that there was something
More than summer going on for all the
Children in the pasture where the waters flow
Sunshine turning shirtless backs to brown
My daddy's hat tipped back to see his kids run wild
Summer time, the water's coming down

Russell, my father, was from Beach, North Dakota. During the Great Depression, he and his family moved to Minneapolis and then out to Southern California. He was a party boy and liked to go dancing on Catalina Island. He had had polio when he was a child and walked on his heels with a limp. Eventually it threw his back out of line, and he suffered a lot of back pain. His grandmother, Maria Peek, had been a socialist and a suffragist, and his great-grandfather, Frederick Near, a soldier in the Civil War with red hair and a long red beard.

Anne, my mother, was raised on Park Avenue in New York City. Her parents, Artemas "Judge" and Dorothy Holmes, were members of the "social register," and made their money in Street and Smith Publishing, which had started with pulps (crummy-paper magazines like *Western* and *Love Story*) and later created *Mademoiselle*. Mom and her twin sister, Ruth, went to Miss Chapin's School for Girls and had coming-out parties, which meant something quite different to them than my coming-out party would mean to me. Mom didn't feel at home in the world of high society, so after graduating from Bennington, she taught fifth grade at the Professional Children's School on Broadway, spent time at the Catholic Worker on Mott Street, and attended Common-wealth College in Arkansas with the hope of finding out more about the world. She swept floors and pulled curtains at The New Theater in Philadelphia, which put on skits for union meetings and performed plays by Marc Blitzstein and Clifford Odets. Then Mom headed for L.A., where she got a job as an electrician at North American Aviation.

There, she met and married Russell, who was a grievance committeeman for the union. They were trying to get child care for the new female work force that had come to make airplanes for the war effort. My sister Timothy was born. The bombs were dropped on Hiroshima and Nagasaki, leading my parents to question their continued participation in the war effort. There was no doubt in their minds that they wanted to fight fascism, but killing 300,000 Japanese people in a weapons experiment was genocide. When more middle-of-the-road leadership took power, Dad lost his job. In search of creative work, they moved north to a ranch in Potter Valley, a small town in Mendocino County. They had three more kids, started a play school, joined the PTA, and learned how political activism worked in a rural town. There were no unions to organize, but they worked to get corporal punishment abolished in the school system. I can't say we were red-diaper babies; it was more as if a red shirt had accidentally gotten thrown in the wash with the whites.

A winding road moves alongside a creek away from the main highway toward a quiet valley—the land of the Pomo tribe before white settlers staked their claim by killing thousands of native people. You can take the west road or the east road—both lead to the main street of Potter Valley, a small town near Ukiah in Northern California. The Methodist Church, the Union 76 gas station selling gas for twenty-six cents a gallon, Dell's swimming pool and motel units, the Garden Club, the Grange Hall, the Potter Valley General Store for groceries, are all here, along with Delight Shelton's Little Deal coffee shop, the grammar school, the old high school converted to fourth and fifth grades, the new high school (destined someday to be the old high school). At the other end of Main Street, set a little apart, are the corner store and the bar. That's the last stop before you head out to the mill. It's 1959. I'm ten years old. I go to fourth grade at the old high school.

The yellow school bus picks us up under the big willow tree. The bus winds around the valley, letting off the other children; and, finally, after the bus grows quiet, it delivers me, my brother, and my sister to Pine Avenue on the west side of the valley. Our older sister, Timothy, comes home later from high school in Ukiah.

Before the old yellow bus pulls over, we look to see if Mom's car is at the end of Pine Avenue. If it is there, we let go a lazy sigh of relief. If not, we gather up our energy, and begin to walk up the lane.

If Mom doesn't show up by the time we pass the dam, the swimming hole, and the bridge, we face the Pembertin! This is a long stretch of land owned by a rancher who raises beautiful, black, muscular Angus cattle that might mistake small children for dogs or other threats to their young calves. It is always frightening to walk the Pembertin. Little legs move as quickly as they can without leaving the littlest legs behind. We crack jokes, sing songs, and clown around to ease the tension, but still our eyes focus clearly on the cattle guard that welcomes us home to the Near ranch, the familiarity of Hereford cattle and grazing deer. Even crossing a cattle guard is a task for our feet in brown-and-white oxford shoes; we step carefully on the iron slats so as not to step in the holes meant to keep cattle from crossing while allowing cars, trucks, and tractors to drive through without gates—a wonderful invention.

We pass the loading chute and corral, where our cattle are driven once or twice a year for shots, branding, and checking for pinkeye or hoof disease. Some are dehorned and castrated. Ranching is not all beautiful horses and calves in the spring.

Down the hill from us lies the quickest route to the creek. In the summer, my brother, Fred, fishes by sticking his head underwater, looking around, and grabbing the fish with his hands. I help him carry his catch or dig for worms that he never ends up using. I like the cool water on my bare feet as I walk from stone to stone without falling in, singing quietly so as not to scare the fish. The field is stickery in the summer and the road is hot, and rattlesnakes are common, so you don't want to get caught without your shoes.

There is the spring-holder up on the hill, a reservoir with a wooden hat on it, screened to keep the raccoons out of the water supply. We are sent up to check it from time to time. First, because it is a good practice to check the water you intend to drink, and second, it is an hour trip if you investigate all the possible distractions along the way, and Mom knows when she needs an hour of quiet.

As we approach the house, we see the wood pile. It gets higher, then lower, then higher as the year goes round. On cold days, we see a friendly column of smoke coming from the chimney. On hot days, the steam rises from the road and we imagine we're in a desert. We who cross the desert know that it is better to drink hot rather than cold liquid in the heat. Home, Laurel reunites with her dog, Trinket, the only pet allowed on the ranch. The stone floor feels cool as we rid ourselves of shoes, books, and finger paintings. Forgetting all our desert training, we raid the icebox for cold lemonade.

The front room is a circle built around a large stone fireplace—kitchen, dining room, living room, all running into each other—a perfect circle to fly around with a new tricycle or in a game of tag that one spring day sent me through the huge picture window. First I cried about breaking the window. Then I cried because I saw blood on my new Easter-bunny white jacket. It wasn't until later that I cried because my arm hurt and because I had to have fourteen stitches.

The kitchen table started out as two saw-horses with four boards laid across to accommodate a crowd. A few nails and some varnish made it a permanent part of the family. Easter eggs would be painted here, engines torn apart and rebuilt, cattle medicines bottled, butter churned, dances choreographed (yes, *on* the table), math problems struggled over, dress patterns cut, and three meals a day for six to fourteen people laid out and gratefully eaten.

The black wood stove marks one point in the circle; on winter mornings we dress there close to the heat and the rich smell of hot milk steaming. Having finished the milking, Mom is making breakfast. Dad has worked for an hour or two and come in for hot coffee, eggs, and bacon. I am just finishing up piano practice or homework. I hate wasting afternoon playtime with such things and prefer to work in the early morning. (Still do.)

The living room houses the piano, a small short keyboard Mom had brought out from back East with her. There is a music corner, with records, tapes, a record player, a Wollensak tape recorder, and a band's worth of instruments—guitars, ukulele, flutes and recorders, harmonicas, a mandolin, hand drums and shakers, a finger cymbal or two, a cow bell, a whistle, a red-and-blue kazoo, a tuning fork, and an accordion. No TV. The thick beige curtains can be drawn to close out the night, but usually they are left open as the huge glass windows provide a perfect mirror when the lamps are turned properly. Here, after we move the heavy iron chairs back, is our stage, and we dance with "Amahl and the Night Visitors." There is a built-in niche with a single mattress and soft pillows where a weary child can fall asleep to the tarantella without having to leave the warmth of the family scene. Before retiring, Mom and Dad carry us one by one into the back of the house, where ice-cold sheets don't seem to wake us. Mom and Dad always sleep in the open-air screened-in back porch, summer or winter. They have each other.

In the back of the house is an outdoor shower, a vegetable garden, and a laundry line forever waving with sheets, work shirts, diapers, and socks of all sizes and colors (seldom two of a kind). Down the hill—and what a hill it is, to roll on and play shadow tag on—is a huge oak tree with a great rope-and-board swing. Just to the left are the cow dogs, each one with a house, and food and water bowls.

A bit lower down the hill is a huge white barn, with milking stanchions on one side, stalls to harbor sick cows or orphaned calves in the middle, and a place for the horses on the other side. Best of all, upstairs is the hayloft. This is a hot and steamy place in the summer, full of bats, mice, and hay stickers. It is empty in June and packed to the ceiling before fall. Here one can dream unobserved or listen to ghost stories if one dares join the older kids on wintry nights when the rain beats down on the tin roof and the wind howls through the slats.

Below the house in the other direction is a cabin where Uncle Lowell lived after he returned from the war. He had been in Africa under General Patton's command.

Next to the cabin are the garage and tool shed. Here is a maze of machinery and occasionally a rack of illegal deer meat hanging in the back where no one can see it except Dad, who plans to feed his family in or out of season. By day the venison is covered with a gunnysack to keep away the flies. By night it's opened to the air so that it will cure.

The dusty road passes through the barnyard and up into the mountains, where there is another cabin: a nice place for visitors from back East to rough it, or where teenagers can play strip poker. William Hinton, the brother of one of Mom's college friends, retreated here to type his notes about his stay in China. Hinton said the FBI wanted to confiscate what he had written. One day he left suddenly, saying Senator McCarthy wanted to talk to him in Washington. Much later, his book, *Fanshen: A Documentary of Revolution in a Chinese Village,* became a widely read intimate view of Chinese society.

The road winds its way along the creek past a bay tree hanging low enough for us to sing to our city relatives in the back of the pickup, "Low bridge, everybuddy down." We reach up and expertly pick off leaves for them to bite or rub on their hands. The leaves release a rich smell to fill them with the country they'd been dreaming about.

Farther up still is Spring Flat, the most beautiful spot on the ranch. Looking out over all of Potter Valley, I would sing out from this natural stage, the valley my audience. But on a good day the valley was only the orchestra pit! Calves are born here on this flat. Christmas trees are discovered in the surrounding forest. Sparse conversations between ranchers are spoken here as they clear out springs. Mom told me many years later that romance and lovemaking took place beneath the May day sun in a hidden swale, while the kids were at school or busy making flower crowns with Grandma.

This is where I lived, where I worked and played my way up to thirteen years old. We sold it in one piece, but it is subdivided now. I hear our farmhouse burned partway down but the present owners restored it in keeping with the old house. There are several families living up on the property now. I don't know them. But I hear they still call it the old Near Ranch.

When it was time to go to high school, like my sister Timothy, I made the forty-minute commute to Ukiah High. It was bigger than Potter Valley High and had more opportunities. Ukiah kids thought Potter kids were hicks, and since I'd gone to school with the same twenty kids for eight years, I didn't know how to make friends. There were so many groups and cliques. Mostly I wanted to sing with the Freedom Singers. But they didn't know I could sing, and I was too shy to tell them.

In December, there was a talent show. I had been performing for years without being scared, but now I was. This would be my introduction to my new peers. I chose three international folk carols and wove them together in a medley. When I went out onstage, I forgot the words and the melody. Instead of stopping, going over to look at the music, and starting again, I began to make up the words and the melody as I went along. The surprised pianist tried to follow me. When I was done there was a big cheer. Dazed, I went outside into the rain to cry.

Water Come Down

How could I go back to school the next day? Maybe I shouldn't try to be a singer. Maybe I don't deserve to be popular. Maybe I'm a worthless nobody. Mom found me in the rain and drove me home.

The next morning the boys from the Freedom Singers stopped me in the hall and asked me to join their trio. I couldn't believe it. Maybe high school would be okay after all. The Freedom Singers had fashioned their arrangements after The Kingston Trio, but now that we were three boys and a girl, we became more like the Weavers. I got to sing Ronnie Gilbert's part.

Forgetting the words onstage has become a tradition with me. I can laugh about it now. But in the midst of a crisis I always wonder if I'll ever want to sing again.

"You know, Holly, you should run for Miss Teenage America. Lots of high school girls do. You could win. The Lions Club would sponsor you. The only thing you would need to do is lose a little weight." I looked at the teacher, trying to grasp his proposal. I had never noticed I was fat. Maybe a little round in places . . . that had happened when my period started. Well, yes, maybe I could lose a little weight. At fourteen I started my first diet, and, for the first time in my life, all I thought about was food. It hadn't been all that important before. I gained weight. The diet lose-gain syndrome began. I asked Mom to help me diet, then hated her for putting vegetables on my plate. My sister Timothy went to modeling school. I watched this five-foot-eleven-inch beauty waste away to 120 pounds. I'd always wanted to be like her. Now what was I going to do? I never ran for Miss Teenage America.

I spent the next years in a love/hate relationship with my body. I went out with the popular boys but it never lasted. I felt I had to act small and a little stupid. Girls had to be cute and thin and coy and wait to be asked. I wasn't good at that. It seemed it was the girl's responsibility to say no to boys. They wanted to feel hot, I wanted to feel hot. They wanted to get laid, I didn't want to be had. I was as curious as they were, but I didn't trust them not to tell. So while we both got into the car on the driver's side, we got out of the car on opposite sides.

I started going out with hoods. They were easier to hang with. We discussed poetry and listened to music and took drives in the country. I continued to play the popularity game as well—vice-president of my junior class, football princess, school-paper staff, French club. I wrote a column for the town paper called "Ukiahi Newsnotes," designed to keep the townsfolk informed about school activities. I would slip in social commentary when I could, like pointing out that the school was letting the recruiting officers on campus but not admitting draft counselors who wanted to discuss alternatives to the military. I was on the dress-code committee trying to get the rules changed so that boys could have long hair and girls could wear pants to school on Friday if there was a football game. The girls who wore their skirts too short had to kneel down on the floor, and if the hem didn't touch, they were sent home. I wore culottes one day to test the waters. They sent me home.

I had some great girlfriends. They were smart and independent and funny. I didn't much like the girls who pretended to be helpless, although I secretly envied them. I wanted boys to like me the way they liked them. I couldn't figure out why it mattered to me so much. I didn't even *like* teenage boys. *Men*—that would help. I needed to meet *men*.

We had dances in the high school gym. The dance committee was doing a pretty good job of bringing city bands up to play for our events. On this night, the band that walked onstage was from Haight-Ashbury. I had watched them in the parking lot from a distance. City bands played the "farm circuit" to make a living. This group was pretty good. Kids started moving toward the stage to dance. Then this woman walked onstage. I'd seen her out back, but since she hadn't come on stage with the guys, I thought she was one of their girlfriends or something. She started to sing. The dancing slowly stopped. We listened and watched as if we were seeing into our futures. It was both thrilling and sobering. The band was Big Brother and the Holding Company. The singer, Janis Joplin.

Finally, my senior year arrived. I had waited four years to get to play Eliza Doolittle in *My Fair Lady*. My dear friend Jeff Langley was to play Pickering. He was perfect. The high school choir director, Mr. Johnson, was in the hospital. David, who was the director's son and was playing Henry Higgins, had been in a car accident, and his face was bruised and swollen.

Mrs. Johnson and choreographer Nancy Hook stepped in to help out as much as possible, but Jeff and I took over. This show was tremendously important to us and we worked to get everyone to take it seriously. They did. It was a difficult production to pull off, even under the best of conditions. We built the set, made the costumes, staged the show, learned the songs, and rehearsed the orchestra. Jeff and I coached and encouraged and pushed. We were exhilarated, overwhelmed, challenged to our limits.

Mom remembers me falling into bed after rehearsal at one A.M., setting the alarm for six so that I could get my homework done before class, and sobbing myself to sleep. I was worried I would gain weight and my beautiful costumes wouldn't fit me by opening night.

The whole town came out to see the production, and night after night I balanced precariously on the edge. My costumes fit, I didn't lose my voice, I remembered all my lines, the songs sounded beautiful. I was the Eliza I knew how to be, the cast worked with amazing discipline and dedication, and, as we did a final reprise, "I Could Have Danced All Night," I truly believed every word.

Jeff and I received letters of praise from teachers and townspeople. Mom was very proud. But she knew what the price had been. When people approached her in the street to compliment her daughter's work, she refrained from saying, "Yes, it was wonderful, but do you know it almost killed her? What would you have done if you were her mother?"

Graduation over, I recovered from a hangover and the disappointment that nothing ever went the way I hoped it would when it came to boys. I had so wanted to have a wonderful romantic finale to high school. The girl wanted to get kissed on her seventeenth birthday! Oh, well. I packed and headed off for White Oaks Theater, in the hills just east of Carmel, California. I didn't have time to linger over disappointments. Adult life was knocking on my door. This would be my first professional job in the theater.

I was in the chorus of *110 Degrees in the Shade* and one of four leads in a new musical called *Eden Skidoo*. Mick, the "leading man," loved to talk politics and smoke marijuana. I didn't try it, but I suppose I inhaled my fair share over the summer just by hanging out with Mick. I constantly annoyed my housemates with my fascination for a singer who had her first hit on the radio. I told them she had played at my high school. I listened to the radio constantly, hoping her single would be played again. The theater's soprano, who had a certain wholesome "Up with People" style, was not impressed when it finally came on. But I lay on my bed, dying over every note of "Piece of My Heart."

3
LONELY DAYS

All those lonely days and broken hearts
And learning to live alone
Lonely days, a child at heart
Learning to leave my home
Lonely days, where to start
It was the first time I had to face the world alone

I wasn't much into rock. With the notable exceptions of Janis, Elvis, and Aretha, I was still living with the "stars" of a generation past. The Weavers and Paul Robeson were my folk music; the great vocal standards and Broadway show tunes of the forties and fifties feit most natural to me. Later Phil Ochs would touch my life, through personal acquaintance more than records. I watched other people go crazy for Bob Dylan and the Beatles, but it wasn't until I heard their work sung by Odetta that I would truly appreciate it. Mostly I loved the standards and musical theater.

Summer came to an end. I hadn't gotten high or laid. The director, Gale Peterson, called me into his office. He had heard a rumor that I wanted to cancel my plans to go to UCLA and stay at the theater for the winter season. He firmly discouraged me. "You're very good, Holly. Don't get stuck here. Go out into the world and find something bigger than this. If it isn't out there, you can always come back." I didn't want to hear that. I tried not to take it personally. But he was right. There was something bigger out there. I set out to find it.

In 1986 I was asked to speak to the students who had set up a tent city at UCLA to protest apartheid. This was not a new issue for me.

Lonely Days

Twelve years before I had done a benefit concert for students in Maine who were calling for divestment in their school. It was frustrating to hear the press talk as if it were a movement recently born. How can we know where we are going if we don't know where we come from?

UCLA. I had been a student here in 1967. It was here I had participated in my first demonstration. We gathered informally in the tent city. I noticed some cautious students standing apart and others who walked by pretending not to notice, their heads tilted a bit to hear what was being said.

"May I tell you a story?" I asked. "When I was in school here, I walked across these lawns every day, right here where you have set up the tents. I studied theater and political science. Well, I didn't really study. I attended classes. When I first got to school, I was so excited, I read all the required books before school even began. By the time finals came I had forgotten everything I'd read and I couldn't seem to find a reason to read them again. But I did learn. I learned about *big*. I came from a small farm town and UCLA was like a huge factory. The university student population was thirty thousand, about thirty times the size of Potter Valley and three times the size of Ukiah. I learned about *tall*. While standing in a lunch line I looked up from my book and saw a belt. As my eyes crawled up and up this magnificent human tree, I discovered it was Lew Alcindor, whose chosen name is now Kareem Abdul-Jabbar.

"I learned about black power and I have trouble forgiving myself for not attending a class taught by a young black woman whose name I later came to know well. Angela Davis is now a friend, but then she was an opportunity missed. I learned that the law school used actors from the theater-arts department for mock trials. Do they still do that?

"And I learned about activism, which had been instinctive to me all my life but I never had a name for it. There was a philosophy professor who led a weekly silent vigil every Wednesday at noon, protesting the war in Vietnam. Yes, Professor Kalish. He's still here? Tell him hello from me. He wouldn't have known me then. I was very shy and quiet and probably never even introduced myself. But you never know who you are affecting, even the ones who walk by or pretend not to listen. I sat and watched that silent vigil from a distance for weeks! I'd take my lunch and a book to sit just within sight of the demonstrators. Some days I desperately wanted to join them but felt too afraid to make such a big leap, even though I'd been opposed to the war for years. Perhaps it is hard now for you to imagine that a silent

37

vigil could have been a big leap for me. I would say to myself, 'Why are they doing that? They look foolish, people are staring at them, laughing at them, or, worst of all, ignoring them. It is ridiculous. They are wasting their time. They have no effect on anyone.'

"Oh, really?! Look who was being affected. One day I gathered every ounce of courage I could muster and joined the line. Only two people were present at the beginning of the hour. When I stepped up, I was the sixth in line. I stood there in silence for one hour, allowing people to stare at me, laugh at me, or ignore me. And I didn't die. At the end of the hour, we numbered thirty. So do not get discouraged by the numbers game. Invite people to visit the tent city, give them an opportunity to protest apartheid, even if they walk by or sit nonchalantly just within hearing distance. You have no idea who may be learning from your example . . . perhaps a young woman who will someday become a political singer!"

I started at UCLA in the fall of 1967. I looked around my English I class and realized it was full of high school kids recently graduated. This undermined my fantasy of college as a bastion of intellectual sophistication, tweed coats, and long, romantic discussions of French poets. But here, at the big UCLA factory, it seemed I was always longing to be somewhere with someone doing something, and except for my Saturday morning musical-comedy class, which I loved, I wasn't going anywhere with anybody.

I watched television coverage of students and police clashing over the war in Vietnam and racism. I was scared. I wanted to go out for a Coke so that I could talk to someone about it. My aunt was a conservative Republican. But I didn't *know* anybody. I went to see *King of Hearts* again and again, and decided I was in love with Alan Bates.

Finally I had a date, with a marine. My aunt's boyfriend was suspicious and critical. He said soldiers couldn't be trusted. He knew— he'd been in the military. I said, "Just because you couldn't be trusted doesn't mean all men are like you." Soon after, I moved out and found an apartment in Westwood Village with a Jewish girl, who later took me to my first Seder.

I sulked around the apartment, listening to the guns go off in funeral salutes across the street in the VA cemetery. Another little white gravestone would be added to the thousands already there. My roommate walked in one day and said, "The trouble with you is you've never been laid!" and walked out. Foolishly, I accepted this analysis. I went home with someone I hardly knew but he would do. We were having a nice time in bed, but just before we "did it," I told him I had never "done it" before. He got very concerned and suggested I wait and "do it" with someone I loved. I assured him "it" was no big deal. Then I took his remarks and twisted them to mean that men don't like to "do it" with inexperienced women. I decided I would never let on from here on out if there was something I didn't know. I would learn fast and fake the rest. Well, you can imagine which part got faked.

The next morning, he went to work and I went to wash the bloody sheets. I ached between my legs so badly I could hardly move. When I walked into the Laundromat, I had this feeling that all the women were secretly saying, "First time, huh?" or, "Well, now you know," or, "Not what you had imagined?" I thought, *We women are so sad.*

I went back to school after the holidays with a commitment to get involved, to let people see me. I went to a sorority dinner and felt completely out of place. I didn't care enough about clothes or place settings. I went to the international-folk-dance night but turned away at the door, unable to face the prospect of walking inside without a partner even though most of the dances were circle dances.

I was surprised to find I wasn't that interested in my theater-arts classes. I wondered if I had chosen the right career. Maybe I needed to stick to musical comedy. I understood the simple relationships and the bold, delightful melodies.

But there was something about theater people. I wanted to be with them. I wanted to break through and try to find myself there. I finally got the courage to walk into the green room of the theater-arts department. I wanted to shout to them, "You should know me, I'm a great singer. You would like me if you knew I was talented!" It never occurred to me that they might like me as a person even if I were not talented.

In order to stay in the department, I had to audition before a panel of teachers and peers. I didn't know any theater pieces, so I decided to sing "Pirate Jenny" from *The Threepenny Opera*. When they called my name, my piano player hadn't shown up. The instructor suggested I reschedule, but I knew that if I waited I'd never return. I walked onto the stage and sang "Pirate Jenny" a cappella. When I finished there was a long silence. I knew I had finally earned my place in the green room with my co-students Judy Kaye, A Martinez, Kathleen Lloyd, Johnny Rubinson, and Colin Higgins. Once again my voice carried me through painful insecurity, assuring me I deserved to be alive. And although the audition forced me out of my isolation, I still have a warm spot in my heart for Alan Bates standing stark naked before the asylum gates.

Gordon Devol invited me to be his partner in a scene from *110 Degrees in the Shade* for the Hugh O'Brien Awards, an acting competition to which UCLA invited the film industry to scout the latest crop of graduates. I finally got to play Lizzy, even if just for one scene. Several agents approached me after the show. I was flattered and exhilarated, but I tucked their business cards into my costume pocket and forgot about them. I was going to be a Broadway actress and was not interested in film and TV. But Gordon had given me a gift I would never forget. It was a much better gift than the kisses I wished he had given me. He had given me a chance to work.

I joined Another Mother for Peace, one of the most powerful women's organizations in Southern California. From its offices in Beverly Hills it called on such celebrities as Donna Reed and Joanne Woodward to help stop the war against Indochina. They had an enormous mailing list, reaching out to women who might never have been otherwise involved in the peace movement. I volunteered to stuff envelopes. The war horrified me and doing something about it made me feel better. I came from an outspoken family. Doing this work helped alleviate my bouts with depression. I was also getting to meet Jews. These women were different from anyone I'd ever met before. As they folded leaflets they talked and I learned. I had not been aware of how powerful the participation of progressive Jews had been in the left. I worked my way up in the volunteer pool and took charge of updating the mailing list. I was proud of my work. These women appreciated me and they had never even heard me sing.

Back at school, I played major roles in *Sergeant Musgrave's Dance* and a TV production of *Gift of the Magi*. I had won the part of Sarah in *Guys and Dolls*. I was worried about my weight, knowing that if I dieted I'd gain weight and if I didn't diet I'd stay the same. I look back at photos of me during that time and am amazed that I thought I was fat. I was simply of a different era. Botticelli or Rubens would have begged to paint a woman like me! Round and red and sturdy. I was five feet seven and weighted 140 pounds. How strange I think it is now to have despaired over ten pounds. It was hard to compete with the small frames of Hollywood ingenues. Harder still was to remember I didn't want to or need to. I was *zaftig,* and I was the one getting the parts.

The rehearsals were fun. But the orchestra played too loud and I had no experience (and no help) in protecting myself from oversinging. A few days after we opened, I lost my voice. My understudy got her big chance and finished out the show. The doctors said I had nodes on my vocal chords and told me to maintain strict silence if I wanted to avoid surgery. Just when I was beginning to feel accepted, the very thing I counted on deserted me. I panicked. Instead of diving into a stack of good books or studying sign language, I went to a weight clinic, where the doctor gave me shots of cow urine.

My paternal cousin was getting married to my maternal cousin, so the families were making a reunion out of it. The Nears headed east for the wedding. I decided to stay east for a while, in Philadelphia. I lived with my grandmother and visited around the corner with my mom's twin sister. I broke my silence with voice lessons from Carolyn Dengler, a teacher at the Philadelphia Music Academy. Carolyn was the best thing that could have happened to me. She was big-hearted and maternal and invited me to dinner sometimes.

I had one date. I was fat. He was fat. I didn't want to go out with a fat boy. My self-esteem was so low that I thought people would look at me and think, *That's all she can get!* I was mad at him before he even had a chance. We went to a Donovan concert. I had called the foreign-student center to offer a ticket to someone who might like to have a North American cultural experience. This guy who worked there had answered the phone and, before I could object, invited himself to go with me. I had wanted to be with a Spaniard, an Iranian, or an African. Instead I was with a fat guy from Philadelphia. Donovan, sitting cross-legged on the stage and draped in white, sang "Mellow Yellow," "Wear Your Love Like Heaven," and other songs of peace and love. I was not in the mood.

Carolyn called me into the director's office and proposed to me that I study opera. She explained to the director that I had a huge voice and extraordinary talent. My ego got a long-overdue boost. Ever pragmatic, I asked how long it would take for me to be ready to audition at the Met. He smiled and said, "You have a highly developed voice. I shouldn't think it would be more than ten years." Ten years! Do you know how long that sounds to an eighteen-year-old girl who has been performing since she was seven? I told him I was honored, but declined. Carolyn continued to give me private lessons until I left town. She allowed me to weep into her grand piano without disapproval, all the while saying with gusto, "Keep singing! It is fine to cry, to feel, to express yourself, but do not crumble . . . keep singing. It is the best time for your voice to grow while you are releasing. Sing, dear, sing!" I did until my voice returned, offering me some hope for the future.

41

For a short time, I attended a dance class. The dance teacher was known as one of the best in Philadelphia. Her name was Nadia Chilkovsky. But I could not go as me. I did not like myself. And that same ten pounds kept me from seeing myself as a dancer. So I cast myself as a strange, introverted character who never spoke, seldom looked anyone in the eye, and was completely unable to keep up with the skinny girls who were consciously competitive and self-centered and in hindsight I can now assume, many had eating disorders. If I had gone as me, I would have felt the need to be the best as I had been in tap class when I was ten, or in modern class when I was sixteen.

My gemini split, my me/she/Holly/I, took over. The proud, confident, beautiful one refused to go to class and fail. But the other one, the scared, homely, shy self, had no expectation of success. It was this little one that walked into class and signed up. The other dancers paid no attention and would simply step around her as if she were not there. She allowed a look of horror to sweep across her face rather than hide behind an air of snobbery. When she felt like crying, tears would well up freely. She got by in the warm-ups, but when it came time to do work across the floor, learning steps and routines, re-creating them with style and grace, her feet would not go where her mind told them to. She could imagine the grace with which she should move. In fact she could remember having danced wonderfully under the watchful eyes of Joyce Trisler, Carol Singer, and others. But she could neither muster the attitude nor execute the steps now. Where was the confidence, the pride, the humor? Lost, the little character stumbled her way across the floor, doing the best she could, which was a sad, paltry percentage of what she knew of Holly's potential.

At the end of class, each dancer found her space on the floor and improvised. No one paid attention to anyone else. Only the teacher watched. The little character gained confidence in this freedom from form. Here, on her own, she began to dance, her beauty blossoming for a moment. One day, the teacher asked her to stay after. The other dancers' eyes all fell on her for a moment, then they moved quickly on. The little character waited for the teacher to speak. "What is going on with you? When you do the floor work you are clumsy and uncoordinated, you are easily confused, you seem to give up. But in the improv work you are a dancer and a damned good one. What? What?" The character was torn between being honored that the teacher had seen through her bumbling self to the real artist, and being horrified that she was going to have to confess that she wasn't really a clumsy fat girl but

42

rather an extremely talented and beautiful woman. She could not confess. "I don't know," she said. "I hear the instructions you give, I can imagine the steps in my mind, but when I go to do them, I fall apart. I will try harder." "Good," said Nadia. "You can dance." Neither Holly nor the little character ever returned to class.

When I returned to L.A. that fall, 1969, I didn't have enough money to go back to school, so I moved into a little two-bedroom cottage alongside Carrol Canal in Venice for a hundred dollars a month. I took a job in the university admissions office. But Kevin Cassleman from the Kurt Frings Agency had seen my work at the Hugh O'Brien Awards the previous year and called me about a role in a film called *Angel, Angel, Down We Go*.

I hadn't planned on being *in* the movies. But I was broke and curious, so how could I turn down an audition? Then life played one of its little jokes. I got the part because I was beautiful *and* because I was "fat." I laughed all the way home from the audition. The director had suggested I try to put on a few more pounds before we began shooting. Hard as I tried, for the next few days I couldn't eat. I called the admissions office to quit my job.

"You hate your parents. All children hate their parents." "No, I don't!" I protested. I tried to explain that my parents were my friends, apparently a contradiction in terms for film director Robert Thom. Maybe he knew about making a movie—that was yet to be seen—but he didn't know anything about me. "I'm glad to *play* a character who hates her parents. Give me direction. I'll play it the way you want."

Robert had rented one of those beautiful homes in Malibu Colony for the summer, with windows open to the sea. I'd never seen anything like it except in the movies. As I stopped at the security gate to get clearance, I became aware that my car was a VW, my clothes were off the department-store rack, and my experience was limited. Was I about to be found out? What would they find? A country bumpkin? Was that okay?

I had visited MGM after getting the part. People smiled and congratulated me and made it clear how lucky I should feel that I had been discovered. Sam Katzman, Jr., said, "This kid comes in and she's all talent. Five grown men walk into a hot office to watch a twenty-year-old girl read a script she's seen for ten minutes and when she was through, we all had tears in our eyes."

I tried to relax. I'd already gotten the job. I was only coming to Malibu to meet Jordan Christopher and his wife, Sybil. When Jordan walked in, I was intimidated, just like my character was supposed to be. I wanted to notice these things so that I could re-create them on camera. Jordan and Sybil were very kind to me . . . and pretty together: he, so young and handsome and quiet; she, older, confident, seemingly settled in her life. I thought, *Good idea. Remember to marry a younger man when you're older.* I found out later that Sybil had previously been married to Richard Burton, and the wig I was going to wear was the one used in *National Velvet.* I wasn't supposed to tell Jordan, or anyone, because it might cause discomfort on the set, but I think hairstylist Sidney Guiloroff was being overly concerned. Jordan didn't seem like the type who would be upset by my wearing Elizabeth Taylor's wig. I think he would have chuckled at another of life's little jokes.

The first day of filming took place down at Santa Monica, on the boardwalk just south of the pier. There I met Lou Rawls, Roddy Mc-Dowall, Davey Davidson, Charles Aidman, and the star of our adventure, Jennifer Jones, who was apparently making a comeback in this film. I immediately fell in love with Roddy. What a dear man. And Lou, well, his speaking voice was as deep and magnificent as his singing voice. I loved hearing him talk. Charles was playing my father. I didn't have many scenes with him, so I didn't get to know him well. Davey was sweet. She drove a leased car. I didn't even know people leased cars. Jennifer was the grande dame that she deserved to be. I watched her struggle with her part, with her role, with her fear. I felt like an ugly duckling next to an aging swan. That is how I was supposed to feel; those were the parts we played. I noticed that Roddy was Jennifer's friend. I was glad for that. I wished he would be mine too.

I didn't feel Robert had much compassion for my character. I did not want her to bear the brunt, so I struggled to give her dignity where there was none, to protect her from jokes and abuse. It was a grotesque story in which the leading man fucks the daughter, kills the father, and seduces the mother. I always wondered why Robert wanted to make this film.

Timothy wisely criticized my performance. She said I was trying to be too pretty in the film, afraid to let the rawness show. She taught me that it was the depth of field and ambiguity that heightens the audience's interest in a character.

My favorite scene was my lovely grand entrance into my coming-out party, when I walked down a long, curved staircase in a silver gown, floating like a cloud on the outside, terrified on the inside. I had taken that walk before as Eliza in *My Fair Lady.* The movie set was more elaborate, but the feeling was the same.

Lonely Days

There was a scene in which I was to be hit. We practiced so I wouldn't get hurt. But when the cameras rolled I did get hurt. I couldn't stop crying. I'd never been hit before. The humiliation was overwhelming. I can't believe people hit their children.

Then there was "the sex scene." The day we filmed the scene, we were to have a closed set, meaning only essential cast and crew would be present—about nine people, as I recall. The AD (assistant director) came to fetch me from my trailer, where I sat alone in a long blue bathrobe. My wig was on, my makeup done. Probably I was nervous, but I don't remember feeling nervous. I was curious—and wanted to be professional. I met Jordan on the path down to the woods, where the shot was set up. We walked quietly along the path on Lot 3. Jordan smiled and took my hand. I wondered if he was nervous. Then he stopped in the path as if he had seen a snake, slowly backing away, squeezing my hand. He informed the AD that we would return to work when, in fact, the set was cleared, but at present it was swarming with people. We went back to his trailer to wait. I was so impressed. It hadn't occurred to me that I could say no.

It was a long day. There is nothing romantic about a character losing her virginity on an MGM set with nine people watching, the cameraman a foot away, the makeup woman moving in and out, touching up the red blotches I get when I'm touched on my neck, the director calling out instructions from the side. We had to repeat the sounds and facial expressions of sex over and over again until they were right for sound, camera, and performance. Of course we weren't really having sex. It was all staged. I faked one orgasm after another (that would not be the last time). I didn't know what the hell I was doing. I'd never had an orgasm in real life and didn't trust anyone on the set enough to ask if I was doing it right.

During one of the many pauses between takes, I was lying on the ground with Jordan stretched on top of me, politely, shyly holding his weight off my body. I looked up into the trees and saw that Lou Rawls had climbed up on a limb for a bird's-eye view. He saw that he had caught my eye, waved, and laughed. It lightened my spirit a lot to see him in the trees. I felt like I had a friend, and the friendship blossomed as the weeks went on. I don't think Lou had spent much time with a farm girl before; I had certainly not known a street kid from the windy city. We got on well, amusing each other with our differences.

I liked my film family and was sorry when the project was over. I was even more sorry when the film opened. It played at the drive-in theater in my hometown, not even good enough to hit the main movie theater. It was trash. My family proudly weathered the storm; they hopped in the car with a thermos of hot coffee and headed for the drive-in.

The critics hadn't liked the film but said flattering things about my work. I was hooked. I hoped my agent would find me another part. I didn't have a lot of competition in the "beautiful fat girls" category, but there weren't a lot of parts for "beautiful fat girls," either. (There was a twenty-year lapse between *Angel, Angel* and *Hairspray!*)

I filled my days exploring the beach community of Venice—a multicultural mix of hippies, artists, dope addicts, poor people, old people, and musicians. I smoked marijuana. It made me paranoid or sleepy. I dropped some acid once with my sister Timothy on Muscle Beach in Venice, once with a rock musician in the forests of Mount Tamalpais, and once with a man just out of prison who disappeared in the middle of a high while I was listening to a Beatles album. I tried cocaine, which I didn't really feel, saving me from a path I might otherwise have taken in search of confidence.

This was also a time of trying to see where I fit into the sexual-liberation movement. It's a shame I had to hurt so many times before I discovered I really didn't fit at all. But, like music, sex took me into other peoples' lives and cultures that I might never have known if I had stayed safe in my own backyard. A tender affair with a jazz tuba player did not begin when he tapped softly on my moonlit bedroom window, nor did it end when he slipped away before morning. He was a drug addict. I watched him go cold turkey long enough to get the evidence out of his bloodstream. I drove him and his trumpet-player friend to East L.A. to "drop some clothes off at his sister's house." I parked the car. They told me to wait. I turned on the car radio and waited. I noticed in my rearview mirror that they had walked several doors down from where they had told me to park the car. They returned shortly and we headed for Venice. "Holly, I think you should try to drive the speed limit," he said. I knew I'd once again been a naïve country girl in the big city. "Tell me," I said. Silence. "Goddamn it, tell me or I will pull over right here." He was not happy that his need had overcome his discretion. "We're carrying heroin." Silence. We fought later.

It was hidden up on the ledge above the bathroom mirror. "Can I see it?" I asked. He yelled at me, "Don't you ever look at that stuff, don't you ever touch it!" Didn't he know I was looking at it and touching it in his beautiful black body that leaned over his horn until two A.M., and then just leaned? Come the day to check in with his probation officer, he poured hot oil on his arm to look like he'd had a cooking accident to cover his tracks.

The last time I saw him he was on his way to Europe to find an audience that appreciated jazz. He borrowed some money from me, to buy his wife a pair of shoes, he said. Many years later I heard the news. Ray Draper. Jazz musician. Dead.

My agent called me to audition for a film called *The Magic Garden of Stanley Sweetheart,* which MGM was producing to reach the "youth market." I quickly discovered Hollywood's conception of young people—just put a headband on them and throw in a little free love and some "I-can't-find-myself" dialogue. I remember wishing someone would do for the seventies what James Dean, Marlon Brando, and Montgomery Clift had done for the fifties. However, I was excited to be auditioning for another part.

I met actor/entertainer Michael Greer in the casting office. He was already signed for one of the parts. He wished me well in my audition and said that if I got the part I should look him up in New York. He would help me get settled. I got the part and tucked his number in my pocket as I left for the airport. MGM was sending a car. I closed my new luggage and waited. The car arrived and a little gray-haired man took my bags out into the darkness. I checked the stove and the iron about twelve times—in my mother's way— and walked out. There before me, shining under the streetlight, was a long, black limo. It reminded me of seeing my first cruise ship with my grandmother in New York Harbor when I was a young girl. It was so long! Bravely, I climbed in. We drove smoothly through the streets, people staring to see if they could recognize a famous person through the darkened windows. The driver asked a few questions at first, trying to find out who I was, why I was being treated to his service, and who was paying the bill. I didn't have an answer for the first one, so I moved on to the money part. But my voice seemed to echo, so I didn't talk much. I started shrinking—my clothes looked cheap, my hair felt undone, my makeup was too Maybelline, my body too round, my shoes too comfortable. I was amazed that a car could do this to me!

The real question at hand was whether I could make it in New York, if I could fit into this movie and walk away from it with dignity, a paycheck, and good reviews.

The car pulled into the airport, and I got out, trying not to feel foolish. The driver left me and my luggage at the curb. I wondered if I should use a porter or carry it in myself. I had always done everything for myself and, unable to cope with the question of tipping or the humiliation of being waited on, I picked up my luggage and strode to the ticket counter. New York, here I come.

When I got to New York, I called the number in my pocket. I was staying at the Delmonico Hotel, but it was expensive and I needed to find somewhere else to live. Michael Greer helped me move into a furnished studio apartment on the East Side. The rent was three times what I was paying in Venice, but cheaper than the hotel. Michael seemed to like me. He said I was the sunshine come to light up New York City. I was certainly developing a crush on him. Although he was always tender and considerate, he would leave me at the elevator and say, "I have an early call tomorrow. I'd better not come up." I started to take it personally. I imagined he didn't like my body. I used this to explain rejection for years to come, even after I lost fifteen of those ten pounds!

One day he asked me to go with him to an interview. I did. It was one of those luncheons with iced tea and expensive lettuce. He was articulate and charming, and when the interviewer asked him whether he was in love or ever hoped to marry, he looked at me with his big eyes, put his hand over mine, and said, "I love this woman and I hope someday . . ." letting his voice trail off. I was very cool, gazing back at him without letting my surprise show. After the luncheon, he raced away to another appointment.

Work kept me occupied for the next few weeks and I had met a friend on the set, so I didn't feel lonely. Patricia was tall and thin and dark. Although she played mysterious, sexy characters on film, it was fun to discover that she was rowdy and mischievous in real life. We became pals. I was invited to a film-opening party put on by MGM to honor Keir Dullea. The studio sent a limo for me and my "party," which included Michael, Patricia, and another *Stanley Sweetheart* cast member, Victoria Racimo. I wore a wine-colored gown. I learned a trick: shopping in the ladies "home attire" department of an expensive store, buying what rich women would wear while lounging. With some costume jewelry and my long red hair, I could make it look chic. I enjoyed being part of the new up-and-comers. At dinner, I was seated next to Andy Warhol and Ultra Violet.

I think it was that night that Michael came up to my room. We held each other for a while and then he said he cared too much about me and really didn't feel he could handle it all right now with his career. I was hurt and confused but not devastated. Michael had introduced me to a lot of nice people, including Sal Mineo and the actors who worked on *Fortune and Men's Eyes*. I had been Michael's date to the opening-night party at Sardi's, and I was starting to understand why Michael could both love me and not be able to be my lover. Michael was gay. I didn't know if Michael knew he was gay. But at least I knew. Now I could love him as a friend.

My co-star in the film was a wild young actor, probably scared on the inside and, therefore, arrogant on the outside. But I developed a soft spot in my heart for him. He worked hard and was very good in our scenes together. I woke up one morning next to him in some hotel. I'm not sure either of us could remember exactly how we got there. It didn't seem to matter much in 1969. Nearly twenty years later, I was speaking at a NOW conference in Miami. When I arrived at my hotel room, the table was covered with a huge bouquet of flowers with a sweet note from Don Johnson.

When I was through with the film, I stayed on to see if I could get work in New York. My East Coast agent, Bill Treusch, and casting director Marion Dougherty both encouraged me to audition for a musical-stage version of the film *Georgy Girl*. I was caught in a tremendous downpour the day of my first audition. My hair was drenched and hung heavily down my back. I tried to remember that Georgy wasn't supposed to be an ingenue but that didn't help: This was my first audition on a Broadway stage. This was it, this was what all those dreams had been about. Several singers went before me. I couldn't decide if I felt better listening to the competition or not. I searched for a comb. But it was too late for that.

''Next!''

The stage manager directed me to a large chalk X that was drawn front and center. A white light threw a cold circle around the X. A pianist sat motionless at his place and simply said, ''Your music and key, please.'' ''I don't have any music,'' I said. ''What?'' ''I am going to sing without accompaniment.'' He shrugged, as if to say, ''It's your funeral.''

I stood where X marked the spot and looked around. There wasn't any set on the stage, which made the place seem especially huge. A voice from the darkness called out, ''What is your name, please?'' I answered. I knew they hadn't gotten it. No one ever believed my last name. Apparently several people were sitting out in the house, but it was impossible to see them. ''Wouldn't you like our pianist to play for you?'' a voice asked. ''If you don't have music he might know the song anyway. He is very good.'' ''No, thank you,'' I answered. ''Okay,'' the voice called back, in a tone that seemed very much like the shrug the pianist had given me. ''You may begin.''

I began to sing, ''Georgy Girl,'' the theme song from the movie. As I found out later, that was a tasteless choice. I sang it slowly and sadly, in the mode of Streisand's ''Happy Days Are Here Again'' or Garland's ''Smile.'' I stood outside myself and watched this young girl, soaking wet and lonely, singing out in the dark. When I finished, no sound came from the theater. The singers waiting in the wings didn't move. I just stood there. I felt chills go up my own spine. I didn't know what it had done for them and didn't care. I'd just sung on the Broadway stage and I was good. Then the voice from the darkness said, ''That was a very daring thing to do. Roger, set up another appointment with Miss Near. We'd like to see her again.'' He'd gotten my name.

I danced all the way home in the rain. A Broadway show! Not only a show, the lead in the show. The lead in a Broadway show in New York City! Well, as I said before, the *thought* of flying is often the best part.

I met with those people who had sat in the dark several more times. The choice was between me and a British girl. They decided to go British. But one of the young writers was very nice to me and expressed her disappointment that I wouldn't be in the show. Her name was Carol Bayer-Sager.

Marion Dougherty suggested I try out for a stint in *Hair*. The show had been running on Broadway for almost two years and they were looking for replacements. Having broken the ice on auditions, I decided to give it a try. They had me dance and sing a song. I decided to sing a cappella again. To this day people say, ''I can't believe you can just stand up there and sing with no accompaniment!'' It's when I have a full band that I say to myself, ''I can't believe I'm singing with all these other people playing all at the same time!'' I sang ''Something'' by George Harrison. Classy audition piece, I thought.

I made a perfect candidate for *Hair*. First of all, I had the *hair*, lots of it. Second, I had a big voice, strong enough now to survive the chorus numbers. Third, I was willing to do the nude scene, which, as anyone who saw the show will remember, was actually very uneventful. There were two places in the show where anyone who wanted to pretend to be outraged could walk out. One was the nude scene and the other was when the American flag touched the ground.

Although the original cast had included hippies, by the time I was in the show, the cast was made up of professional actors who came to work in straight clothes and then, in the magical mystery world of theater, transformed ourselves into hippies night after night, eight shows a week. I would make fifteen braids in my hair after washing it, and by the time it dried and came undone it would explode into a wild mane. I sang "Walking in Space" and "Black Boys."

Since I wasn't making as much money as I had in the film, I was concerned about the Sutton Place apartment I was renting. I had thought I would be in New York for only a month, but now it looked like I was here for a while. One day in the elevator, a beautiful black woman started up a conversation with me. A few days later, she knocked on my door to borrow, believe it or not, a cup of sugar. We started to chat about the expense of the apartments and I explained that I would probably be leaving soon. She suggested I move in with her. She was also having a hard time paying the rent. She had a one-bedroom but promised I could take over the living room, and said that when she was home, she was either in her bedroom or in the kitchen. I moved in. It turned out that she was an African princess, Elizabeth Begaya, exiled by a military coup from Toro, a small nation near Uganda. She had come to New York to try to make a living as a model until she could return to her country. We were strange roomies—she so black, proper and delicate, me so red, wild and *zaftig*.

I arrived at work one evening to find the cast gathering for an emergency meeting. News had just come in that four students at Kent State had been killed by the National Guard during an antiwar demonstration against the invasion of Cambodia. The cast was discussing what to do. I was surprised by their activism. Someone proposed that we cut the grand finale, "Let the Sunshine In," and do a silent vigil. The cast seemed to like this idea. It was put to a vote. I abstained. Fortunately it passed. As opposed to the war as I was and had been for years, I was not good at confronting authority, and this act was going to be both controversial and a breach of our contracts. I also thought it would make the audience mad. They had paid what I considered an outrageous amount of money to see this show, and I thought they should see it in its entirety. We could each be mad about the killings, but I didn't think we should impose our responses on others. In a matter of months, my position would change. A year later I would be commissioned by Kent State students to write a song for the memorial.

We did stop the show before the finale, and one of the leads announced that for as long as the war of aggression against the Indochinese people went on and for as long as American kids were being killed, there would be no sunshine. It was very powerful to stand there in the midst of the audience's stunned silence and feel what we had just done.

A few days later, when two black students were killed at Jackson State, I don't recall us interrupting the show. Some lessons hadn't been learned yet. More than one hundred years earlier, pacifists, abolitionists, suffragists, and labor organizers had missed a golden opportunity to unite into a single movement. It looked like we were going to miss it again.

I received a film offer from California. The script was bad but the money good, and I was ready to go home. I left New York and headed west to do a movie about a guy who killed a lot of young girls and buried them in the desert. I was to play his accomplice.

I kept wondering if I would ever get a part in a *good* movie. *The Magic Garden of Stanley Sweetheart* had not been a success, although once again I had received nice reviews. Victoria Racimo and I were sent out on a promotional tour for a week through the South. We did about six interviews a day, all taking place over drinks: breakfast—Bloody Mary; mid-morning—vodka and orange juice; lunch—martini; midday—gin and tonic; predinner—bourbon and soda; dinner—wine; after dinner—cognac. The first day, Vickie and I drank along with our interviewers. But it only took one day to realize we couldn't keep up. So we shifted to soft drinks until evening. We had fun but I wanted to work. I wanted to do a good film.

4
FREE THE ARMY

TIMOTHY RETURNED FROM LONDON, WHERE SHE HAD BEEN STUDYING at the London Academy of Music and Drama. We decided to live together in Los Angeles. She was the best housemate I ever had, and she taught me how to keep house by example. Mom had been a good housekeeper, ranch-style. Tim showed me how to function in an apartment. Our first place was one room attached to the bottom floor of a two-story house where Jenny Sullivan and Jimmy Messina lived. They told us that the whole downstairs flat would be available in six weeks, so we squeezed into the one room. That's where we learned to really get along.

I had put on about forty pounds in New York and had come to accept that I was a fat person. So what? I asked. There are lots of fat people in the world. Fat women are considered attractive in many other cultures. I tried to ignore the shallow perspective of most white American men. Tim, however, was getting interested in "health foods," which meant things like brewer's yeast on tuna fish. I decided to try it. I stopped eating red meat, and gave up white sugar and processed foods. I ate as much as I wanted, including desserts, as long as they were wholesome and honey-sweetened. I never felt like I was on a diet. I never felt denied. I lost forty pounds that year.

When we weren't working, Tim and I enjoyed going out together. We dated some, but often we would sit on the front porch and make up stories about these two old-maid sisters who never married because they couldn't find husbands capable of pulling off a proper wedding extravaganza: a circus where the bride and groom would swing in on the flying trapeze and the ceremony would be performed in bumper cars; or an opera scene where the vows were sung as an aria. The end of our story would be that the old maids, now in their eighties, were still sitting on the front porch, rocking and laughing at all the men they never married.

Tim and I performed in the Tehachapi state prison, discovering that we were still a good duet. But we struggled to find material appropriate for a predominantly black, Latin, and poor white audience. We decided nothing was appropriate because prison is not appropriate. So we sang the songs we knew and hoped it brought a little temporary relief.

It was a wonderful day when we moved into the main part of the house. Jenny and Jimmy were good neighbors. When Jenny and Jimmy decided to get married, they asked me to sing "Let It Be" at the ceremony. Later, Jimmy started working with Kenny Loggins. I enjoyed sitting outside on hot summer days listening to Jimmy and Kenny practice their vocals upstairs.

Those were nice days, but since neither Timothy nor I were becoming movie stars, we moved into a less expensive apartment. One morning, I woke up exceptionally early. Tim was away and my brother, Fred, was visiting. I heard the birds chattering madly. I fell back to sleep, but a few minutes later the apartment started to rock and roll. I jumped up and ran into the other room to see if Fred was okay. Things were falling off the walls and off the shelves. I turned on the radio to find out what to do when there is a major earthquake. The DJs were making such useful emergency announcements as "Holy shit!"

My old friend Patricia came to visit from New York. She was still playing mysterious, sexy parts in films but getting bored with it. We drove up one of those L.A. canyons to have brunch. It had become a favorite Sunday-morning tradition for me, a nice place to take friends to pick through the newspaper calendar section with all the other working and unemployed actors.

Looking across at this beautiful woman, I remembered how much I had loved her. But it wasn't until that night in New York City, back when I was doing *The Magic Garden of Stanley Sweetheart,* that I realized how complicated it could be to love a woman.

Sal Mineo and several of the guys from *Fortune and Men's Eyes* had come to visit me in my usually empty apartment. After they all left, Patricia and I sat on my bed, glowing and exhilarated. We had talked about homosexuality before—I from a rather intellectual perspective and she from a more curious, personal one. She thought it might be fun to have a threesome with a man and a woman. I think the

54

man was thrown in for safety's sake, and she wanted to come out to me—or to herself.

That night, however, she asked if I wanted to make love. Why not throw myself into the situation with natural curiosity and affection? I did not have a better friend than Patricia. We were a pair to look at—she, mysterious urban; and me, wide-open country. But I guess I wasn't as wide open as I thought. I turned to ice.

My rejection of our love hurt us. We stayed friends and took a wonderful vacation together in Hawaii. Patricia went on to do a film in Asia, and I decided to stay in Hawaii for a few days. I had heard of a collective on one of the smaller islands, living simply, eating fish and fruit. I thought I might visit with them for a day or two. I woke up in the middle of the night, startled, sweating, an inner voice saying, "Don't go. You will never come back!" I packed my bags and headed for the airport in my little red convertible rent-a-car to catch the first plane back to the mainland. I would return to Hawaii but under very different circumstances.

It was good to see Patricia again. She had a lover now, a woman I'd introduced her to. Driving to the canyon café, I had to ask her to pull over. I stepped out of the car, threw up, and got back in. "Car sick," I said. "Drive slower."

Four days later the nausea continued. When the doctor called me into his office, I knew the truth from the look on his face: "You're pregnant." I laughed. My laughter masked complex feelings of disgust, anger, and cynicism. Why me? I had spent one night with a man after nearly a year of being celibate. I had an IUD, which caused me unimaginable amounts of pain for two weeks out of every four. There had not been love. It was a mistake.

At the time, California law required a woman to have a letter from a shrink saying that the birth would be physically or emotionally damaging to the woman's health in order to have an abortion. The clinic provided the whole package—an improvement over a coat hanger in a back alley but still a long step from freedom of choice. It was 1970— three years before _Roe_ v. _Wade_ and a decade before the right wing would start to use the abortion issue to attack women, people of color, progressives, and the poor.

"It is your half hour," he said. "What would you like to talk about. Do you have any concerns about having an abortion?" He was a young doctor who volunteered one night a week at the clinic. "No," I said, my mind running over a phone call to my folks the night before.

They expressed no shock, only concern and love. It's very reassuring to have parents who are not so arrogant about their own choices that they think they should impose them on their children. "No, I don't have any trouble with it," I told the doctor.

I knew that human beings disagreed about how we got here and what we should do while we're here. We were given the complex gifts of heart and soul and brain with which to formulate our own beliefs and make choices. I believed that growing in me was tissue with human potential, but not yet a person. I believed that, regardless, there were so many unplanned children in the world, it was a global responsibility to take care of the living. I believed I was the only one who could decide what to do in this case. I would make the best decision I knew how to make. That is all I would ask of myself. I did not include anyone in my decision, nor have I ever regretted my choice.

"Well, then, what do you want to talk about?" The doctor's gentle voice interrupted my thoughts. I took a deep breath. Why is sex so hard to talk about? I spit it out: "Tell me about orgasms. I can have orgasms when I touch myself, but not when I have sex with a man."

He gave me a basic lesson in body parts and said that intercourse was nature's way to procreate but that heightened sexual pleasure required experimentation and creativity. Then he told me a story. Imagine a little girl and a little boy. The little girl has her arms tied to her sides and the boy is allowed to run free physically. When she is eighteen, her arms are unbound and the world expects her to be as coordinated and muscular as the little boy. It is that way with sex. Most boys are encouraged to flaunt their sexual prowess even though they may not be comfortable with it. However, girls are taught to hide sexuality, to pretend it doesn't exist. They are denied information about their bodies. Some aren't told to expect a period and are terrified when they start to bleed. They are punished for feeling desire. In some cultures the clitoris is removed to make sure there is no pleasure. If a girl experiments with a boy, he is considered normal and she is considered trash. Then, when she "becomes" a woman, she is expected to be a skilled, confident, informed lover overnight. Not fair. But women enjoy a mature and explosive sexuality after men have started to grow weary and insecure. The best is yet to come. He was right.

Timothy and I joined an organization called the Entertainment Industry for Peace and Justice. The impact of the Vietnam War had finally begun to jar Hollywood out of the devastating political silence that had been imposed during the blacklist era. Before the persecution of liberal and leftist artists during the so-called McCarthy period of the late forties and early fifties, entertainment-industry progressives had been active in such organizations as the Hollywood Democratic Committee and the Hollywood Independent Citizens Committee of the Arts, Sciences, and Professions. The EIPJ was organized in that tradition, attempting to regain a public voice for socially concerned artists. Some of the supporters were sincerely concerned about the war. Others were unemployed actors who thought they might get a break in one of the peace shows. I thought of the WPA and the wonderful murals that used to cover the walls of post offices across America. *Why can't we put our people to work?* I wondered.

The EIPJ meetings were spirited and ambitious. That was where Timothy and I first heard Jane Fonda speak about an antiwar show called FTA (Free the Army). She had been doing the tour for GIs and servicewomen all over the United States. Of course, why hadn't I thought of that? I had been concerned about guys my age getting drafted. Girls were getting recruited as well—a tall, handsome woman had come into gym class and talked to us about the fun, travel, and adventure we could have in a military career. To some of the girls, this was a perfect escape from difficult domestic situations. No one told them that they would run into sexism, racism, and homophobia in the service, or that if they were stationed in Indochina they would see blood, death, torture, and hardship beyond belief. They didn't tell the boys that the odds of coming back whole—if at all—were pretty slim. My brother had asthma and a high lottery number, but I was adamant that if he was drafted he should go to Canada and I would go with him.

In 1966, I had argued with my summer-camp boyfriend when Johnson sent more troops to Vietnam. My boyfriend thought it was necessary to defeat Communists. He didn't even know what communism was, but he thought it was the patriotic duty to die fighting it. I said communism was not the opposite of democracy but of capitalism. Tyrannical dictatorship was the opposite of democracy. The United States was in Indochina for economic reasons, not moral ones. He disagreed but got a student deferment anyway. It was mostly poor kids who would go and die for their country. Later, my boyfriend did volunteer to go into the service but stayed out of Vietnam by serving in the trumpet section of the military band. I'm glad he was in the band instead of at the front. I wish all the soldiers had been in the band.

I thought Jane's antiwar show was an amazing idea. Many peace activists saw soldiers as the enemy. Here was a group of entertainers and organizers working closely with legal workers defending soldiers' rights. They were going to the source. Who fights the wars? Soldiers. Who suffers the losses? The soldiers, their families, and the people they attack. Who pays for the war? Citizens. Communication between citizens and soldiers was a powerful idea. Jane's own political development had been encouraged by soldiers who were against the war.

The soldiers were getting organized. There had been massive demonstrations on the *Constellation* and other battleships. Fragging was not an uncommon practice in the jungles of Vietnam. At one point there were thousands of servicepeople in stockades in the Pacific for resisting war. There was also a growing Black movement within the forces, demanding rights that were consistently denied. The makeup of the military in Vietnam was different than in World War II. In fact, at first the Vietnam peasants thought they were fighting a Black country because so many of the soldiers were Black.

The FTA show (it also stood for Fun, Travel, and Adventure, or Fuck the Army) made soldiers laugh and cry at material that objected to war, racism, and sexism rather than perpetuating them. The show was produced by Jane Fonda, Donald Sutherland, and Francine Parker, and during its ten months of existence included such performers as Dick Gregory, Peter Boyle, Country Joe McDonald, and Jules Feiffer.

Although the FTA tour was originally put together to take to Vietnam, the Pentagon refused permission. While that decision was being fought in court, the FTA performers played fifteen cities around the United States and won an Obie Award for their Off-Broadway performance in New York City. The show was not allowed on military bases, but was performed to more than fifteen thousand GIs on sites outside Fort Bragg, Fort Ord, Fort Lewis, Mountain Home Air Force Base, Fort Hood, Fort Sam Houston, and the San Diego Naval Station. The FTA material was based on stories and sentiments culled from the more than seventy-five GI newspapers published by extramilitary GI projects in the U.S. and around the world. I was envious. How lucky the artists in this show were to be able to mix art and politics and do something that was affecting peoples' lives.

Then I got a call from a friend who said a cast member had dropped out and they needed a quick-study replacement before the tour went to the Pacific. I went over to Jane's house to audition. The entire cast was busy preparing for the trip and I was immediately put to work writing out itineraries and buying long underwear for the snowy weather in Japan. The tour was going to Hawaii, the Philippines,

Japan, and Okinawa. Finally, around five o'clock, someone brought in sandwiches and Jane said to me, "Okay, now, what can you do?" The cast taught me one of the song-and-dance numbers, and we read through one of the comedy skits. They had asked me a few political questions throughout the day—they didn't so much interview me as ask my opinion; for example, they invited me to sit in on a discussion about whether John Lennon and Yoko Ono's offer to join us should be accepted. Would it turn the show into a media event? Although Jane and Don were stars, they played against it, trying to avoid glitter and star-type hierarchy. (John and Yoko offered to wear bags over their heads!) My actual audition took about thirty minutes and, seeing that I could sing, dance, and be funny, they said, "Great, here's your script."

I telephoned my parents and we talked into the middle of the night about my going to the Philippines. I had never been out of the United States before and I knew very little about the Philippines. The culture was completely unfamiliar to me. I understood that I had to anticipate trouble—Marcos trouble, martial law, the CIA, and the U.S. military. I had to ask, "Is this worth the risk of never coming back?" and I thought, *Well, I could walk out the door to see a movie tonight and get hit by a truck and never have even seen the Philippines, or the movie!* I began to learn the dance steps.

The FTA show was directed by Francine Parker and written by cast members, with additional material by Robin Menken and a piece from Dalton Trumbo's *Johnny Got His Gun*. It was filmed and later released by American International, which, strangely enough, was the company that had done my first film, *Angel, Angel, Down We Go*. Its cast included Michael Alaimo, a Brooklyn-born actor, comic, and veteran of the San Francisco Mime Troupe; folk singer/songwriter Len Chandler; actress and poet Pamala Donegan; Rita Martinson, the singer and composer who wrote "Soldier, We Love You" for the show; Paul Mooney, a veteran stand-up comic who had worked with the Second City Players in San Francisco; actors Jane Fonda and Donald Sutherland; and myself. Musical accompaniment was provided by pianist/composer Yale Zimmerman.

The FTA troupe warmed up for its overseas venture with a big benefit concert at the Philharmonic in New York City featuring Nina Simone, and a show for GIs outside Fort Dix. On November 24, 1971, the entourage—including a cast of four men and four women (four black and four white), a director, a film crew, a road crew, a nurse, and a press agent—boarded a plane in Washington, D.C., bound for

Hawaii. The entire trip was an education for me. I learned lessons about racism, women, class, music, imperialism, and danger. Naïve at the start, I found I was quite alert and had good instincts.

The tour landed first in Hawaii and met with farmers, women's groups, GIs, and local Hawaiian activists. I hadn't realized the true nature of the relationship between the United States and Hawaii. We met a pig farmer whose family had lived in Hawaii for several generations and was being forced off his land on Oahu. Housing developers were gobbling up the property and attempting to move small farmers to the big island. Since corporate farming was displacing family operations, such small farmers as George Santos were losing their social and economic role. Consequently, food had to be imported. Whether of Japanese, Korean, European, or indigenous Hawaiian descent, the local population was being forced into service jobs, from tour guides to waiters to nightclub performers. Not only was Hawaiian culture being grotesquely exploited but the orientation of people was being altered, and a rich, self-sufficient island was becoming dependent on the mainland.

GIs were being sent from the battleground in Vietnam to Hawaii for "rest and recuperation." They were told, "Oh, you're going to Hawaii to lie in the sun, drink wonderful rum drinks, and the beautiful Hawaiian women will welcome you." But when they arrived, they were welcomed only by military personnel and prostitutes. Many of the guys were shell-shocked. They were used to turning on a dime, pulling a gun, and shooting to kill the moment they heard a twig crack. They had been conditioned to mistreat Vietnamese women. They transferred their hostility to Hawaiian women, creating a great deal of tension between the locals and the soldiers. That was the beginning of my first trip out of the United States, and it was a microcosm of the impact of economics, sexism, imperialism, and cultural disruption, all laid out in a vivid picture . . . right there in someone else's paradise.

The Philippines were not prominent in North American people's consciousness in 1971, although Ferdinand Marcos's regime had long been important to U.S. strategy in the Far East. Before the FTA troupe arrived in the Philippines, its members had agreed to conduct group press conferences so that we could present a unified front and avoid all the attention being focused on Jane and Donald. When we landed in the Philippines, we were met by a huge press corps. I was still begging off participating because many of the questions were way over my head. I didn't even know what the military-industrial complex *was*, so I would sit in the back and hope that I didn't have to say anything.

Free the Army

Cameras were clicking and questions were flying. I was terribly excited. Then a disembodied voice from the press called out, "Miss Near." Adrenaline shot right up my back to the top of my head. I stood up nervously and said, "Yes," and he asked, "How do you think traveling with Miss Fonda is going to affect your career." *My career, I thought, my career? What is this man talking about?! I've made a couple of bad movies.* So I asked him what career he was referring to. As it turned out, my grade B movies had been playing in the Philippines and, unbeknownst to me, I was a movie star. I felt embarrassed. This wasn't how I wanted to be seen in the world. Nor was it how I wanted life in the United States to be perceived. I was sad to discover that some of our worst films and music were being exported and young kids there were buying it. The weight of this discovery never left me.

I have referred back to this moment often over the years when facing my responsibilities as an artist: rewriting the words to the song "Old Time Woman," changing words that were demeaning to old people; becoming aware of the use of blindness as a poet's metaphor for ignorance; noticing how many folk songs have a jealous man murdering his love and throwing her into a river; evaluating the manner in which art is presented as well as the content; trying to read the effect a piece is having on the audience in order to improve the presentation. Even as a child I knew the power of art, but it was becoming more clear how its power could be used against a people as well as for a people. A lullaby can put a child to sleep. However, Muzak can be used to put a whole nation to sleep. Music can rouse people and inspire action. But witness the use of the brass band to call men and women to war. And so I return to his question. How will this work with Jane Fonda affect my career? Completely.

The symbols of U.S. cultural imperialism were everywhere, from Foremost ice cream to rock 'n' roll. Driving into the mountains in the Philippines, we reached the crest of a hill, then headed down into a valley. There, looming over the rice fields, was a giant cardboard Coca-Cola bottle. The FTA show was designed to satirize just those aspects of U.S. culture and ideology and to present alternative perspectives on the policies that the armed forces were being asked to implement.

One of our skits shocked me at first, although the GIs thought it was extremely funny. The skit was about fragging. What the hell was fragging? Everybody in that audience knew. Stories had come back from the front about units that apparently had an agreement with the Vietnamese that neither would shoot first. They would sit on one side of the river and the Vietnamese on the other. If a newly arrived commanding officer ordered them into battle, the unit refused and told him to relax. If he insisted, his tent might accidentally blow up that night. That was fragging. Yet reports were sent back that the battles were going fine and the GIs were winning.

In one song-and-dance number, Jane and I were dressed as "the military-industrial complex," which I now was beginning to understand. Jane was big business and I was the military. We sang, "Nothing could be finer than to be in Indochina making money." The audience loved to watch Jane clown. She was good at it too. I was supposed to sing two musical solos, but I had a hard time finding the right material. I tried to sing John Lennon's "Imagine," but I found singing about a world without countries inappropriate for the Filipinos who were not only fighting for their country, but for their very lives. At one gathering I sang, "I'm gonna lay down my sword and shield . . ." I looked up and this Filipino woman had tears streaming down from her eyes. After I was done she said, "You know, it would be great if someday we had the option to sing a song like that, but if we lay down our sword and shield, we'll be run over." This was the beginning of a lifelong dialogue I would have with myself about pacifism and armed struggle.

Two of the songs I sang were already in the FTA script. They were both feminist songs. I was completely unprepared for this, as my own feminism was underdeveloped. In fact, I had recently been heard saying, "Feminism is all right for those women who need it, but not for me. I am a strong, independent, working woman!" Little did I know how strong a woman had to be to identify herself as a feminist! But I was a professional actress, and I played my part, and my part in the script was that of a feminist.

I thought the soldiers would object to the feminism in the show, but they related to it. They were feeling one down too, and when all four women in the show sang Beverly Grant's "Tired of Fuckers Fucking Over Me," they gave us a standing ovation. I also sang another Beverly Grant song: "I Can't Be Yours and Still Be Me."

The women of the FTA show were all feminists, but they had come to it through different doors. Before the tour had left for the Pacific, there was a women's luncheon for all the women from the cast and the road and film crews who were going on the trip. Some called for an agreement among all the women that none of us would sleep with any of the men while on the tour. I was astounded that this was being discussed and that women would even consider making such a pact. I didn't understand it, but I sat quietly. I knew that I was in for some lessons. They explained that on previous tours, men had vied for women's attention and had played the women against each other, creating a lot of bad feelings.

There was very little energy spent on sexual positioning and partnering, although there was an affair or two. It is not surprising that the song "More Important to Me" was included in my first album in 1972.

It's more important to me that we stay friends
It's more important to me that we make amends
So if he's the man that you're after
That I can understand
It's more important to me that we don't fight because of a man.

The most dramatic lessons about women's roles and feminist consciousness, however, were to be learned from women in the countries visited by the FTA show. As we got off the bus in one city, the first person to greet us was a little girl who looked like she was only about eight or nine years old. She approached Paul, lifted her skirt, and said, "Peace, man." We all froze for a moment while Paul explained who we were and why we were there. The little girl did not show much interest. She wanted money. In Subic Bay, we had a very hard time finding a hotel because the rooms were rented only by the hour. We ended up negotiating something with a hotel owner and paying high rates in order to be able to stay there overnight. I was in a room that had a small bed and a pair of buttons. If you pushed one button you'd get drinks, and if you pushed the other button you'd get a girl. I sat on the bed for a long time, feeling sick to my stomach. I kept thinking of the women and soldiers who passed through this room. The soldiers were kids, younger than me, and I was only twenty-one. The women were peasants, the daughters of farmers who had lost their land to the military base (which, I recall now, had a golf course for the officers), and they had no way to make a living to raise their families. I was the daughter of a farmer.

Later in the day, we met with a group of prostitutes who had organized themselves and were part of a coalition of Filipino revolutionaries. They would greet men coming off the ships, sleep with them, be paid for a service, and talk to them about the GI movement, about how it was not good for them or for the Filipino people to have U.S. bases in the Philippines. The women used part of the money to support their families and the other part to support the revolution. I went to sleep that night feeling the power and the courage of these women, these farmers' daughters, these prostitutes, these revolutionaries.

Touring with a group of people from diverse ethnic, cultural, and political backgrounds made me aware of how differently people perceive life. One time we were guests at a restaurant and were served a big buffet. Afterward some of the people in our group noticed that there were a lot of kids on the street with their noses pressed up against the window. They took the leftover food out to them. The restaurant owner was furious because he usually put the food back in the pot and sold it again; we were giving away food he didn't think was ours to give. Our Filipino host said, "How can we teach our children to grow up and be revolutionaries if you teach them to take handouts from colonialists?" Some of the cast were angry and said that it is a terrible thing to be hungry and that kids should not be the tools of revolution. You feed them first and talk about colonialism later. I didn't know what I thought.

Traveling in the Philippines meant not falling out of favor with the Marcos family government. We had to have lunch with a relative of Ferdinand Marcos in order to stay in the country. He wasn't really interested in our group—he wanted the prestige of having lunch with Jane. I sat next to her and he sat on the other side. Every once in a while she would reach over and squeeze my hand and turn back to him and force a smile. We knew what Marcos and his "followers" were doing to the citizenry, but this was the price we had to pay for our visas. Later that day we met with the legal-aid workers who had been facilitating meetings between the soldiers and the local Filipino political organizations supporting the GI movement, counseling and defending the GIs who resisted going to Vietnam.

The tour attracted not only GIs who wanted to see the show but the nervous attention of the military authorities as well. They made bumbling attempts to disrupt the performances. They would advertise our show at the wrong place and the wrong time to confuse the men. But we would wait. Someone would direct the crowd to where we were. The show went on late, but it went on. In Manila, two GIs from Clark Air Force Base were discharged within seventy-two hours of meeting the FTA at a press conference. In Subic Bay, home of the Seventh Fleet, the USS *Coral Sea,* due to sail in on the day FTA arrived, was kept outside the bay, and the USS *Chicago* sailed out twenty-four hours ahead of schedule so that the men couldn't meet with us.

Free the Army

We did concerts in a bullring, on a floating stage, in a field, in a theater. We moved the sets, the costumes, the props, the lights, the sound, the film equipment . . . setting it up, taking it down, moving on to the next site. We attended a rally at a university in Manila. I looked up and saw Marcos's soldiers with machine guns on the rooftops. I'd never had a gun pointed at me before.

Sometimes GIs would pull us aside and give us information about their work, then disappear into the crowd. One man said they were backdating death certificates and changing the cause of death, trying to keep the death count down in Vietnam.

In Olongapo, an all-Black meeting was arranged. Rita learned to do the sound for the film since we didn't have a Black sound technician. One soldier said he shot off his own foot so that he could return to "the world." He had been sent to Nam because he wouldn't cut his hair. The Black GIs said they were called "boy" or "nigger" all the time, and if they replied they were sent to the brig. They could be busted for doing the Black handshake, but if whites did it they were "cool." At another time, Black soldiers explained the handshake—the dap—to us . . . four slaps for four hundred years of oppression.

In Manila, during one of my solos, I introduced myself as being from a small town in California. Out of the darkness a voice answered me. It was a Potter Valley storekeeper's little boy.

From the Philippines, FTA was scheduled to go to Japan, but the show was turned back at the airport. Japan barred our entrance and we got a lot of press. First they put us in a holding room, and then, when they didn't approve our visas, they put us up overnight in a hotel, bused us back to the airport, and sent us away.

We altered our itinerary and went next to Okinawa, where the military high commissioner, General Lampert, put the island on condition green, which meant that all military personnel had to be off the streets by six P.M. and during the day could only be in closed vehicles going to or from base. The order effectively barred the soldiers from seeing us. At the time, the people who worked on the army bases, most of whom were Okinawan, were on strike, demanding minimal increases in what were already very low wages. FTA members joined the picket lines and sang labor and solidarity songs with the strikers. While walking around with a new Okinawan friend, we saw kids coming down the road, swinging something, playing, and I asked, "What are they doing?" He said, "Those are hearing aids." The children came over from the island, Iwo Jima, where pilots still did cannister-bombing practice runs. The bombing went on twenty-four hours a day, and many of the people who lived there went deaf. They sent their kids over to mainland Okinawa to go to school and get hearing aids.

The FTA was finally able to enter Japan after successfully negotiating cultural visas for the performers and crew. The press almost killed us trying to get to Jane, "the sex goddess." Then they wrote half their reports about how "sexless" she was. The show was not permitted on a single base in Japan. Nonetheless, the FTA continued to perform for and meet with GIs off-base.

In Hiroshima, the cast toured the museum that memorializes the tragedy of the atomic bomb. We learned that Hiroshima had been picked as the target because of the weather—the sky was blue over Hiroshima that day. I came out of the museum feeling overwhelming guilt.

Our Japanese host reminded me that I wasn't even alive yet when the bomb was dropped. He said that I couldn't be responsible for that which had gone before, but could look around and see what was happening in my own time. Vietnam was my Hiroshima.

Once again, soldiers approached the FTA members with stories that were not being disseminated by the press back in the United States. While Nixon and the Japanese government were assuring the public that the United States had no nuclear weapons in Japan, soldiers told us that they themselves were moving nuclear weapons through the country, all in secret and all illegal.

By no means did all the soldiers approve of us. In one city, a GI blues band asked if they could come onstage and play. When those men walked onstage, the other GIs loved seeing their own guys up there. I sang a couple of songs with them. The next morning we heard that the musicians had been beaten bloody on the snowy streets by prowar fellow soldiers.

At one show, Don Sutherland was onstage reading his monologue from Dalton Trumbo's *Johnny Got His Gun,* and suddenly these big, burly guys came up onstage. I don't know how they got past security, but there they were, yelling disjointed insults. It looked like war was imminent between the FTA cast and the U.S. military. We came out onstage to be with Donald. It was revealing to watch our different reactions. Donald and Jane became very verbal and very calm, trying to talk to these guys. Some of the cast reached for weapons, Coke bottles, hair picks, quietly preparing for battle. Others started to lead the audience in song. You could tell which street corner each person had grown up on. I joined Len Chandler in singing "Move on Over, or We'll Move on Over You," which Len had adapted to "The Battle Hymn of the Republic." Soon, unsolicited and unorganized, GIs from around the hall just stood up and slowly moved onstage to stand between the cast and the angry soldiers. Outnumbered, our critics backed off. The program went on. Then one of the men started running around the back of the hall flashing a gun, threatening to shoot. Somehow our Japanese hosts got him out.

These hostile men moved me deeply. I wanted to say to them: "Look what's happening to you. We don't want this to happen to you. That's why we're here."

When we came back to the States, I continued my work with GIs and vets, learning from such Vietnam vets as Ron Kovic and Scott Camille. Americans felt uncomfortable around men who had been in Vietnam. For the most part, we didn't know much about the women who had been in Vietnam. The world still doesn't quite know how to handle "the Vietnam experience." I learned most of what I know about war from the soldiers in the GI movement. I thank them for that.

We continued on our journey across Japan. I watched women in the Japanese peace movement struggling to redefine their role as women, but determined to retain their culture. I think we were often arrogant and insensitive, imposing feminist conclusions on them. I understood this. I had felt a lot of "feminist conclusions" imposed on me as well. This women's-lib stuff was testing me to the core.

The FTA members were also constantly learning from one another.

Poet Pamala Donegan offered me a profound introduction to the Black American woman's experience of racism and sexism. Until then, my contact with Black people had been mostly with Black men— musicians and men I had met in the prison work. Pamala wrote powerful and relentless poetry, challenging and unforgiving. She dressed sharp, beaded her hair, and called me on my racism. I felt myself be hurt by her criticism rather than value it. I wasn't used to being accused of racism. That was for those other white people, from the South. I loved her and feared her.

Michael Alaimo was the first comic actor I had ever worked with whose face and body seemed to be able to go in several directions all at once. He talked about Marx, socialism, and class when he talked about Vietnam.

Yale Zimmerman brought his candles with him on the trip and

celebrated Hanukkah. He explained the traditions, the prayers, the symbols. I wondered if there had been many Jews in Ukiah and I just hadn't known. My sister Timothy had gone out with a guy named Jack Cohn. Kathy Zimmerman had been in the class before me. Why hadn't I known they were Jews? Why hadn't we celebrated their holidays and learned about their culture?

And then there was Jane. She was a superb teacher. She didn't even know that she was a teacher or that I was watching. She was doing everything she could to hang on. There was so much pressure on her for being famous, for being known as a sex symbol. Men were mad at her. We talked to soldiers who explained that they had pictures of her, virtually naked, hanging in their lockers. Now, all of a sudden, she's not a sex symbol, she's a person. The men who couldn't deal with her transition from being a dumb blonde to being an intelligent, outspoken feminist and activist tore her posters down. It made them angry and they didn't know why. Others, however, had taken those posters down and put up FTA posters. One soldier told us he had had an FTA poster in his room and was ordered to take it down. The officer said the FTA was opposed to the war; the soldier said, ''That's why I put it up.''

Over the years of my work with Jane, I listened to her do media, I watched her deal with people. I watched her jump into the deep end and learn to swim, not always gracefully but staying above water. I watched her become touched by an incident, and the next minute, when she was speaking to two thousand students, integrate that experience into her presentation. She learned how to tell real stories and gave up some of her early rhetoric, which she herself had only recently learned. Since then I've heard her say how she wished she hadn't used the rhetoric in the first place because it sounded silly coming out of her mouth. It did. But soon the work became her own. She took the world into her life and was at her best when she was telling stories from the heart.

She became the target of government surveillance and harassment. She had to live with highly organized campaigns against her as well as anonymous threats against her life. Both the FBI and the CIA monitored her activities as well as the activities of her child, Vanessa. Conservative politicians painted her as an ''anti-American dupe.'' When she visited Hanoi in 1972, some politicians called her trip an act of treason, although hundreds had made the trip before her. For some time, Jane was one of the most hated women in the world, and, simultaneously, one of the most loved.

Free the Army

Why did they pick her to call traitor? I think a lot of it had to do with her being a woman, a movie star, a sex symbol. She is passionate and very visible. This was not somebody who came back and just said the war is bad. This was somebody who poured her guts out in every American town. She was asked to go on television—on *Meet the Press* and *Face the Nation*—to debate theoreticians, historians, and political strategists. These men, their dry voices void of feeling, tried to convince the American people that this was a moral war, a valiant attempt to free the Indochinese from the Communist monster, when, in fact, U.S. interests had more to do with real estate, resources, drug running, and investments. Jane, her voice full of emotion, tried to encourage the American public to question the war. Is it rational to bomb a nation in order to save it? Does it make sense to imprison a people in order to free them? Why were Vietnamese women getting operations done on their eyes and breasts so that they could look more Western? Was this a war of liberation? Why did U.S. corporations build "tiger cages" for the Thieu regime prisons, little boxes to hold Vietnamese people suspected of opposing the government? What was the moral reasoning behind making antipersonnel weapons not strong enough to blow up a tire but big enough to blow off a child's foot? Where was the model of democracy we were presenting when the U.S. dropped tons of Agent Orange on Indochina? Who thought it was humane to destroy the ecosystem of an entire nation, creating even more hunger and despair? These were the questions Jane asked the American people as she traveled around the country. And she dared to offer some answers to the questions, answers that embarrassed the government and challenged U.S. foreign policy.

I will always value those lessons that I learned from Jane Fonda— her courage, her heart, her energy, her humor, her beauty. We may approach politics somewhat differently now, but she set many standards in my early development. When we worked together, I was for the most part "unknown." But she saw me as a friend, someone she could trust, who was paying attention and didn't need to be spoon-fed, who cared deeply, who after a long day would not need more from her than she had already given.

The FTA tour ended in December 1971. We got home before Christmas, which I spent with my family in Ukiah, pouring out the stories. As the New Year turned, I found myself sitting back in my L.A. apartment wondering what the hell was going to happen next.

5
IT COULD HAVE BEEN ME

I TRIED TO RETURN TO THE LIFE I HAD LEFT ONLY A FEW WEEKS before. Landing a part in *Slaughterhouse Five* helped, for it was a film with integrity, directed by George Roy Hill. I became seriously ill during the making of *Slaughterhouse*. Strep throat knocked me to my knees. I showed up for work every day and fell onto the cot they had there for me, feeling I would never get up again. Yet when the assistant director would call me to the set, energy from somewhere would fill my body and I would become the nagging daughter of Billy Pilgrim. The hospital scene—in which I had to learn from a doctor that my mother had died in her Cadillac—was technically difficult to film. We did dozens of takes. I had to react to the news of my mother's death each time, knowing I'd better get it right because if they finally got the technical part together, they would probably use the take. I played twelve years old and forty years old and all the years in between. They asked me to sing "Happy Birthday" without hitting any of the right notes. I got well fast and had a wonderful time working on that project, thrilled to finally be in a good film—not only a good film but an antiwar film.

The Partridge Family provided a different challenge. I played the part of a bright, scholarly high school girl (described in the breakdown as shy and homely—you know, any girl who is smart is probably homely!). Susan Dey, who played the eldest daughter in the family, encouraged my character to run for student body president against her brother, Keith, played by David Cassidy. The basic premise was brains versus beauty—not an unrealistic situation for high school kids. But the ending was atrocious. Keith wins, of course, but Gloria Goldstein

70

(interesting casting!), who should have come back at him and said, "Okay, I was shy and inexperienced but I have learned a lot doing this and I'm going to run against you next time and win!" instead went to the Partridge house in tears. Ma Partridge (Shirley Jones) comes to the door and asks, "What's the matter? Are you crying because you lost the election?" And good ol' Gloria has to say something like, "No, I'm crying for joy because with all the attention I got running for president, I just got asked out by the school-paper editor."

On the first day of shooting, I tried but failed to change the last line. I hated the thought of putting such a message out to all the thirteen-year-old girls from around the world who would watch this: "Don't worry about becoming the president, just go for the guy." The director said he wasn't authorized to change the script (which may or may not have been true), but he did let me read the line with a kind of bitter sadness, as if I were thinking, *I know this is what I'm supposed to say, but, boy, I'm not happy about it.*

Sometimes people see that episode on TV, not knowing it is a rerun (have I not aged in seventeen years?), and ask in a somewhat accusatory tone, "What were you doing on *The Partridge Family?*" I used to feel defensive. Now I just say, "What were you doing *watching The Partridge Family?!*"

I still hadn't assimilated the FTA experience. I would often wake in the middle of the night and sit up wondering, . . . *but, then, why is it that so many of the soldiers stationed in Vietnam are Black or Latin? . . . And why did I meet a Puerto Rican soldier fighting in the U.S. forces? Puerto Rico isn't a state. Are Puerto Ricans subject to U.S. draft?* I would jot down these thoughts so that I could remember to ask someone. Or in the middle of writing a chatty letter home I would go off on a tangent about how war affects women—in Vietnam, at home, all over the world; that maybe women's liberation was bigger than I had ever imagined; what would be the effects of global feminism? And what about the men? And what the hell did all this have to do with Gloria Goldstein and Keith Partridge?

I started to write songs. I wrote like I was on fire. All the material that would eventually end up on my record *Hang in There* came pouring out. I was trying to name the experience that had just completely changed my life. But I couldn't sit at the piano all day, so I volunteered some time at the downtown L.A. defense-committee office of the Pentagon Papers trial.

The office was in disarray, staffed by volunteers and always short of money. I looked around to see how to make myself useful. No one was sitting at the receptionist's desk and the phone was ringing. So I answered the phone and sat down. And stayed. As the days went by, I grew fond of the times when Dan Ellsberg, Tony Russo, Leonard Boudin, Stanley Sheinbaum, and Leonard Weinglass would pass through the office on their way to court, followed by young legal assistants who were not getting much sleep that year.

One day Tom Hayden walked in. I didn't know who he was. He introduced himself and said that Jane Fonda had suggested he come talk to me. He and Jane wanted to take a cultural and educational presentation across the United States to make the war in Indochina a major issue in the 1972 presidential campaign. They wanted me to help them develop the plan and take part in the tour. I took this to mean that Jane had respected my work on the FTA tour. This made me very happy. We went through many "what ifs" and "how abouts," which included ideas as big as a political circus and as small as Jane and Tom doing a speaking tour. We were most excited about forming an Indochina Peace Campaign that would not simply be a cultural tour but would become a national organizing campaign with regional and national headquarters. It would be run like a presidential campaign, but instead of running a candidate for president, we would be putting forth a concept—peace in Indochina. Tom, Jane, and I, along with road manager Ruby Ellen Lustbader, would be the spokespeople for the concept. We hit the road.

We did the tour twice, once in the fall of 1972, coinciding with the presidential campaign, and once a year later, for, despite Nixon's "secret plan," the war was still not over. Among the people who joined the tour from time to time were Dan Ellsberg, Ramsey Clark, and Dick Gregory. For the whole second tour we were joined by my longtime friend and piano player Jeff Langley, and a newborn baby boy named Troy Hayden.

I kept notes. I learned how to network. I studied the organizers who were effective and those who were not. I kept the names and numbers of people I would like to work with again. I watched the effect music had on an event, how it was used or abused, the craft of putting together a good program, and the lost opportunity when the order of the event was left to chance. I discovered an empty space and moved forward to fill it. With the support of Jeff's friendship and extraordi-

nary musicianship, I began to develop an audience and a unique singing career.

Day after day, city after city, we traveled, speaking/singing to
people about the war in Indochina. Jane showed slides from her trip,
and spoke of the Vietnamese people and their culture and of Vietnam
vets and their broken lives. Tom Hayden spoke of Laos and Cambodia,
providing updates and analysis, using the daily news as a starting
point. I sang songs I had written about the war and how it affected
American and Vietnamese people, putting forth a kind of progressive
patriotism. Sometimes Vietnamese students who were studying in the
United States would speak. The students were very brave, knowing
they could lose their visas and end up in the Saigon prisons they were
decrying. They spoke about torture in the U.S.-built "tiger cages" in
South Vietnam. There was no way to soften the blow of their information. They said the Thieu regime guards would play loud American
rock 'n' roll to drown out the screams. The guards would laugh,
"Where are your peacenik friends now? They can't hear you." The
Vietnamese students spoke so gently. Then I would sing a song Jeff
and I wrote specifically to help the audience through the horror. I had
known a singer could be a teacher. I was learning I could also be a
healer.

"Oh Come Smile with Us"

Take my hand
Or I may have to leave the room
Please end your story soon
It's not like me to run away
But I don't think that I can stay
To hear your story

Knowing your name
Ties my heart around each tortured cry
And you didn't die
Let me keep looking deep in your eyes
So I have no chance to break the ties
Though the cage is locked the spirit flies
The prison song escapes—the truth defies

Fire in the Rain ... Singer in the Storm

Oh come smile with us
It helps to make the days seem less like years
Oh come smile with us
Smile beneath your tears

Don't turn away
There are things in life my heart must know
Though feelings tell me go, hurry go
Words that startle my waking dreams
But if you have lived it then it seems that I must hear it

Feeling your hand resting on my shoulder to ease the pain
To ease my shame
Have we forgotten or is it just too hard to feel
Protecting tenderness with steel
And with the rarest kind of smile you help me heal

Oh come smile with us
It helps to make the days seems less like years
Oh come smile with us
Smile beneath your tears

We traveled for nine weeks with only one day off and three to five events a day. At night I would dream: *We were sitting in the lobby of what they called the movie room, Jane and I and one or two other North Americans. The rest were Vietnamese. I knew what the movie room was—a torture chamber that was quickly turned into a theater when human-rights observers came to inspect the prison. Jane took my hand and quietly reminded me of things to do in order to get through it—how to breathe, what to think about, what to remember. I squeezed her hand. The door opened and a guard appeared to call in the next victim. . . .* I woke up.

I was lonely. The work was hard, the pressure high, and sometimes I just needed to be held. I wrote letters home to my boyfriend, Michael, in Ukiah and looked forward to sleeping with him out under the stars, when I got home. I didn't want to have affairs on the road; it didn't seem dignified. We usually stayed in people's homes and I wouldn't have felt comfortable having my affairs so closely observed. I felt sex was a private thing.

I focused on the work—trying to find a reasonable role to play in Jane and Tom's shadow; trying to learn the million lessons handed to me each day, regardless of whether I had energy to accept them; trying to keep my health together under the stressful schedule. On our day off I slipped and broke my elbow.

Still, we laughed a lot. Jane was trying to get pregnant. Most of the people planning the schedule didn't even know Jane and Tom were in a relationship, much less that they were in the midst of a serious timing crisis. They kept being scheduled to go to different towns after the last event of the day. It was hard to explain that they didn't want to be separated without coming right out and saying, "Look, we have to go to the same bed. We're in the process of making a baby in the middle of all this!"

Before the tour set out, I had tried to memorize all the appropriate names and historical events related to Indochina—French colonialism, the difference between the north and south, what was the PRG, U.S. policy-makers and military figures, battle dates and locations. I was learning about strategic thinking, germ warfare, psychological warfare, air strikes, and world economics. I'd never studied war before.

There were very few restful moments on the tour, but I do remember one lovely afternoon spent with Leonard Weinglass at the Washington zoo. The panda, a gift from the Chinese, had given birth and we went to see the new life. I had had a crush on Leonard since I first met him during the Pentagon Papers trial. He was exactly the kind of man my parents would have liked me to bring home. But I was very young and shy, so I didn't tell him I liked him until many years later after the crush had passed.

The tour was becoming more successful and controversial every day. We arrived in Rochester at the venue for the last presentation of the day. A group of people in the front row were holding up an effigy of Jane with a rope around her neck and a sign that read, WE HANG TRAITORS. Their rage was frightening. The auditorium was full to the back row of the balcony. The disrupters shouted every time Jane tried to speak. She asked me to sing, and she left the stage to go discuss the situation with Tom and security. Sing? I did. The screamers quieted. But the moment Jane returned they started up again. She tried to speak over them and couldn't. The crowd tried to shout them down, but that only created chaos.

I stayed on the stage with Jane, moving closer as the hostility mounted. She smiled at me and suggested another song while she went off to confer again. I noticed that some people in the balcony were leaving. I didn't want this disruption to be effective. But then I noticed that they weren't leaving at all. They had descended from the balcony and were walking down the aisle to the stage. As they got closer, I could see they were a group of young Puerto Ricans. They walked to the front row, stood in front of the hecklers, one-on-one, and said, "Sit down and be quiet or we're gonna sit on you!" The disrupters, all of whom were white, were afraid of the Puerto Ricans and sat down and were quiet. Jane walked on to see what was happening. The Puerto Ricans turned to her and said, "Now talk!" And she did.

We received a series of bomb threats while speaking on campuses. The halls, filled with students, would have to be evacuated so that a bomb team could sweep the building. No bombs were ever found, none ever exploded. Finally, Tom got annoyed. He felt quite sure it was just a disruptive tactic to keep the students from hearing the program. One day, he was in the middle of his talk when a representative from the university handed him a note saying a bomb threat had been called in and we had to stop the program. Tom told the audience of the threat but explained that he thought it was a scare tactic. He said that by law he had to advise the audience to leave, but that we were not leaving. Although we could not go on with the program, we would stay in the building and silently demonstrate our opposition to the war. He invited the students to join us at their own risk. Out of three to four thousand students, only a handful left. The rest of us sat there waiting for the nonexistent bomb to not go off.

George Smith, a former POW who traveled with us, made me laugh. George had been captured by the PRG in the southern part of Vietnam. He was an unlikely hero, a postman now living with his wife and family in West Virginia, opposed to the war. He said the Vietnamese sometimes gave the prisoners little treats for the holidays, so the prisoners tried to think of as many holidays as possible: birthdays, Valentine's Day, Columbus Day. In September, the prisoners told the guerrilla soldiers that they wanted to celebrate Labor Day. The soldiers laughed. "Oh no, we're not stupid. We know Labor Day is May first!" The POWs said, "No, really, it's September." Neither knew what the other was talking about. I doubt the POWs had ever heard of the Haymarket incident that led to International Workers Day celebrated on May 1.

It Could Have Been Me

Madison, Wisconsin, was a city of activists preserving a long tradition of midwestern radicalism. We arrived in the middle of a block party, and I got a sampling of the city's political exuberance that challenged my coastal chauvinism. The speeches were sharp and to the point. The dancing was wild and joyful. The political actions were diverse and complex, including a recent bombing of the university math building, which was known to be a focus for the development of antipersonnel weapons. David Armstrong and David Fine had watched the building for some time to make sure no one ever entered it at night. They weren't planning an attack on human beings, but rather on the institution that promoted the terror. Tragically, on the night of the bombing, a professor uncharacteristically entered his office to retrieve a file. He died in the blast.

Defenders of Armstrong and Fine's actions were present at the street fair, and I was confronted with a new moral dilemma. What did I think of the tactic? There was a war going on! Buildings got blown up during wars. I'd seen it in the movies. Was the war okay as long as it was kept neatly on someone else's land, disrupting other people's lives, not ours? Was it okay for Vietnamese and U.S. soldiers to die in the war but not college professors? But he was innocent. He didn't work on the antipersonnel weapons. Well, the Indochinese children are innocent too. War kills. War hurts. War is a horror. It is a horror in Hanoi. It is a horror in Saigon. It is a horror in Madison. I did not reach any conclusions overnight.

David Fine went underground. Years later, when he was facing trial, his defense committee asked me and Jeff Langley to do a benefit for court costs. We decided to judge the reason they had blown up the building rather than the tactic itself, realizing that it's hard to know what is a reasonable response to genocide. I did not believe in violence or destruction. I did understand Fine and Armstrong's need to find a response proportionate to the destruction going on every day in Indochina. As some activists were pointing out, the government that was committing genocide in Indochina was the same government that was committing genocide in the United States against Native American leaders and Black Panther leaders. We did the benefit.

We faced a similar question when we supported Inez Garcia's case. She had been raped, and then later went out and killed her rapist. I did not believe in revenge killing, but I understood her desire to kill the man who had raped her. Once again we evaluated the crime that had caused the crime.

One day, several years later, a young man walked up to me and said, "Hello, I'm David Fine." This gentle, lovely man told me stories about how he had come to my concerts when he was underground, but, of course, he could never introduce himself. He said the music had helped him through that difficult time.

The first tour was winding down. It had been a huge success. I went home to Ukiah, and after telling stories of the journey to my family, I went to sleep, for days. My mother would bring me hot soup, which I would sip before drifting off to sleep again. I was so tired, I couldn't even cry when I heard that Nixon had bombed Hanoi. I could only sit in front of the winter fire, trying to get warm in the face of this news, listening to the wind outside in the redwood trees.

Back in L.A., I did a bit more film, television, and theater work— John Cassavetes's *Minnie and Moskowitz*, Norman Lear's *All in the Family*, an episode of *Mod Squad*, which we affectionately called "Three Little Pigs," and a few others, but my energy was going into political music and peace work. It was not the music of the sixties. It was not exactly folk music in any traditional sense. I didn't play the guitar and my singing style was a mixture of folk, pop, and musical theater. The lyrics and presentation were becoming more feminist-oriented, and I was finding a hungry audience.

The Ash Grove, a folk club in L.A., harbored the sounds of great folk and blues musicians. It was funky, but when the house filled up with a capacity crowd, the roof was raised. I started a mailing list at the shows so that I could let people know when and where I would be singing next. Jeff and I played there many times in a variety of double bills, including a night with Sonny Terry and Brownie McGhee and an all-day benefit concert where I sang in a trio with Linda Ronstadt (still barefoot in those days) and Maria Muldaur.

I learned how to invite music-industry people and press to my shows. David Braun, a well-respected entertainment lawyer who represented such performers as Bob Dylan and George Harrison, agreed to help me find a record deal. I cut demos for record companies, but I didn't know anything about the record business and apparently I was asking for the moon by industry standards.

Timothy, Jeff, and I performed at a benefit to save the Santa

Monica Pier. We wrote a song for the occasion and sang it as people went round and round on the beautiful merry-go-round. It was there I met Alex Hassilev of the Limeliters and his friend Julie Thompson, which led to the recording of my first album in his home studio. Julie became a long-term friend and co-producer of some of my early albums, and for a while, my manager.

It's not that I didn't want a major recording contract. I did. But I wanted to record the songs I had written after my experience with FTA and the first Indochina Peace Campaign tour. The majors didn't seem very interested in that material. They were interested that I was selling out the L.A. clubs. They were interested that I wrote good melodies and strong hook-lines but thought the lyrics too political. They were interested in my singing—although one label representative told David Braun that I wouldn't become a successful pop vocalist because there was no element of submission in my voice.

I decided to make an album of political songs and get it out of my system. I don't think I really had it in me to rock 'n' roll. But I might have made my way back to Broadway, or maybe, once country became more mainstream, I could have moved in that direction. But none of that happened. Instead, I quite innocently went dancing down a different path, made my own first record and started Redwood Records.

Had I been wiser, I would have traveled around to other alternative record companies to see how they were doing it. But I didn't really think I was forming a record company. I thought I was just making a record. I had received lots of letters from people who had heard me sing when I traveled with Jane and Tom. They wanted to use one song for a church program, another for a radio documentary, another in a school presentation, another as part of a thesis. I was making homemade tapes—singing a cappella into a small tape recorder—and sending them out to these dear hearts who wanted my songs to help them do their work.

I didn't think making a record would be so hard. High school bands and summer camps made records. I'd made those little direct-to-disk records for Grandma when I was a kid. But now I had to form a business. I went down to the Board of Equalization and applied for a business license. I took out an ad in the *Ukiah Daily Journal* announcing my fictitious business name—Redwood Records—named for the beautiful trees of Mendocino County. Mom and Dad agreed to be the "home office"—the mail-order address on the albums.

Jeff and I began to practice, planning a piano-and-voice record. Before we knew it, we were arranging a bass part here, a violin line there, and some background voices, which my sisters added. The little record grew and grew. We called it *Hang in There,* after one of the songs I had written for the Vietnamese. I learned all the steps as I went along: arranging, recording, overdubbing, mixing, sequencing, mastering, pressing, artwork, and all the paperwork for royalties, taxes, and insurance. Dad set up some simple bookkeeping for us. Mom organized a system for packing and shipping on the long sawhorse table that was still in the family. She also helped me put together the mailing list I had been gathering over the years. When the record arrived, we were so happy with our new ''baby.'' We didn't think about having a record company, but we had a record!

While the factory had been pressing, I had been busy finding other club work for Jeff and me. In addition to the Ash Grove, we developed a nice audience at the Icehouse in Pasadena, the Troubadour in West Los Angeles and McCabe's in Santa Monica, where I always had unique opening acts, one a handsome singer named Al Jarreau and another strange fellow named Tom Waits! We played a few gay clubs. For that, I put together a more cabaret-type show, but I couldn't resist standing up onstage in my long gown and singing ''No More Genocide in My Name.'' Audiences would sit silently, then explode in applause, and I knew it was wrong ever to make assumptions about people's responses. I had to learn to dare to be me despite advice to the contrary. I began to look for concert opportunities outside the L.A. area. Maybe I could do a national tour, perhaps not as big as IPC—I wasn't Jane Fonda—but I was willing to start small.

Friends kept advising me to give up the political material, assuring me I could be a big star if I would sing commercial songs. However, they, with their commercial songs, were unemployed and I, with my political songs, was working.

As summer arrived, Jeff and I were invited to the Placerville Fair. Jeff arranged material for the Placerville High School band, which had just returned from Europe after winning a state band competition. We would rehearse with the band and do two performances at the fair. We left Ukiah in a tiny four-seater airplane, our parents watching nervously as we loaded in our luggage, amplifiers, and instruments.

Whenever I worked with Jeff, it was more than the music. He made room in the rehearsal space for me not only to work on dynamics but to pause and explain the word *genocide* to one curious young musician. Placerville was a right-wing, Republican-dominated area, and we were there with a certain understanding that we would not be too political. I wanted to answer the child's question in a way so that when the story was repeated at home, we wouldn't have a swarm of parents on our heads the next morning. There were several ways to answer. *Webster's* says genocide is "the systematic killing of a whole people or nation." But I went on to describe how the Europeans who landed in the Western Hemisphere—what is now known as the Americas—killed off most of the indigenous people in the race for natural resources, land, and wealth. And that it hadn't stopped. When groups of people are "in the way" of expansion, they are systematically "removed." When women are economically strangled, humiliated, ignored, put in mental hospitals, administered drugs, beaten, raped, and accused of being immoral and unfit, that is not called genocide; it is called misogyny and sexism. It was a lot to hand to kids. But I had loved that kind of talk when I was sixteen, so I decided not to be patronizing. The kids were great and the parents did not come storming down.

Marianne Schneller, whom I'd met in Ohio while on tour with Jane and Tom, had since moved to California and was working as my assistant. I liked that she was a Judy Garland fan. She came to Placerville to help out. We were all put up at the fair board director's house, girls in one room, boys in another. The director probably thought that was morally correct for young people. What he didn't know was that one night on our double mattress Marianne leaned over and kissed me. She meant it to be a warm and lovely kiss between friends that left the door open if there was more than that. She knew she was kissing a straight woman and I knew she was a lesbian kissing a straight woman. I felt the ice come over me like it had with Patricia. Marianne didn't push it but I was left wondering why I felt so cold. What was wrong with me?

We did a wonderful show and everyone's parents—including ours, who drove over to see us—were very proud. The child behind the tuba was a shining star of discipline. Jeff stepped in front of "his band" and lifted his baton to begin the overture in the Broadway tradition. I sang pop songs, peace songs, country songs, feminist songs, and a great medley of old jazz standards. We blended love songs (pronounless where possible), political material, and funny personal stories. We received several standing ovations. Jeff and I were taking a giant step into a career we couldn't even begin to imagine.

That night, Jeff and I drove back to Ukiah, worn out but happy. We talked for hours of our future work together as the car sped through the night. I decided to have Jeff take me to Michael's instead of home. It would be fun to surprise him in his bed at dawn. Michael lived up on a hill. He planned to build a cabin soon, before winter set in, but for now he had a tent and a wonderful bed hung between two trees. The night skies were magnificent, making it hard for me to close my eyes for fear I would never see such stars again. Soft breezes and lovemaking rocked the bed gently. In the mornings we were burned out of bed by the bright sun.

Jeff left me off on the mountainside. The last quarter-mile up the hill had to be made on foot. I grabbed the huge bouquet of flowers that the high school band had given me and headed up the hill. It was a dreamy walk, through the mist that was rising to let in the dawn. My whole body was tired. I couldn't wait to take off my wilted clothes and relax into Michael's warm and naked body. As I came close to the top of the hill, I felt a strange sensation. I was out of breath, but not from the climb. Something was wrong. I paused to listen. Maybe there was a wild animal crossing the path above. There was motion, but I couldn't place it. I walked on. I could see Michael's bed now.

I backed away quietly, unseen by the lovers in the beautiful bed that was swaying in the wind. When I reached the road, I laughed until I cried and cried until I laughed again. It was five-thirty in the morning. I was ten miles away from town or a telephone. I was dressed in fancy white clothes with a bouquet of flowers in my hand. I began to walk down the hill, my hair flying behind me. I'd gone about two miles when I heard the sound of a Volkswagen, and I hitched a ride.

Humiliation hurts, but commitment is frightening. Michael and I had never agreed on monogamy. I was on the road a lot. It was hard to find a man who would wait at home for a career woman to return. Michael and I had a good time when I was home. He was a good dancer and we could spend the whole night happily at a country bar. But I was starting to read more feminist literature. I didn't know what to think. And there was this new sensation I was beginning to feel at the most unexpected and untimely moments.

Rage.

It Could Have Been Me

Then I hurt my back lifting a railroad tie while helping him build his cabin. I went to doctors, surgeons, back specialists, neurologists, holistic healers, and chiropractors. I was impatient and wanted this "fixed" before my upcoming tour. I spent a couple of weeks in traction at the hospital, where I took up knitting and became a TV junkie after years of having not watched television at all. I read a biography of Edith Piaf, which spoke to my self-destructive side and triggered my interest in the astral plane—Edith had become obsessed with a dead husband speaking to her through a Ouija board. The traction didn't help. I was a lousy knitter. And I discovered that I hadn't missed much from not having TV all those years.

I went to a specialist. "Dear doctor, what can I do to ease my pain?" He said I could rest it away or he could cut it out. "Why, of course I will rest, then," I said. But I did not understand the meaning of rest. He did not mean a short nap. And after a few months of working only full-time rather than time-and-a-half, I decided rest was not the answer for me. I said, "Doctor, cut away my pain so that I may go on with my work."

After surgery I would have to learn to walk again, but would I learn to walk differently?

If I'd known then what I know now, I would have kept looking for an alternative solution. But I was young and impatience ruled. My mother came to San Francisco with me. Of course I was concerned about my back and the possibility that I might never walk again if the knife slipped. But I was more worried that I might not sing again if the anesthetist goofed while putting the tube down my throat. We had a long, serious talk with him. Mom took a motel room a few blocks away and I checked in for my ten-day ordeal.

I contemplated what I would do if surgery didn't work. I tried to forgive the doctor in advance. Early in the morning they came for me. The inquisition from *The Man of La Mancha* came to mind. They gave me drugs and I grew drowsy. The anesthetist came in and affirmed that he knew he was dealing with a prized instrument. The doctor came in to say good-morning and reassure me. The nurses were attentive. This was an expensive private hospital. My care was being paid for by my Screen Actors Guild health insurance. It was far different from the time I went to Detroit General with a broken elbow. There, I sat for hours as exhausted doctors, nurses, and staff met one crisis after another—murder victims, drug-overdosed kids, women cut up in domestic vi-

83

olence, children accidentally poisoned from household chemicals, hysterical parents.

I was rolled onto a gurney and, as we rode down the hall and through the swinging doors, I could feel my mother's rough, callused hand still in mine, even though she'd let go several minutes before.

I became aware of being awake but didn't open my eyes. Somewhere in the distance a sweet voice called my name. "Holly, it's okay, you can wake up now. Everything went fine, Holly." I opened my eyes but the lights were too bright. The person with the sweet voice put something cold and wet on my dry lips. Later—was it later?—I woke in a softer room. My mother's hand was still there. "Hi, Hol, how you feeling?" I moved toward her voice. Oh! Excruciating pain! I started to cry from confusion. That hurt too. I tried to breathe slowly and deeply but achieved only little gasps. I was afraid to look at Mom for too long. Her loving face made me cry. She asked if I hurt. I nodded, and for a moment it crossed my mind that it is as hard to observe pain as it is to feel it.

The doctor came in. I was polite and in charge, as usual. I talked with him as if I were the public-relations manager at a bank. *For god's sake, Holly, fall apart. There is no need to please this man. He is getting paid thousands of dollars for this operation. Even if he wasn't getting a dime he is your doctor and is supposed to be taking care of you, not the other way around.*

The doctor took my mother aside in the hall to tell her I should not be feeling this much pain since it was a simple and successful operation. He asked her to describe my personality a bit. She told him I was an extremely responsible and mature person, used to being in control of my life and . . . He stopped her. Say no more. He explained that it was the control aspect of my behavior that was keeping me from recovering. "Unless she relaxes and lets us take care of her, she isn't going to feel good." He took matters into his own hands. "Holly, we're going to give you a little something for the pain," he said as the needle went into my arm. I asked what exactly it was. I was out before I heard the nurse say, "Morphine."

Jeff came to visit me the day before I was released. He arrived just as I was learning to walk again. I was in good spirits. "Let's see if I can remember how to do this!" My legs did work, one leg in front of the other, as I held on to the railing.

Jeff glowed. "I guess I'll be on that next tour after all." I was happy. I was going to do another IPC tour with Jane and Tom and, this time, with Jeff and baby Troy. I started to get excited about the songs we might do. Jane and Tom decided to get married. They asked me to sing. I wrote them a special song, and Peter Fonda and I sang together. As I watched the ceremony, I wondered if I would ever fall in love enough to get married.

The second IPC tour gave me the foundation to return to each city again apart from IPC. I booked a national tour, often pretending to be a booking agent. It was easier to negotiate money as "Martha" than as "Holly." Jeff and I worked hard, and thought that tour life was supposed to be as rigorous as we had experienced it working with Jane. I pushed myself mercilessly. Sometimes we drove, sometimes we took Greyhound, mostly we flew. We stayed in people's homes. The audiences were small in number. We sang in churches, schools, clubs, small concert halls, and at rally sites in empty lots, parks, fields, city-hall steps, and from platforms and truck beds. We sang for labor organizations, farm workers, Native American groups, and prison projects. Soon ten people became hundreds of people and then thousands. There was excitement about our work. I still have people come up to me to remind me of ". . . that night that you played in the basement of the Redbook Store in Boston? People were crammed inside to the ceiling, and although it was cold, there was a bunch of us who huddled outside, our ears and noses pressed against the glass to hear. Everyone had a sense that we were part of the beginning of something very important. Now, fifteen years later, we know we were!"

Wherever we performed, we carried *Hang in There* with us and sold records after each show. We sent around legal-size pads for people to sign up on our mailing list. In airports, I would tear out the record-store listings of the yellow pages and send each store a note saying I had just performed in their town and if anyone came in looking to buy my records, it was available from us . . . and I gave all the pertinent information, including a request that they consider stocking my record.

For our first pressing of *Hang in There,* we ordered one thousand copies. Anything less raised the unit price to something unaffordable. But we were quite certain we would be eating off those records for years to come, and I don't mean off the profits, I mean literally—using them as plates. But in no time at all we were reordering. To the record industry, we were nothing. But to Jeff and

Mom and Dad and me, we were a hit. And it was fun to be a hit on our own terms.

Then we became more of a hit than we expected. Maybe commercial radio and the mainstream industry were not interested in political music or a big, strong woman singing out, but the peace movement was. People came faithfully to hear Jeff and me perform, bringing new friends each time to share their "discovery." This reassured me. I felt part of a long and essential tradition. And yet, at the same time, I felt something new was happening. I noticed I wasn't in a big hurry to get back to the music industry.

I had been asked by one of the wounded to write a song for the students killed at Kent State by the National Guard in 1970. I had tried to finish the song. Everything I'd written sounded shallow to me. Here I was on the plane to Ohio for the memorial service and I still didn't have the goddamn song!

Okay, Holly, write. This shouldn't be so hard for you. After all, four college students shot . . . it could have been you. As the plane landed in Ohio, I finished the last verse. Yes, it was okay. This would do.

The crowd gathered at the site of the killing, standing in silence. Ironically and tragically, some of the students who were shot had not even been part of the demonstration, but only passers-by, not unlike so many Vietnamese who had died of the crime of being Vietnamese; cause of death . . . passing by. Since the Kent killings, more students had become the objects of federal violence, including the black students at Jackson State in Mississippi.

I heard the introduction. I stepped forward, and feeling the weight of my co-activists who graced the platform—Ron Kovic, Jane Fonda, Jean Pierre Dupris, Judy Collins, Julian Bond, Daniel Ellsberg—I sang:

It could have been me but instead it was you
So I'll keep doing the work you were doing as if I were two
I'll be a student of life, a singer of songs
A farmer of food and the righter of wrongs
It could have been me but instead it was you
And it may be me dear sisters and brothers before we are through
But if you can die for freedom
Freedom, freedom, freedom
If you can die for freedom, I can too

6
HANG IN THERE

DAD HAD COME TO MARCH WITH ME AT A PEACE DEMONSTRATION IN Washington, D.C. It was a long, cold day. Miraculously, he met up with my aunt Ruth in the huge crowd and they set out to find me.

But a demonstration doesn't *require* a hundred thousand people. I remember hearing about a man who stood day after day within view of the Oval Office, wearing an antiwar sandwich board. Some thought he was crazy. But later, when Nixon's notes were revealed during the Watergate crisis, this man's daily presence was reported to have been driving Nixon mad. He apparently discussed with his staff how to get rid of the man, contemplating the hiring of thugs to beat him up.

I walked into the church where the marchers were gathering and found the bathroom. I went into one of the stalls, dumped my stuff on the floor, sat down on the loo, and felt like crying. I was tired. I hoped Dad was somewhere in the city. I hoped the war would end soon. I hoped there was coffee. Then from the stall next to me I heard a woman start to sing quietly to herself, "Hang in there, a little bit longer, though I know it's been too long. For so many years, we have been fighting, for so many years we have been strong." A wonderful, warm grin swept over my whole body. "That's a great song," I thought. I picked myself up and went out to the registration table. There was my dad. Joan Baez was there too. I felt she didn't like me much. I was not a pacifist and was becoming a more outspoken feminist. But we didn't need to be friends. I enjoyed talking to a woman who was a legend in her time.

A young girl, maybe ten years old, asked me to sign my album. I was in a phase of being uncomfortable with stardom and explained to her, as I did to all autograph seekers, that her name was as important as mine and that autographs just perpetuated a star system. I could see her brain working on this one. "Well, just say something on the album, don't sign it," she said. So I wrote "Work to free political prisoners in South Vietnam." She read what I had written, sighed, and looked at me as if I were hopeless, saying, "I'm already doing that!"

Something happened to the U.S. citizenry when we watched the Vietnamese child running down that road, trying to get one step ahead of the napalm that enflamed her body. Something happened when we watched a monk immolate himself before the world in hopes that someone would come forward and put out the fire that burned the world. Something happened when we watched the SLA desperadoes, enraged by those who lit the fires that burned the child and the monk. Now, caught in a house in Los Angeles, they burned right before our eyes on live TV. In that moment something happened to U.S. citizens. There were those who watched, unsure whether it was the six o'clock news or the six o'clock movie. There were others who grabbed their hearts and turned away from the screen so that they might retain the ability to feel the difference. There were those who went to the street to see for themselves, to feel the heat of the fire, smell the burning flesh, let their eyes sting from the smoke, hear the screams direct, heart to heart, cry out, and know that they might be heard, at least by someone crying out next to them. Others stayed by the screen and soon became accustomed to seeing blood without the smell mixed with that of burning flesh lingering in their nostrils. Something happened.

Have you ever sat too long curled up before the TV until your foot goes to sleep? You don't know it's asleep until you try to stand, then there is that painful sensation as the nerves untangle and the blood rushes in. You fear that your body will fall from under you. Then slowly you recognize the feel of your toes again as they touch the cold linoleum of the kitchen floor. Relief. To feel again, even forgetting that for a moment you could not find your balance.

I started to work with independent distributors, who would buy the record from us and place it in stores within their territories. Mom handled distributor orders as well as individual mail orders. She was also Redwood's public-relations department, and good at it too, personable and efficient. Dad bought a bigger set of books and assumed the task of expanding our ledgers to help us better understand inventory, cash flow, and international money exchange. We were now selling to people in Canada, Europe, Australia, Japan, and Mexico.

In 1974, Jeff and I toyed with the idea of going for a major record deal. We made a demo for Epic and met with A & R representatives from A & M, but we decided to make another record on our own. This time, we would do a bigger, more "produced" album. We let ourselves be talked into recording all the musicians at once to get a "live" feeling. Understandably, our co-producer wanted to work with some of the best studio players in town, which cost us triple scale per musician. We didn't really need "the best"—we needed good players. This wasn't going to be a landmark mainstream album, and we couldn't afford that kind of talent. I got swept into it. However, the first day I knew we were in over our heads. That night I called off the project, paid everybody, parted ways with our producer, and kicked myself for a day and a half.

I listened to the tracks we had recorded to see if there was anything we could salvage. I didn't think so. The musicians may have been the best in town, but we hadn't created an ensemble feeling. It was an expensive lesson. Jeff and I decided we could recoup our losses and keep costs down by recording a live concert. Julie Thompson would co-produce the album. We hired a good "unfamous" bass player, Rob Moitoza, and called it a trio.

We returned to our old stomping grounds, the Ash Grove, which had been renamed the Pitchell Cabaret after a fire, and recorded two shows a night for three nights, using that tried-and-true mailing list to invite all our Los Angeles-area friends and supporters.

My music began to have its own personality. It was not quite folk because piano was the dominant instrument and not really cabaret because the lyrics were so outspoken. I was becoming a storyteller, documenting people's lives as they passed through my own. A mixture of world view, feminism, and romance started to be the identifiable characteristic of my songs. The songs were alive and fresh, the arrangements were tight, the audience was excited, and I was in good voice. Everything went smoothly except my pitch on the song I'd written for the students at Kent State, "It Could Have Been Me." The arrangement called for me to sing several verses a cappella. Then, several minutes into the song, the bass would enter, and, finally, the piano. Each show my pitch would slip a bit before the bass entered. I was so frustrated, but we had more than enough songs. If we had to cut that song, so be it. On the last show, however, the bass entered and I was right on. The song went on the album, which we called *A Live Album*. And live it was. To date, that album has sold more copies than any of my other albums, rivaled only by *Fire in the Rain* and my first duo album with Ronnie Gilbert, *Lifeline*.

One Sunday morning, I opened an imported copy of *The New York Times* and turned directly to the theater section. As I looked at the ads for all the Broadway musicals, I was overcome with sadness. Wasn't I supposed to be there? Growing up, I had listened to a lot of styles of music, but none had grabbed my heart like the musicals. I seldom knew the whole story, but had lived and relived the huge dramatic conflicts again and again as if they were my own. Acting out the parts as briefly described in the album jacket-liner notes, I played them all: the king at the round table and the carnival barker, the street girl taught to speak proper English and the nun who falls in love with an Austrian resister; a gang member on the West Side and a young soldier from Alabama who finds contradictions in the Pacific; an autistic child who plays the trumpet in an Indiana marching band and a gambler who takes a lady to Cuba; a prostitute who dreams them all dead and a union leader who hands out dangerous leaflets; a woman whose beauty is confirmed by a rainmaker and a woman raped on Kitty Hawk Island. These were my playmates in that hot and dusty farm town—life with all its truths, its misinformation, its warped perspective, its dreams and disappointments. But I held on tight, like the cowboys I'd seen at the local rodeo, riding to the bell and sometimes beyond because it was safer to hang on than to get off. And Billy Bigelow asks, ''What if *he* is a *she*?'' I put down *The New York Times* and went to the travel agent to pick up our tickets to Vietnam.

Jeff and I waved to our parents, who saw us off at the San Francisco airport. I wonder now at our folks' support and courage as we flew off into the unknown. We stopped to refuel in Alaska in the middle of the night. I remember the shimmer of the snow outside the window in the cold dark night and the thought of the people whose job it was to refuel our plane. What were they doing here? What were their hobbies? What music did they listen to? How did they feel about the war in Vietnam?

We landed next in Hong Kong, where Jeff and I made our way to a YMCA hotel. We would spend one night here before heading for

Hang in There

Saigon. We dropped off our bags and headed for the wharf and the marketplace to see as much as we could of this city, which, until then, I knew only through novels and films. The streets were packed with people buying and selling. We were not on the tourist side of town; that was across the bay. I felt the stares at the big, red-haired white woman. Animals were slaughtered before the eyes of the buyer to assure freshness in a community that lacked refrigeration. On the water thousands of junks were anchored nose-to-nose, filling up every space from the dock well out into the bay. In order to get out to one's boat, one had to hop from boat to boat, a most extraordinary system of co-existence. People lived, cooked, and dumped their waste on these waters.

The next morning, we left Hong Kong. I had no idea if I could get into Saigon, given the work I had done with Jane. But Tom Hayden had thought that even though our invitation was from Hanoi, we should witness the differences between the two Vietnamese cities and systems, so I was going to try. I thought Jeff would probably get in fine, so he carried the cameras and the letters we were delivering for friends. We arranged to meet in Vientiane, Laos, if we were separated.

There was a man from the Saigon police on the flight. He kept walking up and down the aisle, scrutinizing the passengers from behind his Thieu-regime dark glasses. Jeff and I had intentionally sat apart. I tried to busy myself with a fashion magazine. I wondered who the hell he thought I was, coming to Saigon. Well, maybe the daughter of embassy personnel or an anthropologist en route to Thailand. This would be my first trip to a war zone. Under the leadership of five U.S. presidents, 50,000 North Americans had died, 415,000 Vietnamese from the south, and 924,000 from the north, and several thousand others from Australia, Puerto Rico, New Zealand, and Thailand, and three to four million Cambodians. That's nearly five million people! As I got off the plane, I felt the weight of death.

We had no trouble getting in. Saigon was about to fall and everyone wanted money. Money seemed to be the bottom line. We caught a cab and went to find our friends.

The bombs were falling fifty miles outside the city. There was a sense that the South Vietnamese PRG would take the city soon. Many revolutionaries were operating clandestinely in the city. Much later I heard that a woman inside the Thieu regime, who served refreshments to high-level guests, supplied information to the resistance on a regular basis. I wish I could have seen the look of surprise on the faces of those who had been served when she took off her apron and escorted her bosses off to jail, although I imagine many of them got out of town long before it was too late, relocated by their U.S. cronies.

Poverty and mistrust were everywhere. A little girl holding a baby came to our table as we were having coffee with an American journalist. He advised us not to give her money. "She's a professional," he said. "She has been working these tables for years." He had grown cynical in his stay with this war. I gave a little money to the girl anyway. So what if she was a pro. I doubted her profession had made her rich. I decided I didn't like cynics and would try not to become one.

Saigon was decorated for Christmas. It was bizarre to walk around in eighty-degree steamy heat and hear Christmas carols blaring out of the shop radios, then to look across the street and see young boys being picked off the sidewalk by Thieu's soldiers "drafting" them into the army.

The next morning we walked through the streets of Saigon, picked up a loaf of freshly baked bread, a papaya, and a lime, and headed for my friend's house. He was setting up a meeting between me and a Buddhist nun who had escaped from a Thieu-regime prison and was operating underground. She wanted to update me about the conditions in the prison so that I might tell the story when I returned home.

The war in this land had gone on for so many generations, with the Chinese, then the French, and now the United States. Perhaps Saigon would be liberated soon. What will that mean? What will happen when the city is taken back by nationalists, and the foreigners and puppets are kicked out? So many people fall between the cracks. Will they flee and be lost in the streets of Oakland, Seattle, and Los Angeles? Will the new government be able to preserve the dances, the songs, the instruments, the poems, and the traditions after people here have Americanized their lives in order to survive? How will these people ever find themselves in the midst of all this cultural confusion, compounding the economic and environmental havoc of the war?

I had reached my friend's house. He directed me to a small street and told me to go to the third house, step inside, and wait. How did a farm girl from Potter Valley find herself in a clandestine meeting with a Buddhist nun in Saigon? I waited. Next door, Buddhist prayers began, the chant, the drum. A small figure entered the room, a light and energy around her that was like a mystical clear bubble. I was accustomed to shaved heads and Buddhist garb; it was the light that

Hang in There

startled me. She embraced me and pulled a stool up to my chair, and we sat so close, knee to knee.

She took my hands and looked at me very intently. "I hear you do work for peace. This is good. This is good work." Her eyes sparkled. "You know things are very difficult here. You can see that." She proceeded to tell me in great detail about the conditions in the prisons, always talking clearly, precisely, quickly, with no wasted words. There was no despair in her voice, no request for sympathy, only direct information with a look in her eye that assured me I could handle the task. How was she able to transmit such confidence? Though she spoke almost in a whisper, I heard every word. And when she was done she handed me a small etching that had been smuggled out of prison, and she placed it in my hand like a contract. The prayers next door were coming to an end. She kissed my cheek and said, "I must go." And she was gone.

I sat for a moment, unable to move or breathe. She had come with the sound of the drum and left just as it ended. Of course. This way, no one could hear what she was saying to me. There would be many Buddhist nuns and priests moving in the streets just after prayers. She would be less noticeable when she left. I looked down at the contract. It was a drawing by Buu Chi, a student political prisoner who was in Chi Hoa prison. Dated 12/74, it must have just been smuggled out. He had drawn a beautiful woman with deep black eyes, one long and graceful hand holding her hair away from her face, the other holding an apple so that the dove of peace might taste its precious sweetness: this beauty created inside a prison where torture took place daily, where live eels were jammed up women's vaginas as a gruesome extension of rape, where three to four people were crammed for days and weeks at a time into boxes so small they could not stand or sit but had to curl up in little balls. What goes wrong with human beings that they will inflict such horror? What goes right with humans that, in the middle of the nightmare, they are artists who draw pictures of women and doves and apples or they are nuns who travel with the speed of light, expecting the best of one's human potential? I took the contract seriously, and I believe my follow-up work would not have disappointed her. But it was years before I could see or hear about eels without hearing women scream.

On our last day, Jeff and I wandered down to the docks and saw the weaponry stocked up—billions of U.S. tax dollars that could have built schools, health centers, and cultural programs standing there before our eyes. Some soldiers came toward us to tell us to move on. Jeff and I started to kiss and flirt and behave like honeymooners. The soldiers laughed and turned back. What in God's name would anybody be doing honeymooning in Saigon in December 1974?!

We bade farewell to our friends and caught the plane out to Vientiane. This plane would make one stop, at Phnom Penh in Cambodia. At the time I didn't realize how close the Khmer Rouge were to taking the city. Our plane dropped down and took off at steep angles to avoid their guns. Jeff observed the whole thing and later told me how dangerous it had been, but I escaped by sleeping through the whole flight. I had this idea that all the Communist forces in Indochina were united in their fight against imperialism. I found out how wrong I was when a few years later the Vietnamese moved into Cambodia and defeated the brutal Khmer Rouge.

We stopped in Laos to get our visas from the Vietnamese embassy.

Hanoi was a mixture of the old Vietnam and the new, war-torn but proud, with vestiges of China and France: The older generation of intellectuals spoke French as their second language; the younger generation was learning Russian and English. But the people celebrated being Vietnamese and were aggressively preserving their traditions.

Our translator and guide, Quock, adopted us for the next two weeks and showed us his country . . . or half his country. He spoke longingly of the day when the two parts would be united.

It was a city of bicycles and bustle. Children followed us as we walked around the city, young girls pulling at my braids to see if they stayed on like theirs did. Many had never seen a redhead before.

We were free to wander wherever we wanted but were asked not to take pictures of military installations or bridges. I made a stupid mistake one afternoon and took a photo of a lake, not seeing the bridge in the distance. Within moments I was surrounded by children trying to tell me something. A kind policeman arrived, pointed at my camera and then at the bridge, and I realized my error. I saw how the citizens, including the children, had united to protect their country from the bombs. I gave up the film. They developed it and returned my pictures to me, all but the bridge photo.

When we drove anywhere, we were given a running account of life in Vietnam: "That's where the bombs of December fourteenth fell. . . . That is where Ho Chi Minh used to talk with the university students. . . . That is the hospital that was bombed. . . . That is the music school.''

We visited factories where child care was on-site for the workers. Women could take breaks to go nurse their babies. The workers had athletic teams that played each other or those of other factories during break times or after work. There were cultural groups and study groups. The work itself was tedious, but they were making the best of it.

We heard funny stories about previous visitors from the United States, one of whom was Pete Seeger. They said he hated to be driven places. He was always leaping out of the car with his banjo over his shoulder even though it might throw off the whole schedule. Pete wanted to walk. We laughed. Yes, that's Pete.

On the night of our concert, we were each presented with a gift. Jeff received a jacket from the youth brigade and I received a traditional Vietnamese dress made out of silk. The concert hall was empty as the time to perform grew closer and closer. I was concerned that no one was coming. Quock assured me not to worry and, as usual, he was right. About five minutes before curtain, well over a thousand seats filled up rapidly, and the concert began on time—to a full house.

We performed a high-energy concert, often drawing gales of laughter because we were so different from the Vietnamese, who often stand very still and formal while performing. We rocked and rolled. I clowned and pranced around the stage à la Judy Garland. We sang soft folk songs, powerful peace songs, and rhythmic gospel tunes, and even a few show tunes, trying to give the people a wide variety of musical styles from America. I sang one song in Vietnamese. They adored it—very few Westerners even try to learn simple Vietnamese phrases much less sing a whole song. I had been well coached by one of their national composers. Grammar is impossible for me, but accents are easy . . . so melodic.

We got a roaring standing ovation, and as I stood with Jeff before these glowing faces, I thought, *My God, I've just done a concert in Hanoi!*

We left the stage. Our hosts greeted and congratulated us backstage, and then I went out to meet the audience. But when I got there, the theater was empty. I looked at Quock with astonishment. Where did they all go so quickly? He explained that the Vietnamese were skilled at coming and going from buildings quickly because of bomb raids.

We traveled to several other parts of the country, meeting with artists and government delegations all along the way. In one province, we had dinner with ten men from different government offices. They toasted me and the women of Vietnam. I felt Jeff's foot under the table gently kicking me in hopes I wouldn't launch into a feminist tirade. I smiled and lifted my glass to the women of Vietnam.

The next morning, I walked out of my little room into a large courtyard. I heard two women's voices coming from the workers' quarters. As I strolled over, they came out to greet me. I had been on television and everyone in the country knew who I was now, a peace activist visiting as a guest of the musicians' union. I didn't speak Vietnamese. They didn't speak English. We all spoke a little French, but we quickly departed from language. They sang me lovely Vietnamese songs and I sang them some of mine. Then they unraveled my two long braids. Each women kept one of the rubber bands. They petted my hair and cooed over how different it felt from their own. When they rebraided it, they took the band from each of their single braids and resecured my hair. Then they took my bands and tied up their single braids. They went off to work arm in arm, humming a song I had sung to them, and I knew there were other ways to solve world problems. We had to find a way to remove the war-makers and make room for the long-haired women.

Back in Hanoi, we stayed in a beautiful old hotel left over from the French colonial days. At dinner, one had a choice of Vietnamese or European food. I ordered Vietnamese. I became addicted to a coffee drink made with sweetened canned milk. I sat sipping my drink, writing in my journal, when the Chinese soccer team came downstairs and entered the dining room. They moved with a certain graceful arrogance. I laughed out loud. No matter the politics of a country, a jock is a jock.

Late in the evening we were called over for a drink with the editor of the party paper. We dressed quickly and went to his house. It had grown chilly and, as we sat around a little oil heater, he brought out a bottle of Cuban rum. He apologized for not having a ladies' drink to offer me. Jeff, having reached his own limit, said, with a lovely gleam in his eye, "Don't worry about Holly. She can probably drink us both under the table."

Jeff and I spent most of our time with artists—filmmakers, musicians, painters, poets, and dancers. We went to the circus and to music schools. We heard professionals and local community bands. East Germany had just donated instruments to Vietnam for a full symphony orchestra. I met a beautiful actress, who sat next to me as I watched her film. I had to pee so bad I thought I would die, but I couldn't leave her side in the middle of the film. Jeff and I had long debates with intellectuals over the subject of art and politics. Dear Quock was exhausted after such conversations, trying to translate ideas that were even hard for each of us to express in our own languages.

I learned the concept of "cultural worker" in Vietnam and I thus returned with a new sense of how I hoped to serve music and humanity. I learned about time. The Vietnamese artists had three intentions: to preserve the past; to honor the present and help people in their daily lives; and to create a vision of the future. Behind them lay the understanding that if you don't know where you come from, it is more difficult to know where you are and where you are going.

We met artists who called themselves professionals and those who called themselves amateurs, and the distinction wasn't based on skill. Professionals made a living doing their art but might also work in a related field. The government, for example, would subsidize a poet. She could write her own poetry for two months out of the year, but for the other ten months would teach poetry in school or work in a library or a publishing house. In this way, she was supported for her art but she also put time back into society. An amateur did art for free and made a living elsewhere. I met a man whose musical group went down to the docks to play lunchtime concerts for free. His craft, however, was as a machinist—a work he said he loved. "I could not live without my machines, but I could not make the machines work if I didn't have my music."

I liked the value that was placed on the arts. Art and money didn't get all mixed up. Art had to do with ideas, love, expression, immortality, and talent. Money had to do with the obvious material necessities.

Theater people talked about the war's effect on their work. "We cannot really create good theater at this time, for theater requires deep study of personal conflict. Our whole lives are mobilized for survival and we cannot pause to do such internal investigation. War destroys everything on every level. It will take us a long time to recover from this war."

We heard debates about censorship, abstract art, freedom of expression, and moral responsibilities.

Driving from one meeting to the next, the composer who had taught me the Vietnamese song told me a story.

"Long ago, before Vietnam was called Vietnam, the ancient people of the land lived peacefully with each other, farming and caring for one another. But this peace was disrupted by word that the Mongolian armies were heading for their home with the intention of taking it from them. The people were not warriors, they were a gentle people, and the Mongolians rode large horses with weapons that could kill. The gentle people gathered to discuss what they should do, for they had only their hoes and their hands. One of the wise ones knew a little about these great people who would come to dominate them. He revealed to the gentle ones that the Mongolians were superstitious. And so a plan was devised. The gentle people went to the edge of the forest and wrote in calligraphy on the leaves of the trees with honey. The caterpillars came out and ate the honey, engraving into the leaves the message, 'The invading army must go home or our land will swallow you up.' The army arrived, full of themselves, the smell of victory in the nostrils of their horses. But when they saw the forest, and the message written on the leaves in calligraphy, they fled in terror."

Clearly, if the presidents of the United States had known any Vietnamese history or folklore, they would have known it was a bad idea to invade Vietnam.

I was fascinated, challenged, and delighted by the Vietnamese. I thank them for the thoughts they put in my head. I think I have done well with what they taught me. That is the only way I know to truly thank my teachers.

The coming together of such lessons with feminist sensibility was the basis for the song I wrote a year later with Meg Christian: "The Rock Will Wear Away." "Can we be like drops of water falling on the shore, splashing, breaking, dispersing in air, weaker than the stone by far, but aware that as time goes by, the rock will wear away."

Jeff and I left Vietnam vastly changed by the experience. Our parents waited to hear from us when we hit Bangkok. First we had to *get* to Bangkok. We departed from Hanoi to Vientiane, but our connecting flight to Bangkok had been canceled. Flights out were infrequent and the train took a long time. An experienced traveler suggested we rent a cab. I looked at him in horror, knowing that it cost well over twenty dollars just to go from downtown San Francisco to the airport. We were going to another country! He assured me that we could go for less than the cost of our plane ticket and explained the route. We would need a car to the river, a barge across the river, and another car on the other side that would take us to the airport. Jeff and I negotiated with a driver and settled in with all our "stuff" for a long journey across Laos and Thailand.

When we arrived at the river, we carried, with difficulty, all the things we had gathered in our travels—including hats, Vietnamese instruments, and a variety of gifts we had received. We bought our tickets and were directed down a set of stairs. Well, these were thirty steep steps straight down to the barge. We balanced our loads and headed down. Somewhere in the middle, Jeff said something funny and we got the giggles. I thought I would die, trying not to drop everything and fall headfirst into the river, knocking down old women along the way. We looked like such clowns in our American clothes and our rice-paddy hats, our arms loaded down, laughing out of control with tears streaming down our faces. The peasants who had been waiting quietly for the barge watched us in disbelief. But it was contagious. Soon everyone was laughing. No one moved to help us because everyone was loaded down with chickens and vegetables.

Our parents met us at the San Francisco airport. At the checkpoint, we were asked what we had been doing in Saigon and Vientiane—the Vietnamese of the north had not stamped our passports. We said we were ethnomusicologists doing research on the cultures of Indochina. No truer words were ever spoken.

The peace agreement was signed in the spring of 1975. But the war wasn't over. The Vietnamese had to heal a nation divided and feed a hungry people from fields that were still laced with explosive mines and poisoned with Agent Orange. With huge problems of their own, which included self-defense, they sent thousands of their soldiers into Cambodia to fight the horrific Khmer Rouge, the Pol Pot regime that plagued Cambodia with an unprecedented nightmare. Thousands of Indochinese people fled their war-torn nations in search of new life in America, but it was a long journey—especially for the "boat people."

The war was not over for North Americans either. U.S. soldiers returned to a nation with gravely underfunded veterans' hospitals and high unemployment, homelessness, racism, and union-busting. Many of our children were now men addicted to war and heroin.

And as peace activists turned their attention to the CIA's activity in Central and Latin America, the U.S. continued covertly in Indochina to undermine Vietnam economically and politically and to secretly support a Cambodian opposition that included the Khmer Rouge—even as U.S. audiences watched *The Killing Fields*.

*   *   *

Pat lived in a little trailer house. In the heat of Ukiah's summer of
'75 it was like being in a metal box. But there was something I liked
about it—it was his and it was temporary. Pat had always caught my
eye. In fact, the whole Hook family had charisma. The boys invariably
seemed to be getting into one kind of trouble or another, but I think it
was just that they had a lot of creative energy and nowhere to direct it
other than sports. They were all superior athletes, and after you are the
best, what is there to do but get into a little trouble?

I met Pat at a dance when I was in high school. Pat was a jock, full
of physical self-awareness and pride. Why not? He had won the California Golden Gloves Boxing Championship! He and his brothers were
friendly and charming but dangerously tough. Pat was a good dancer
and liked to dance with me. He was smart enough never to take me out
or drive me home. He was "an older guy" and I was "jailbait."

But here we were   lmost ten years later, making love in a steaming metal shelter. I   found Pat exciting. We lay wide open, hoping
the fan would co   sweating bodies. But my hands were burning
from a differen.   at. I had been to Clark Air Force Base and to
Okinawa; I had listened to the torture stories; I had met clandestinely
with people struggling for their freedom; I had been to Hanoi and seen
the bombed-out hospitals and the effects of antipersonnel weapons; I
had sat up night after night listening to vets telling their stories; I had
met Vietnamese women who had lost their lovers; I had met American
women who had lost their lovers. But my hands burned from having
touched the body of this broken man who was scarred inside and out,
lucky that he wasn't dead but afraid to be alive. I had gone to the world
to find the war: Now the war had finally come home. Pat began to talk.
I recognized the sound in his voice—it was a sound that vets made as
they struggled to decide whether to talk about the Vietnam experiences. Or to talk of something more "acceptable."

We came to a small village. We were tense, we were
always tense. With these people you couldn't tell who was a
soldier and who wasn't. They were all in this together and
they hated us. Why shouldn't they? We were about to destroy
their village. We dug around for a while. I don't know what
we were looking for. Then our instructions were to burn the
place down. So we did. This one young woman, she was
really beautiful, she yelled at me, pointing to the old people

100

and the babies who were so scared and confused. I don't know what she said . . . but I knew, you know? Then, in her rage, she cut off her long black hair and handed it to me.

Pat got wounded. They sent him home. He had been in a stupor when they asked him to sign papers allowing them to amputate his leg. He doesn't know how he'd had it together enough not to sign. They would often suggest amputation because artificial limbs were cheaper than physical therapy. Pat now walks without any noticeable limp. But his state of mind deteriorated. He was in and out of recovery centers for drugs, and he hit bottom when he found himself drinking some kind of toxic chemical to get high.

Another ten years passed and he called me from a treatment center to say he was getting out. He felt he had a new lease on life and wanted me to know he would be working at a V.A. hospital and going back to school. I saw him a few months later at a concert in Ukiah. He looked great. He told me his son was thinking about joining the marines. And my hands burned again.

7
You Can Know All I Am

I LOOKED BACK AND FORTH IN THE REARVIEW MIRROR AND AT THE road so that my eyes wouldn't get stuck in highway stare. Meg Christian and I were chatting and enjoying some rare time alone together. But then it dawned on me that something more was behind us than the road we had just covered. I looked again. "Meg, do you see what I see?" She turned and said in her wonderful Southern drawl, "Yayus, I do believe we are bein' followed by a tornado!" I stepped on the gas. "Hold on, darlin', we are going for a ride!" I drove hard for the next hour, depending on the road signs to assure me we were getting closer to Ames, Iowa. We laughed at the people who don't want to live in California because of earthquakes. We beat it to town, but no one seemed as concerned as we were. Meg and I proceeded to do our sound check. The wind howled and the rain pounded on the windows of the little club. Apparently the heart of the storm had passed by some distance from town. Secretly, I was a little disappointed. I have a passion for being in the heart of the storm.

Such passion for life can get you in trouble. I watched Meg's hands as she tuned her guitar and my mind drifted backward . . . was it only a little over a year ago? The L.A. Women's Building had asked us to do their major fund-raiser for 1975: Meg Christian, Margie Adam, Cris Williamson, Lily Tomlin, the Alice Stone Ladies Society Orchestra, and me. It would be the largest gathering of feminist performing artists ever presented in L.A. In hindsight, the omissions are obvious . . . the extraordinary voices of Vicki Randle and Linda Tillery come to mind. Still, I had never been part of an all-women's production before, and I was excited.

There had been disagreement over my participation. Some of the organizers liked the presence of so many lesbian performers and didn't see why they needed to invite another heterosexual woman. Those in favor, led by Bobbie Berleffi, who was an old friend of Cris's, argued that I drew a broader audience, which included the music industry, the "straight" press, and the peace movement, and besides, I sang strong songs about women and sold a lot of tickets. The critics pointed out that most of those songs were about women in relation to men/patriarchy. "Can't we for once have a major event without having to ask, 'What about the men?' "

I heard about these discussions from acquaintances who were at the meetings. I was fascinated by the debate and the level of its intensity. It served to notify me that these questions were not to be sidestepped.

The vote led to an invitation, and I, in turn, invited Meg, Cris, and Margie to my home for the first music rehearsal. The word was that Meg and I were not going to like each other. She was part of a lesbian separatist collective called Olivia Records and had not wanted me to be in the show. I discussed this with my lover, Arthur. He was visiting me from New York. We decided, in the interest of keeping the peace, that he would stay out of sight, so he curled up in my bedroom to learn the lines of a play he would be rehearsing when he got home.

The women arrived in good spirits and in their respective cars: Meg in her Toyota, Margie in her Volvo, and Cris in her VW. I was sporting a Rambler American at the time. I had prepared snacks and everyone had brought their refreshment of choice—beer, wine, marijuana. We tuned the guitars to my piano and picked a song. After the first few lines we fell apart, delirious over the delicious sound we had just created. It was, naturally and effortlessly, a magnificent quartet.

Margie was outspoken, articulate, and opinionated, and she played the piano with gregarious personality. She seemed to fall in love over and over again with the beauty of women making music together and agreed to accompany me on my solo songs. She liked Jeff's work with me, so she took his basic approach to my songs and elaborated on it. I appreciated this respect. Cris had a voice that combined the cry of the wolf and the lullaby of the spirit mother. She was also writing some magnificent songs that later became part of the classic recording *The Changer and the Changed*. It was hard to know which of Cris's songs to choose. Each one was a singer's dream. Cris also had a comic locked up inside her that seemed unable to control itself in Meg's presence. Between the two of them, we laughed as much as we sang. Meg, "little Mayug" as we came to call her, played the guitar as if she were sculpting. I can still remember watching her hands and fingers, so alive and strong. But behind her Southern articulation, her impish sense of humor, and her commitment to lesbian music, there was a huge sadness I could feel in her songs. With all our differences, I felt moved by her.

The all-women cast, crew, and staff gathered for dress rehearsal. Seeing someone make a mistake, I found myself blaming it on the fact that she was a woman. I love to catch myself being small-minded or acting out on a stereotype. I grin, close my eyes, and erase that tape from the library. The sensation of feeling my consciousness being "raised" is superb entertainment if I stay free of guilt.

Dress rehearsals take time, so I had brought a biography of Judy Garland to read. I found a place in the carpeted stairway to cry over this child star who took uppers and downers to make sure her moods were compatible with the heavy shooting schedule at MGM. How is it, I wondered, that I had turned away from being a child star, had avoided drugs and alcoholism, had made these peculiar choices to work outside fame and fortune? Why was Judy so important to me lately, as if she sat on my shoulder warning me, imploring me to be happy?

I looked up and Meg was standing there watching me. Her guitar was nowhere in sight but her hands were alive, as if they were making music. I wondered if she would approve of my book. Why did I care what she thought? Why was it hard for me to be myself with these women? Meg always seemed to be saying, "You fascinate me . . . if only you were a . . ." I knew lesbians had been forced to live as outcasts, to create a world outside the world, to hide from hostile eyes. I knew lesbians had trouble finding their literature and music, and, once found, would have to receive it wrapped in a brown paper bag to avoid the postal worker's silent accusations. I knew lesbian bars were often owned by the Mafia, and women had to depend on and pay for the protection offered by men who would just as soon kill them. I knew lesbians had to drive for hours to the nearest major city in search of Daughters of Bilitis or the Metropolitan Community Church. I knew some lesbians thought they had to choose roles, to be butch or fem, in order to survive in the heterosexual life model.

But courageous and creative women, following in their foremothers' footsteps, were changing that. Meg was one of them. She had found a home in the lesbian feminist community. Olivia Records was her new self-created family. I felt she mistrusted me as a heterosexual but admired me as a woman and an artist. I didn't want to be one of those straight women whom lesbians talk about with disdain. I wanted to be an ally.

Flirting is a complicated game between women. I had picked up that some lesbians didn't like straight women who flirted with them. Women inherently like women's energy, whether it is girl-talk in the kitchen, going out shopping, or playing sports together. Women can be sensual and physical together. Straight women can linger in that delicious place because they have a self-imposed cutoff. Lesbians know there are no limits to how women can love each other and must take greater risks. A straight woman can always decide it was just a game all along, leaving the lesbian broken-hearted, humiliated, or simply pissed off that she wasted her time on a woman who is going to take it home to a man.

So I was determined not to flirt. On the other hand, if I gave the cold shoulder, I might be seen as being critical of the wonderful physical exchange of joy and love between talented and creative women. I tried to find a balance. One woman, another redhead, seemed not the least bit concerned that I was straight. She came on strong, with grace and humor. I couldn't help but admire her courage as she flirted shamelessly in front of everyone, even while the others laughed openly at her efforts.

Lily Tomlin did several sketches in the show. I felt she was one of the few comedians who knew how to be funny with love and not at someone else's expense. If Don Rickles is hell, Lily Tomlin is heaven.

The show was a great success. Jeff was in the audience. It was the first time since I was a sophomore in high school that I had worked with a pianist other than Jeff (except in the FTA show). He had brought our friends Robben Ford and Rob Moitoza. I was so happy that these men in my life had attended, supported, and loved this show. I was also aware that there were some women who wished they hadn't come. I was concerned that in this complex world there was no way to meet everyone's needs all the time. What could be done? The answer didn't come easily or soon. In fact, it never came.

After "The Building Women" show, Cris, Margie, Meg, and I collaborated with TV producer Lynne Littman on a musical special entitled "Come Out Singing," for which we won a local Emmy in L.A. For years, gay artists had been part of heterosexual artistic events and did not say, "Oh, but I'm gay," so I decided that while I participated in these productions of women's music (which, as far as I could tell, was a safe code word for lesbian music, with the exception of a few women like me and Kristen Lems), I would not cling to a heterosexual safety net. I avoided heterosexual songs, which left me songs without pronouns or lesbian songs. I learned that "out" gay and lesbian artists are very brave.

Curiously, at this time I was more in love than I had ever been in my life. But because my lover was a man, I didn't feel comfortable sharing my happiness with these new friends. I didn't think, for example, that Meg wanted to hear about my wonderful man and his two beautiful sons. For the first time in my life, I felt a man loved *me,* not his image of me or his fantasy, but me. Arthur didn't seem threatened by my work, but admired it. He took responsibility for birth control. He liked to talk after making love. He made himself vulnerable, sharing his love for and confusion about his Jewish culture. We were talking about living together and he had offered to move out to California, acknowledging that it would be very difficult for me to move to New York with my record company. I wanted to glow, but now that I was aware that even ten years after the so-called sexual revolution, lesbians couldn't comfortably stand in a movie line snuggling and kissing on a cold Friday night with all the other dates. Straight folks had kept that liberation for themselves. And if I were a new ally, it felt inappropriate to be a blatant heterosexual if blatant homosexuality wasn't okay. I have since learned that I could hate racism and still feel fine about being white; that I could have worked with these women for lesbian rights and the development of lesbian culture and still be thrilled in my love and passion for Arthur. But, at the time, I was breaking new ground and felt a responsibility to rectify past injustices. Arthur continued to be patient, stretching his own perceptions as I stretched mine.

One night . . . where were we? . . . we were sleeping on the floor in a house that was neither his nor mine. We awoke in the middle of the night and made love. Arthur and I were wonderful lovers together, sometimes slow and dreamy, other times wild, adventurous, and athletic (he had a black belt in Aikido!). This was a dreamy night. I asked him if he had ever had a homosexual relationship. He said no. Although he had made love to a man once and it had been pleasant, he said it had not led him to homosexuality. I asked if he thought people were basically bisexual or either one or the other. He said that he didn't know, but that if I found myself wanting to make love with a woman I should follow my instincts—it would probably be a worthwhile experience regardless of what I discovered. I was very touched by his response and fell asleep wrapped up with him, feeling that I wanted to be there for a long time.

After the TV taping was over, Meg, Cris, Margie, and I went our separate ways. Margie was co-founder of a company called Pleiades Records, along with attorney Barbara Price. Margie was their only artist. Cris and Meg were on Olivia Records. Some women from Washington, D.C., had fallen in love with Cris's music and had befriended her after a concert. They'd told Cris they wanted to start a women's business that would be an economically viable tool for organizing, and that would be good for lesbians. They had discussed everything from Laundromats and restaurants to old-age homes. Cris had said, "Why don't you start a record company?" And they did. They'd formed the Olivia Collective. Cris was not a member of the collective (Cris isn't a joiner) but had agreed to record an album on their label. Meg was in the collective and, along with Alix Dobkin, who had recorded Lavender Jane Loves Women (on Women's Wax Works), was fast becoming the darling of lesbian music.

In the summer of 1975, I was invited to perform at the San Diego Women's Music Festival. I'd never been to a women's music festival before. In fact, I had never been to any kind of music festival. I had never even been to the desert. I wondered what this would be like. What did lesbians *do* when they gathered together in the desert? I wasn't used to going places without Jeff as my pianist, but this was a women-only festival. Cris, Margie, and Meg would be there. We would sing together, and Margie agreed to play for me on a few solo tunes. This was to be an adventure.

I found women walking around looking tan and healthy and relaxed. Small groups were singing or fiddling under a tree. One woman was stretched out on a rock like a snake drying its skin and another woman recited poems to her, dancing gracefully around the rock. I discovered lesbians could be hippies too! There were softball games and craft areas and serious debates. They were trying out new ways— most had never been out in the desert with hundreds of women, either.

The stage was built in a natural amphitheater and women sat on the slope, leaning against rocks, trees, and each other to listen to the music that many had waited all their lives to hear. I sat alone most of the time, listening or writing in my journal. Women came and sat next to me from time to time, concerned that I might be having a hard time being around so many lesbians. I didn't try to explain that the only trouble I was having was being around a large crowd. I assured them that I was enjoying myself. But maybe I *was* having trouble being around so many lesbians. I didn't feel the way they did about women. And that bothered me. If this was something so many women felt, why didn't I? I wasn't used to seeing women kiss each other and didn't quite know where to look. Out of curiosity, I wanted to watch, but I didn't want them to feel me staring. I watched Meg with her lover, Ginny, leaning against each other lovingly while listening to one of the afternoon concerts.

When it came time to sing, I finally felt a little bit at home. The harmonies we had created months ago were still fresh in our minds. The beauty of our voices together surprised me once again. We entertained, out there under the sky, but we also invited these women to discover their lives apart from men, to blossom in self-esteem. We were part of a long tradition that we hadn't even begun to discover. We were the footsteps in which the next generation of women would walk; we sang in the desert so that they might sing in the world. All that in a song? To my continued amazement, all that in a song.

I toured heavily that fall, integrating a stronger feminist perspective into my show and singing one of Meg's songs. It seemed I was touring all the time now, as my reputation grew and the opportunities expanded. Jeff and I talked about my desire to work more with women. He wanted to pursue his own classical and composing career. We had been together for so long, it was hard to imagine working with anyone else. We had about six months of commitments before us, but we decided at least to think about a break. We had an album to do first of the year, but maybe after that.

People started asking, "How's Jeff?" as if my pianist partner were deathly ill or we were being divorced. Clearly some thought I had "dumped" Jeff at the altar, in favor of this radical lesbo crap. They didn't seem to understand that Jeff and I were not struggling. Jeff was my friend. He loved me and was not threatened by homosexuality or strong women. We were fine with each other. It was our friends and fans who were having the trouble.

I received letters responding to the more radically feminist show that Jeff and I were presenting. Of course, many were letters from women who were thrilled with the integration of feminism. However, some letters arrived from men, expressing feelings of exclusion, resentment. Other criticism came from men and women, political activists, who had expected the focus to be on Chile and other international issues and felt alienated by the emphasis on women's struggles.

> *I am feeling both disappointed and resentful . . . re-*
> *sentful because as a man, I felt nearly totally excluded from*
> *what your songs related to the audience.*

> *I resented feeling like it was an exclusive women's con-*
> *cert tonight when it was billed as a benefit for Chile.*

> *To have been recognized and exhorted during the con-*
> *cert last night would have been quite powerful. Please be*
> *more gentle to my people, men. Some of them want like hell*
> *to be on your side.*
> *Men are part of the struggle too. I felt a silent slap in*
> *the face . . . I heard no thanks for their support . . .*

Here are excerpts from a journal that led to a letter I wrote in response:

> *I received letters from men and women who felt the*
> *concert was the most complete political concert that Jeff and*
> *I have ever done in our work together. So combined with the*
> *letters of criticism, my first sadness is that there are not*
> *enough cultural workers who have been given the opportu-*
> *nity and privilege to serve the needs of the people. Conse-*
> *quently, people are forced to put all their hopes and needs on*
> *a very few artists. However, experimentation has been es-*
> *sential to the work I do. Please do not demand that we, the*
> *artists, always be the same as we were the time before. Do*
> *not feel ripped off by our changing and growing. We work in*
> *a movement which means to me, motion. And given the state*
> *of affairs, it is best we not stay where we are at present.*
> *The concert that Jeff and I did was full of strong, rich*
> *songs, global and domestic, some of which spoke specifically*
> *of women's lives. Are men in the audience so insecure and so*
> *tender that they cannot go for one evening seeing the world*
> *through women's eyes? Must they be constantly stroked?*
> *Can they not celebrate "Nicolia" as she joins women in*
> *taking over a factory, even if she doesn't say to the men,*

109

"You too"? Can men not see themselves as part of the revolution in songs that have no pronouns or do not linger on brotherhood?

In truth, not one of my songs excluded men. Most of the songs were without gender and extended themselves to the broadest definition of humanity. A handful were specifically about women and if they offended you, then perhaps it is simply because you are unaccustomed to seeing women take their rightful place in society. I suggest then you get used to it. There is more of the same yet to come.

Men can learn from reading books and listening to records and concerts presented by women. See it as a unique opportunity to get to know us. Men cannot be liberated by women. Men must confront the deeply bred sexism inside and when that has been done, men will not feel excluded by the inclusion of women.

The issue of women is an international issue. Women are the largest oppressed group in the world, and for the most part, are poor. Neither labor unions nor the organized Left have shared space on this earth equally with women unless they needed their blood, their feminine wit, their office skills, or their courage in the face of confrontation. When women confront sexism, you may feel it harsh. But sexism is harsh and the power of it must be matched in our struggle against it.

Women have asked me why I do benefits for Chile if my commitment is to women. Leftists have asked me why I am no longer concerned with global struggles and I am just doing women's music. Both questions astound me. Are there not women in Chile? It is important that the women's movement develop commitment to ending racism and class oppression, the very things that have kept women divided. When I sang "Sister-Woman-Sister," one man called out "But what about men in prison?" I wrote the song while working in a women's prison. There were no men there. And what kind of question is that? Do we have to keep defending ourselves so hard that we don't have any energy to get on to the creative leadership that is ready to burst inside us? The FBI used that tactic against the anti-war movement and the black move-

ment . . . keep everyone so tied up in court defending them-
selves that they can't be out on the street organizing. . . .
Just as whites must protest racism and genocide without
wanting approval from people of color, men must attack
sexism and patriarchy without wanting approval from
women. Men must do this for themselves and for the quality
of their own lives, not for "their women." And brothers,
when you truly oppose sexism, I do not think you will feel
alienated by my anger. I believe you will match it with your
own liberation.

That was around 1975. When I read it now I am pleased. I was
learning to live out on a limb in the middle of a storm. I was part of
the peace movement, learning from Vietnam vets coming home to a
nightmare; part of the solidarity movement, working for human rights
in Chile, and I was just beginning to know about Central America; part
of the growing feminist movement, working for changing roles and
economic equality; part of a handful (if that) of heterosexuals being
outspoken supporters of lesbian culture and women's music; part of the
long tradition of leftist radicals trying to stay in touch with the farm
workers, Native Americans, Puerto Rican independence, and Black
Power, trying to find unity so that all that we are could move through
the world as one rather than be ripped into little pieces.

8
IMAGINE MY SURPRISE

I GOT A CALL FROM MARIANNE SCHNELLER, THE WOMAN WHO HAD worked with me and Jeff back in our Placerville Fair days. She had seen the Building Women concert as well as other smaller women's music events and felt the music was far superior to the production. Marianne proposed a seven-city tour in California with Meg, Cris, Margie, and me. And she would see to it we had good lights and sound and promotion so the music could be presented in a professional context. We all met once again at my house, each exhausted from our individual work. We needed sleep. But we said yes, sure that when we were all more rested, we would think it was a great idea. Marianne's father would loan her five thousand dollars to front the tour. However, something quite more than a great idea lay before us.

I finished the fall tour and raced into the studio to record *You Can Know All I Am* so that I could be done by February. Cris was just across town recording *The Changer and the Changed*. She was doing the record with all women. I sang backup on one of her songs. She came over and sang backup on one of mine. I asked Meg if she would come sing as well, but she said no. She wanted to do only projects that were with all women. I tried not to take it personally. I knew one shouldn't take separatism personally. But Meg was not a political party or a movement. She was a new friend and she could hurt my feelings. I could not completely dismiss the logic of her perspective. In fact, it haunted me. Separatism is usually a necessary historic position that can be seen in almost every minority movement for dignity while counteracting a dominant culture and its institutions. It was one of the "largest" ideas I'd ever examined since taking a look at imperialism. I had read *Lysistrata*, but that was a tactical threat. This was not only a strategic choice, but a personal preference.

When I spoke to Jeff about it, he considered the concept. He seldom confronted me. Jeff had some strange sixth sense about my work, knowing there was always something interesting to learn on the other side of my explorations. But some of the musicians working on my album were not so open-minded. They immediately started ranting on about discrimination and unconsciously put forth a strange defense of the existing separatist system of record making in the music industry . . . men-only records.

The more they argued against radical feminist perspectives, the more I began to be excited by them. "More Important to Me" on *Hang in There*, "Get Off Me Baby" and "Free to Grow" on *A Live Album*, and "You've Got Me Flying," "Sister-Woman-Sister," and "Nicolia" on the record I was in the middle of making were just the beginning of my artistic expression of understanding sexism. We called the album *You Can Know All I Am*. Little did I know how prophetic that would be!

Jeff, Rob, Julie, and I worked together easily. We found a small studio and worked with players we could afford, starting with just the basic tracks, and adding layers as we went along. The only "star" we hired wasn't a star yet—Lee Rittenour.

Everything went smoothly until I had to sing. I found I didn't like how I sounded outside a live environment. I stopped trusting my instincts, I started combining vocal tracks together, one verse from this take, one from that. Why couldn't I just sing the song!? I left the studio at one point, throwing my arms in the air in frustration and screaming, "You decide. I don't know what sounds good anymore. My voice doesn't, that's for sure. Why don't you go find a lead singer who knows how to do the job!" I was so hard on myself. I didn't know that most contemporary records used vocal compilations. Very few singers could sing it perfectly from top to bottom. Not only did I think I should be able to sing it in one piece, I thought I should be able to do it first take.

In the beginning of the new year, Cris, Margie, Meg, and I regrouped to rehearse. Slowly, the issues that tore society apart day after day began to wear us away too. We were women in search of a new world. We asked hard questions of ourselves. How could we call this a tour of women's music if we were all white? What about Holly being straight? This wasn't a lesbian concert. Or was it? So we should call it a lesbian concert? No, many woman wouldn't come if we called it that. It was too scary. Should it be for women only? Yes, it was time that lesbians had a safe place to come together without fear of reprisal. No, it should be mixed. This was an opportunity for women's music to be acknowledged by everyone. A lot of women, straight and lesbian, wouldn't come if it was for women only. What about lesbians who have men friends? What about gay men?

The debate went on. What about ticket prices? It couldn't be too expensive. Poor women wouldn't be able to afford it. A sliding scale would solve that. No, people didn't value culture enough to have a sliding scale. They would just as soon pay for beer rather than music. That wasn't fair to say. The production couldn't afford low ticket prices. This was a large tour. It would be nice for us to make some money. These women would pay to hear Linda Ronstadt, why shouldn't they pay to hear us? But what about poor women, what about children? What about child care?

The discussion went on. Should we invite the press and really make this into something? The lesbian press, yes; the straight press, no. Why not? The straight press reached a lot of people, including lesbians who were in the closet. Yes, but it would bring this music to the attention of a lot of men and this music wasn't for men. That was not true for all of us. Some of us wanted our music to be for everyone. Well, *everyone* could listen to it another time. This was a women's music tour.

The search went on. We should record this and have it filmed. What company should record it? Olivia would do it. Some of us won't do an album on Olivia. Redwood could do it. No, Meg and Cris recorded for Olivia and Margie was on Pleiades. Maybe we could co-produce it? How was that possible, we had gotten too angry with each other and now there was mistrust.

For my try-to-fix-it attitude I ended up being accused of playing both ends against the middle. The disagreements, the exhaustion, and the hurt feelings made it difficult to reach any agreement. The greatest casualty was that the tour was not officially documented. I wish we had asked an outside party to tape it and then put it away in a locked box for twenty years. But there was no recording of this magnificent collaboration, only a bootleg or two. And it *was* magnificent.

Some may have called our process foolish, struggling over details when we could have been getting rich and famous. Yes, maybe, but we were asking the essential questions of the decade, and if one doesn't try to act on one's beliefs, then it is a parlor game of mental exercise, not social change. And despite the conflict, night after night the music soared. The concerts were open to the general public and the press. The tickets were four dollars compared to the going concert price of five dollars. There was child care. We played San Diego, Santa Barbara, Oakland, Los Angeles, Santa Cruz, and Sonoma. Oakland and Santa Cruz sold out and extra shows were added.

We stood in the wings in Sonoma. More than one thousand women plus my father (and perhaps a dozen or so other men) filled the hall with a vibrancy I had never felt before. Closet doors were swinging open; women who had hidden in the shadows were strutting around, proudly and defiantly in love. We were welcoming in a new era and it seemed that women's culture would never be the same again. We were not the first feminist musicians to sing out, but this tour jump-started a cultural phenomenon that would change the lives of hundreds of thousands of women and men; it laid the groundwork so that a dozen years later, young independent women could dominate the music industry. At the same time, millions of people never even knew it happened.

But that night in Sonoma, we knew we were in the middle of something unprecedented. I think we were scared to walk out to meet it. We stood quietly together, speechless, breathless. The audience was clapping and stomping. We walked onstage. The place exploded. I thought for a moment, *My God, we are the Beatles of the women's movement!* Only when we began to play did the screaming subside so that they could hear the words. But they were too excited, and when a particularly beautiful phrase or harmony flowed out from us, they leaped to their feet again as if to grab it.

The next day, we were in Sacramento doing a sound check. Meg and I had remained friends despite all the struggles. Although we disagreed politically, we had great respect for each other. I looked forward to seeing her each day, and perked up when I heard her Southern twang. Sitting at the loading dock, waiting for my turn to sound check, letting the winter sun warm my cheeks, I heard Meg begin to sing "Valentine Song." This was a song she had written for her lover, Ginny. I moved inside to watch her from the wings. Yes, Meg was a special one.

Night after night women gathered, the music soared, and lives changed. During the days off, I missed doing the show. I laughed at myself when I noticed how happy I was to see Meg again when we regrouped. I was like a little kid when her old buddy greets her on the playground after summer vacation.

The tour was almost over. Our last concert would be at the California Institution for Women, a women's prison in Southern California. Karlene Faith, a supporter and scholar of women's music and a central organizer in prison work, set up the concert at CIW. We had collected musical instruments to take into the prison so that the women could be part of women's music from within. Going to a prison for the first time is intimidating, even if you have no intention of staying. Prison is authoritarianism that cannot be escaped; it is not helpful or reasonable. But there were people inside who had been badly hurt and we went to heal, to sing . . . "Sometimes it takes a rainy day," sang Cris. The women danced, laughed, cried, and sang. A young guard stood in the wings while Meg sang "Valentine Song." I became concerned that the lesbian nature of the song and the closeness the women in the audience were feeling to each other and to us were going to make the guards nervous. But the young woman in uniform was smiling and swaying. "The girls are having a good time," she said. "They need a little valentine." Maybe the guard needed one too.

My thoughts returned to Meg. Driving out to the prison that afternoon, we had let our hands rest dangerously close to each other, my hand on my knee, her hand on her knee, our eyes watching our hands to see if they could resist the urge to hold each other. I tried to focus on the clever conversation that bounced around the car, but my mind kept screaming, "What are you doing? What is going on here?" I would answer myself with imposed calm, "It is just a fun flirtation. This happens a lot when people work together. It's simply an extension of creativity. It is nothing to worry about. She is a married lesbian separatist; you are a soon-to-be-married heterosexual. This is as safe as it gets. Nothing could possibly happen."

Karlene had invited us all to her house for a party. I said I would come but I needed to stop by my house. Meg asked if I could give her a ride. I said of course. I could not bear the thought of saying good-bye to her. The tour over, we would have no reason to see each other.

We sat in front of Karlene's house for four hours and never went inside. Somehow we didn't worry about being missed. We talked around it for a while, but finally Meg asked me if I had or would ever consider making love with a woman. That broke the ice, and soon I got to hold those beautiful hands. The problem, I said, was not whether I would make love to a woman, but whether she would make love with a straight woman and cheat on her marriage. Would I become a lesbian? I thought not. Would she leave Ginny? Of course not. So it was undoubtedly safe. And it couldn't have been more exhilarating.

Our first rendezvous was in the afternoon at a motel. I couldn't eat or sleep for days in anticipation. I had never felt so excited in all my life. I'm sure it had something to do with the clandestine nature of our meeting. Also it was like having a second chance at virginity, older and wiser at twenty-five than I had been at eighteen. And I was in love.

My hands could feel her even before they reached her. How soft her skin was, how strong her muscles, how sweet her shyness, how amusing my bold desire. This is what men get to have? This is what I have offered them and then wondered if they liked it? These are the smells and tastes I have felt insecure about and tried to wash away? This is how breasts feel rising? This is the beauty of a round belly and voluptuous thighs? The wonder of this woman's body . . . of *my* body. I knew exactly what to do to bring her pleasure. It was my pleasure. I was making love to her and to myself and I was essentially and forever changed by the experience. This will be my memory, but lesbians will smile and straight women may wonder if it is not time to give themselves the gift of self-love. The diet cycle that had started in high school ended abruptly. My body was happy. In the years ahead, I would come out to people all over the world. But it was in this moment, as I made love without fear or shame, that I came out to myself.

The next week, one of the women from Olivia asked if she could come over to talk to me. I should have said no. It was not a good time for me to talk to someone I barely knew. In fact, I should have left for New York City immediately. But I said yes. The Olivia rep said that they (meaning the collective) were of course supportive of my having a relationship with a woman, but they feared this might cause Olivia to fold. Why didn't I say, "If the collective is stronger than the individuals in the collective, it will not fold, and if it isn't, then perhaps folding will be the best thing," or "People fall in love and break up, people are born and people die; it is not a good idea to build a dream, a business, or a movement on the premise that there will never be crisis or change"?

But I did not know to say these things. All I knew was that I had "accidentally," and without malice toward anyone, fallen in love with a woman who was in a committed relationship. We hadn't meant for anyone to find out. We had meant for it to go away. But it didn't. And someone did find out. Ginny and Meg had been curled up in bed watching *The Sound of Music* on TV. During a commercial, Ginny had asked Meg if she had a crush on me. Meg was silent and then chose not to lie to her best friend. Now everyone was scared.

If I had been wiser—if, if, if—I would have called Meg and said, "It was wonderful and exciting to meet you clandestinely in motels, to feel the spontaneous power of this infatuation, to feel like a teenager in love for the first time. I do not regret it. But the purity of this love will be scarred by conflict and guilt. So let's not see each other anymore. If one day you decide to end your relationship with Ginny and I am not still with Arthur, then we can meet again."

Instead, I lived in a state of denial—telling myself that this was just an affair, that Meg was with Ginny and I was with Arthur, and if everyone would just leave us alone for a while it would blow over. I couldn't sleep. I couldn't eat unless I was with her. I lost weight. Out on the road, I sat for hours in dark corners missing her. But there was no escape. It seemed every household I stayed in was playing her records. Finally, I became very sick with a high fever. I had to cancel one concert and ask Cris to substitute for me in another. Julie Thompson, my manager and housemate, did not know but she *knew*. She called Meg to tell her I was sick and gave her the number of my hotel up in the Northwest. Hearing Meg's voice was the air I needed to breathe.

Meg and Ginny decided to give their relationship another try. But Meg wrote me a letter from somewhere on the road. She intended it to be a simple, friendly letter, but it revealed that she was having as hard a time being away from me as I was from her. Things were not going as I had planned. Arthur was being very supportive. We talked every day on the phone. He could tolerate my having an affair, but he was afraid he would lose me. He also felt it was not the affair with a woman that would take me. It was an affair with a movement, a time in history. With that, he did not stand a chance. I could feel his sense of helplessness. I guess I tried to assure him that I still loved him, but I also tried not to lie. I was coming to New York City soon and maybe things would be better if we could see each other in person.

When he met me at the airport, he handed me a letter that had arrived from Meg. I put it in my purse and we headed into the city. At some point I slipped away to read the letter. In it Meg said she had been thinking about my trip to New York to see Arthur. I obviously had to do what I had to do, *but* if I continued to be lovers with Arthur, she could not be lovers with me again. She had known I was straight when we first began this affair, but she realized now that she did not want a relationship with a straight woman. I needed to decide if I was a lesbian or not.

I put my head down on my lap and wept. How could she do this to me? It wasn't fair. And the frightening part was that I felt so powerless. I was in love with Arthur—we deserved a chance just like Meg and Ginny. Arthur and I did make love, but it was filled with confusion and left us sad. Why had I hurt this man I loved so dearly? Why was I so in love with this woman I barely knew? I went back out on the road the next day with Jeff for concerts in the Southeast. Somewhere in South Carolina, Jeff and I searched unsuccessfully for a gay bar. I needed to take a look at this life that was calling me.

Meg and Ginny broke up. Arthur and I parted ways. Meg and I were together for three and a half years. I loved that woman to dis-traction and made choices I never would have made had I not wanted so to please her. It complicated matters that she was in a collective. It was like having a dozen in-laws. Meg weighed every choice against the good of Olivia. Even when she paid for dinner, it was collective money, and she felt buying me dinner was not the collective's idea of well-spent funds! Meg lived in a room behind the Olivia Records office, so I had to go through Olivia to get to her. Ginny was still her manager. It must have been terrible for Ginny to have me there. We all tried to be civil, but it was an unreasonable expectation.

It was impossible not to work together in some fashion. Olivia had lesbian feminist priorities and believed in world peace. Redwood had world-peace priorities and believed in lesbian feminism. I wanted to feminize the peace movement and globalize the lesbian movement. Olivia wanted to build networks that would serve the lesbian commu-nity and bring lesbians to that newly created cultural base. Neither idea was right or wrong. We tried to be compatible but instead we were often at odds. However, in what we felt was in the best interest of "sisterhood," we seldom aired those differences publicly. As we be-came more visible, we were thrown into one lump . . . "those lesbian separatists." This was especially difficult for me, because Redwood was not a separatist company. My father was the business manager! But at the same time, I did not want to be on the defensive saying, "Oh, we're not one of those!" and thereby perpetuate homophobia. Olivia and Redwood didn't like or trust each other much, but we were in the forefront of women's music together. It was, in this Dickensian tale of two record companies, the best of times, it was the worst of times.

I was looking forward to the National Women's Music Festival in Champaign-Urbana, Illinois. Kristen Lems was the moving force behind the festival, struggling on the one hand with the university to keep subsidizing this unique extravaganza, and on the other hand with lesbians who wanted the festival to be more woman-identified. She hung in there year after year despite it all.

The first year, there had been men onstage supporting women headliners. Then the organizers had agreed to have only women onstage. Several years later, in 1976, I was invited. Meg agreed to play for me in place of Jeff Langley. We decided that, rather than do two separate sets, we would put our two sets together, with a song-swap feel. I would have preferred to have had Jeff with me, but I was trying to respect the identity of the festival. Jeff and I used to joke about dressing him up in drag.

The festival organizers were excited that I had agreed to attend. Kristen was not only involved in the women's movement, she was a world-view peace activist. My music represented a holistic perspective. I think she hoped I would introduce some world-peace ideas to women who had recently been politicized by the women's-liberation movement. They also wanted to present a heterosexual artist who openly opposed homophobia. (They did not know that Meg and I had just become lovers.)

The promotion already out, Meg remembered that I drew a very mixed crowd—that meant there would be a lot of men in the audience. She was committed to singing for women-only audiences whenever possible. I should have suggested we return to the idea of separate sets and I find a different accompanist. But I was in love. I wanted to support Meg's desire for a separate lesbian space. I wanted also to challenge my own deeply ingrained heterosexual and male-identified training. I have always felt the only way to appreciate someone else's shoes is to try them on, or at least get close enough to see the soles. So I decided, okay, here we go. I tour a lot. Men can see my show another time. I will ask that our show be for women only. Well, all hell broke loose. The very reason I had been invited to the festival was to present a bridge between lesbian feminists and the progressive mixed community, and here I was suggesting my presentation be women-only.

Not unlike the folk/rock world or the world at large, in 1976 many of the participants in women's music were using drugs or were alcoholics and/or co-dependents. The movement for sobriety had not yet surfaced. The idea of "co-dependency" behavior was relatively unknown in the world and completely unknown to me. I didn't even know my new lover had a drinking problem. And I certainly didn't recognize that I didn't need to be the one drinking the alcohol for it to affect my behavior.

Kristen tried to understand our request for women-only space even though she knew it was inappropriate. This was a college campus and the festival was open to the public. Her co-producer was causing even more difficulty by making homophobic remarks, which sent Meg into a frenzy and strengthened my belief that I should back Meg on this one.

The saddest part was that Malvina Reynolds, who was a friend of mine, took the other side, and we were pitted against each other. She accused me of discrimination, saying she would never participate in any event where her husband, with whom she worked for peace and justice, would not be welcome. I thought my heart would break. My father understood the concept of women-only. I wished he had been there to talk to her. I was surprised by her defensive stance. After all, she had written the song "We Don't Need the Men." Tempers flared out of control.

I tried to explain that women-only concerts were not a form of discrimination but rather like self-help clinics. A man wouldn't demand to be in the gynecology office, nor would he holler discrimination if he wasn't allowed in. Most women get together alone to heal, to change the world, not to steal or dominate it. That is different from some men's social and athletic clubs. Women lose jobs, money, and power as a result of being excluded from them because men do business there. That's why ambitious men want to be in them. But women-only space was not discriminatory. I felt absolutely sure about that, though I did not feel absolutely sure that it was correct at this festival, at this time, and in this fashion. I had gotten myself into a bind.

I searched for a compromise and wrote a letter that we handed out at the concert explaining why, historically, women needed their own space and that it was not an antiman but a prowoman request. I asked that men, if they understood this need, voluntarily choose not to attend the concert. I asked that those men who did not understand or who disagreed take the seats in the back of the auditorium so that women could fill up the front and feel surrounded by women during the concert. I heard an inner voice say, "This will get you through the night but you are not done with this one yet." It didn't feel good but it was the best I could do at the time, and word of my position raced through the country. I started getting calls at my office, "What is this we hear that Holly won't let men come hear her music anymore?!" It was already out of hand, and I hadn't even come out yet! But in spite of the controversy, some beautiful music was made. And if there were some unhappy folks, well, I understand now that sometimes we have to be willing to try it someone else's way, or at least acknowledge that there is another way, hoping that new solutions surface from conflict.

A few months later the for-women-only Michigan Women's Music Festival was born, followed by western, southern, eastern, and European women's music festivals. The NWMF of Champaign-Urbana moved to a campus in Bloomington, Indiana, and continues to this day as a women's festival open to the public.

The wet August heat defined the first Michigan Women's Music Festival in the summer of 1976. Meg and I had been together seven months, the first few of which had been riddled with the conflict of breaking up with our lovers. I hadn't really come out yet in public. *The Lesbian Tide* was publishing an ongoing dialogue criticizing the paper for putting me, a straight woman, on the cover. Many lesbians felt that because there were so few outlets for lesbians to express themselves, it was inappropriate to devote that precious front-page space to a straight person. I read the dialogue for a few months and then wrote them, but my response hadn't been printed yet.

I didn't believe in secrets. I wasn't ashamed of my love for Meg, but I was private. I hadn't announced my boyfriends from the stage. I had seldom discussed my heterosexual relationships in the press. But because of the nature of this particular oppression, coming out seemed important, and how did one come out without it being identified with sex? I couldn't find a way around it. Being a good post-McCarthy child, I had vowed I would never do anything that I wouldn't talk about on the Johnny Carson show or in court. Well, I was about to come out in the lesbian equivalent of Carson and court—a women's music festival.

I was still trying to pretend that Meg was only a social drinker. I sat on the edge of the bed thinking and trying not to think. The trick was to keep going, not to slow down too much, or else I would lose control and the world would crash and crumble around me. If I kept moving . . .

I packed water, Kleenex, a flashlight, little cans of deviled ham and chicken, and protein candy bars to get me through the day. I was horrified at the thought of hundreds of urban women in the woods without any country skills! Hundreds became well over a thousand. No one had dreamed that this many women would show up. The town cowboys went berserk, some even going so far as to rent planes so that they could fly over and swoop down to look and harass. Security groups were formed to surround the camp and protect women from men who had, after a keg of beer, decided to come play with the girls. The guys did not realize that this was not like the girls' camps they had seen in *Marjorie Morningstar*. They were coming to mess with fifteen hundred dykes.

When we arrived at the camp, tents and campers covered the grounds. I enjoyed seeing women shed their defensive postures and their clothes. With a sigh, they melted into a self-created world that for this moment in time they would call their own. Naked bodies danced in the sun, strong arms threw footballs, the timid became courageous, the courageous were able to rest for a moment. I doubt anyone imagined that it would become an institution and that eight thousand women would show up for the ten-year anniversary.

The stage was built and the sound and lighting equipment was up, but no one was prepared for the rain and wind that were on the way. Canadian women announced that they had been harassed at the border coming in, some skin-searched. A small group of women begged for a chemical-free camping space. Most of us didn't know what that was; many laughed at their request. If there was a problem, it was theirs. A space was carved out for them, but it was constantly invaded by those who came to encourage them back to the "good times." (A decade later, a small group of women ask the festival for a place to get high. Some laugh at them, some sigh and walk away, some go off to a campsite AA meeting.) There were no Porta-Johns, there wasn't enough food and water, there were arguments about whether boy children should be able to come and at what age a boy is a boy.

I had recently cut my long hair, and in my new, "stripped" persona—fingernails gone, makeup gone, the security of a heterosexual career gone, my old sense of self gone and no new sense filling the void—I stood in front of fifteen hundred women in the heat and dust, and with good humor accused them of having placed bets on me. "But you can stop now. I have fallen in love with a woman!" They gave me a standing ovation. I went to the piano and, accompanying myself (something I had rarely done and have seldom done since), sang "Imagine My Surprise," a song I had recently written for Meg. I thought of all the women whose lives would have been so different if, instead of losing family, jobs, children, and self-respect, they had been cheered by fifteen hundred people when they came out. Later in the day, Linda Tillery, Teresa Trull, Meg Christian, and I sang a mighty version of "You Make Me Feel Like a Natural Woman."

I loved watching new feminist square dances that had three in a "couple" instead of two and included the calls "Sisters in the center" and "Come out to your family." The delight of "redoing" was everywhere. Women who had always thought they were the only ones found that they had a family, and marveled at the possibility that there were lesbians everywhere in the world. Someone was suggesting that more than 10 percent of the population was gay, not counting bisexuals. This was a mind-boggling discovery for those who had grown up on *The Well of Loneliness*. As night fell on the festival, I sat alone in the dark, letting the music and starlight wash over me. Despite my joy for these women who had seemed to come home, I did not share this feeling of relief.

I had never been a singles queen by any stretch of the imagination. But I had sat in my share of bars and gone home with a few strangers. I had been to gay bars but never a lesbian bar. I was excited, nervous, curious. Most of all, I was feeling overwhelmed with respect for these women. They had not made their choice out of political awareness. They found each other without any help from feminist bookstores or lesbian music festivals. They took greater risks than I shall ever have to take in order to hold a woman's hand. It was in their footsteps I was about to walk. I thought I had better pay tribute.

I changed clothes about three times. Then I drove out to a country bar in North Hollywood, parked my car, sat there for a long time, took a deep breath, and headed for the door. As I got closer, a policeman walked by. I felt myself gasp and then laughed at myself. *The policeman knows about that bar, it's on his beat. He knows it's filled with lesbians. Who are you hiding from? He probably knows more about lesbians than you do. He may also harass the hell out of them, ticket their cars, check more IDs, maybe even beat up some women some-*

times. I've heard stories. But you are going in there and you are going to feel all the fear there is to feel, all the discomfort, all the panic. You are going to watch all the eyes turn and look at you when you come in, as they check out the new baby queer. No matter that you are wearing jeans and jacket, you are a fem through and through, girl, so keep walking.

I went through the door. There was nobody there but the bartender, who was a bleached-blond butch talking to a skinny gay cowboy. It didn't matter. I had just experienced plenty of feelings to sort through. And I had learned that no self-respecting dyke shows up at the bar at six P.M. on a Friday night!

But I would have other chances. I would come to feel easy in a lesbian bar, especially if I wasn't recognized or if I came in with a bunch of friends. I would enjoy watching women, and try to imagine what their lives were like. Some who came in directly from work still had on nylons and heels or their nurse's uniforms, shattering my assumptions about what kind of a woman a lesbian is. Strikingly beautiful, well-dressed women would saunter in with their lovers, who were equally striking and beautiful. Athletic women in running shorts and muscles to die for would stop by. Women who I imagined rode up on motorcycles (but may have had Volvo station wagons with car seats in back, for all I knew) would roll up their sleeves and shoot a hell of a game of pool. Older couples who had fallen in love back when role-playing was an essential part of survival would come in and celebrate their thirty-fifth anniversary, one with a butch haircut, pants, and comfortable shoes, the other in a dress, makeup, and teased hairdo. It was often the case, as it is in heterosexual relationships, that the fem was the stronger of the two, and the butch a marshmallow. I saw integration take place naturally, not out of political awareness about racism, but because women fell in love first and had to figure out what to do with their racism second. There were also the sad and lonely women, the ones who never quite got what they had hoped for, who no longer fell in love, who weren't invited home for Christmas or Hanukkah, who were the leftover victims of the time just short of the rubyfruit jungle. They looked on with sad confusion bordering on fear as they watched the new, young baby dykes flaunting proud and radical gay slogans on their T-shirts—bold, sexy, free-spirited.

There were the bartenders who tried to keep an eye on their flock, who faced the law and the mob and anyone else they had to deal with to stay in business. They would discourage the straight men who came in to gawk, harass, or work out a threesome. There were also the straight couples who came in to find a woman who would do it with them, just to liven up their dying sex life. Sometimes they found what they were looking for, but for the most part they missed the point. Lesbians didn't come to lesbian bars to do it for men or with men or with straight women. They came because they enjoyed the company of other lesbians, and they would prefer that all the riffraff start their own bar.

There was always talk about some Hollywood actress or other who had been in a few nights before. I felt bad for these women who had no privacy. I also marveled at their courage. A general rule did seem to be in effect that if you were going to pass on that kind of gossip, you told only other queers. It was not meant to be malicious; finding out a famous person is gay or a lesbian is felt to be a validation in a homophobic society. You could tell yourself, "You see, she is a lesbian and she is beautiful and respected and famous. She's okay, therefore I'm okay." Of course, everyone knew that if she was out of the closet, she would no longer be respected and famous, but damn, she would still be beautiful.

I went to a disco once by myself. It was the *Saturday Night Fever* era. I found a post to lean against and watched the dancers. Shortly after I had arrived, I saw a man staring at me. I thought, *What a drag. I come to a gay men's bar where I ought to feel completely safe and unbothered, and damned if there isn't some straight guy here come to bother me.* He slowly worked his way in my direction. I tried to ignore his approach, hoping to discourage him. I didn't want to leave the comfort of my pole. For a moment I didn't see him, then there was a tap on my shoulder. I jumped and turned toward him. He looked so startled. Now that he was up close I could see that he was a young, frightened gay man. He said, "I'm terribly sorry, I thought, I thought you were . . . a boy." He looked excruciatingly embarrassed and disappointed. I laughed out loud and he slipped into the shadows of the crowd.

I never picked up a woman in a bar. Somehow making love with a woman is so personal, it never seemed appropriate to treat a woman like a stranger.

Amid the struggles at the National Women's Music Festival, I had reconnected with Amy Horowitz, who had produced a concert for me

126

in Ashland, Oregon, in March 1976. Amy had founded Women's Space, one of the oldest women's music festivals still going. Amy was also Redwood's independent record distributor in the Northwest. I liked Amy. She was a little more spiritual than I, into astrology and such things, but she also had a passion for hard work and I was looking for someone to work with who had experience in feminism, lesbianism, and the left. I said to her, "If you ever want to leave Ashland . . ."

Sitting in Champaign-Urbana over coffee and home fries, which she ate with an incredible amount of catsup, Amy told me she was ready to move away from Oregon. I offered her a job. She arrived in Los Angeles in August and moved into my house, which also harbored my office. She introduced me to sucking on lox wings, told me stories about her adventures as international president of B'nai B'rith youth, and fed off my addiction to long hours, telephones, booking systems, and ice cream. She became my assistant, booking agent, and valued political friend.

I was completely dedicated to the long-overdue celebration of women's culture, of lesbian and feminist song, but women's music cramped my style in its narrow approach. On the other hand, mainstream culture was so sexist and capitalistic and the folk music scene so male-dominated, I was not drawn (or completely welcome) to enter those circles on any full-time basis. Perhaps it was our discomfort with private party politics or maybe it was our fascination with diversity that drew Amy and me to coalition work. We began to work with artists and organizations that stretched out into the world. Jeff had moved on to focus on his own classical career, and I began working with pianist Mary Watkins, who brought more of a jazz influence to my music.

The Wallflower Order Dance Collective was co-founded by my sister Laurel, Krissy Keefer, Nina Fichter, and several other women who were dancing in Eugene, Oregon. They combined forms like Aikido, ballet, modern jazz, and American Sign Language to put forth a vision that included feminism, world politics, and spirituality long before such integration was popular. In my opinion, they were the most daring and entertaining dance company in the country. Amy and I decided to book their first national tour. We also produced a benefit concert in Los Angeles that brought together the Latin and women's communities in defense of José Medina, a Mexican attorney who was seeking political asylum in the United States, and we booked a tour for Iris Films, which had made a film about lesbian parents, *In the Best*

Interests of the Children, produced by Liz Stevens and Frances Reid.

Then Amy and I heard an extraordinary record by Bernice Reagon. While in Washington, D.C., visiting her parents for Passover, Amy set up a meeting with Bernice to find out what she was doing and to tell her about our work. Bernice had been in the original Freedom Singers, born out of the civil rights movement. She had since founded an a cappella group called Sweet Honey in the Rock, self-described as "Black Woman Sound." They had been scheduled to come to California, but the event was canceled. Amy called me to see how I would feel about us taking on the tour. It would mean putting all other work on hold for six weeks. We agreed to do it. Amy booked the tour having never seen the group perform, with one album and two press clippings to work with. In the spring of 1977, Sweet Honey in the Rock did their first California tour. The tour broke new ground and broke even!

In Los Angeles, I welcomed the group to my home and made them a turkey dinner. Of course, the best part was hearing them sing. Bernice laid down the foundation, Evelyn and Pat soared through the middle, and Yasmeen took the tops of our heads off with notes I couldn't even imagine. The young black students at the community college found Africa, Selma, and Santa Monica all in one song.

I was invited to the 1977 International Conference Against A & H Bombs in Japan. I said I would attend but wanted to bring a small women's delegation. The organizers agreed. Our delegation was made up of me (singer/songwriter/record company exec), Amy Horowitz (organizer, poet, booking agent), Dr. Bernice Johnson Reagon (singer/songwriter/Afro-American cultural researcher at the Smithsonian Institution), and Sally Savitz (athlete, member of Iris Films).

In Tokyo, we stayed in a Buddhist temple. We were provided mats and slept in the open air. Early in the morning, the monks began chanting. We rose quietly and each did our own version of waking up. Then, when the chanting stopped, we joined the monks in the kitchen, where they were eating peanut butter and jelly sandwiches and watching daytime soaps on TV, thoroughly smashing any preconceptions we had of Buddhist monks. There was one young woman we liked a lot, wrapped in bright yellow robes, her bald head shining so soft and perfect, her arms burned inside the elbow where she had done her penance by pouring hot wax on her skin. Sally gave her a T-shirt that said "Sisterhood Is Powerful," with a clenched fist in a red circle. Bernice refolded the young nun's yellow robe so it could be worn African-style. Wearing her T-shirt and African clothes, she put her fist

128

in the air and said, "Sisterhood is powerful." I love how women find their way across the borders.

That afternoon, Bernice suggested we practice the song we were going to sing at the conference cultural event. I met her at the temple, ready to learn a song. We sang about two bars of something and she said, "Come here." She sat down cross-legged and pointed for me to sit across from her. I did. "No, come closer." I moved in until our knees were almost touching. "Now," she said, "meet my voice in the middle." I didn't know what she meant. "No, right here," she said, pointing at the space between her mouth and mine. "Push my voice back with yours. Do not let it go any farther than halfway between us." Afraid that not trying would be worse than failing, I pushed her voice and my own grew to twice its size, not so much in volume as in power. We sang Bernice's song, "They are falling all around me, the strongest leaves on my tree."

Our hosts included Buddhists, Socialists, Communists, and two feminists who had found us. The latter introduced us to other Japanese feminists and organized a women's gathering in Tokyo after we returned from Hiroshima. It was lovely. About thirty women sat in a large circle, each of us in turn telling a little about herself, her work, her ideas. Then Bernice and I each sang and the Japanese women sang for us.

Our Buddhist hosts took us around Tokyo and on a field trip to the mountains to see some of the magnificent temples. I could have stayed there forever, surrounded by the mighty snow-capped mountains and a breathtakingly blue sky. I needed some peace. I was having a hard time with my life. Fortunately, I was "built" so I could carry on, sidestepping my moods just enough to keep going. But at night, or in quiet moments, the discrepancies attacked. At the moment, I did not know where the peace would come from. I felt a responsibility to be out as a lesbian in Japan, and yet it felt inappropriate. Not everything can be done at once or in order. Change is both slow and rapid and humanity is defined by centuries, not decades. But I was still young and wanted "everything" to be okay and now! I wasn't sure where my career was going, or even what "career" meant. I worked "frantically" for peace and justice, feeling torn between the Left and the lesbians and not understanding why it wasn't one and the same.

The conference itself was huge. People from all over the world gathered to remember and to assure that the horror of atomic war would not happen again. I had assumed that all who attended would be united around this issue. But I discovered that unity existed only on the surface. Beneath was a maze of debates and negotiations. Grass-roots organizers discussed the effect nuclear war has on human life, mother earth, and world peace. They proposed alternatives. Doctors, scientists, and religious leaders engaged in heated discussions about nuclear power and the economy, as well as about whether nuclear power and weapons were okay for some to have but not for others. I recall one man suggesting that nuclear development was safe in the hands of the developed countries because we had the skill and the political sophistication to see that it was used only for the good of humanity. Another countered with the argument that the Socialist countries, particularly in the Third World, were the only ones who had the best interests of the working people at heart. I left that meeting quite early on. I knew they were all going nowhere.

Then there were the meetings behind closed doors that involved world leaders—not the presidents and prime ministers, but their representatives. I doubted they thought that multicultural feminism was essential to discovering solutions to poverty and strategies for world peace. But our hosts did. It was no accident that they received our delegation with enthusiasm. They wanted us to return to the States and impact our work on feminist and black culture. They would not be disappointed. As a result of this visit to Japan, all of us became more committed to a nuclear-free world. While still in Japan, Bernice began to write a superb anti-nuke song called "B'lieve I'll Run On . . . See What the End's Gonna Be." Later Sally would put together an educational slide show, and Amy and I would originate the first national anti-nuke tour ever presented in the United States. The evening cultural event was breathtaking. I was especially moved by the Taiko drummers, a mixture of men and women who all stood in powerful stances before huge drums and used their full strength to beat the rhythms. Bernice and I sang, separately and together, but there was smoke and dust in the hall, and before the night was out I had no voice at all.

I returned to the hotel, hoping that a good night's sleep and a lot of water would heal me for the next evening's performance. Instead, I got a high fever and became extremely sick.

I asked first to have an acupuncturist come to my hotel. An older man arrived on the arm of his young assistant. He was blind. He began work on my body, and as he commented on my condition, she translated. He said my legs were very tired. He also shook his head when he worked on my diaphragm and lungs. "Very tired," he just kept saying, "very tired." He worked his way up my body, and when he got to my throat area he put a needle in my neck. When he was done, I slept for a long time.

In the morning, I still had a high fever. I was sweating and shaking. The hosts would no longer tolerate my holistic approach. They felt responsible for me and insisted that I go to the hospital. An ambulance arrived. Into my room came five men dressed in what looked like riot gear, including helmets. They were running. They carried a stretcher. I was ordered to get on it, and they carried me out of the hotel as if I were being arrested and locked me in the ambulance. With the siren screaming, we raced through the streets of Tokyo to the hospital. When at long last a doctor came to see me, he was very curt with his explanation to the interpreter. I wasn't really sure what I had, what I was taking, or why. I didn't die. In fact, I got well quickly. But I knew that my life was running away with me, and I didn't know how to stop it.

When I returned to L.A., I had only one day before I had to board a plane for Iowa to speak at a Socialist conference sponsored by NAM, the New American Movement. But I was having what might be called a nervous breakdown. I couldn't move. I couldn't stop crying. I couldn't function. Meg suggested I talk to a counselor. Roslyn was a big, striking black woman with a smooth voice. Just being in her presence was calming. I sat in a big, cushy chair and she sat across from me on a couch. "How are you doing?" she asked. I probably said something like, "Well, really I'm fine, it's just that . . ." But within a few minutes I had shrunk and crumbled down into the chair. She asked me if I really had to go to Iowa. I said yes. In an hour or so, she had me sitting back up, at least looking like I was all in one piece, but she warned that this was temporary. She told me I had better make some plans for the future. I nodded and then proceeded with my life, conveniently forgetting those wise words for many months to come.

I walked off the plane in Iowa and was met by a bright, energetic woman named Torie Osborn, one of the conference co-coordinators. I watched her throughout the weekend. She was good. I didn't want to forget her. Torie was possibly the only "out" lesbian in NAM. Someone had given her a copy of *Hang in There*, but she hadn't liked it

131

much. When she heard she was to pick me up at the airport, she listened to *A Live Album* and *You Can Know All I Am* over and over again, and started to like the music.

I had been invited to join a panel focusing on art and politics. Apparently my participation made this a pivotal conference for NAM, as it had just begun acknowledging the presence of lesbians in the Left and integrating lesbian feminism into leftist theory. I gave a radical speech about lesbianism, feminism, separatism, and the arts, stirring things up a bit for 1977. A lot of Socialist women were apparently experimenting with lesbianism, that is, sleeping with each other, but not many were talking about it. I think my speech embarrassed some, threatened others, and thrilled a few. Interestingly enough, some of the older Communist party veterans were glad I had come. They had been badgered mercilessly in this country by the Right during the forties and fifties and by much of the New Left in the sixties. They could relate to the radical nature of my speech.

In the evening, there was a dance. Torie brought tapes of the Shirelles and Elvis. We sang along and then Torie and I danced together. The spirit took over. Women danced together. The men danced together. (Torie says I was bold and fearless. I don't remember that part. I like it when she reminds me of things like that.) We would not be wallflowers waiting to be asked, or hussies doing the asking. We danced with ourselves and with any other selves who wanted to share the dance floor.

I hadn't been scheduled to sing at my workshop, but at some point talking about what I do doesn't work as well as just doing it. So I sang "Mountain Song" and ended with a long poem, parts of which went:

My eyes blink
My pupils grow large then small
As she turns from light to dark to light
She is all around me
A protective layer of air worth breathing
In this world of gross destruction
I not only touch the velvet and silk of her body
I defend the fire and steel of her heart . . .

We love each other as no man will ever love a woman
We love so much we have hidden like guerrilla soldiers in sub-
urbs, in factories, universities, marriages, gymnasiums, cotton

132

*fields, the radical Left, convents, med schools, and the dark-
ness of theaters.*
*And now, as we grow stronger, we are coming out
Coming out all over the world to defy your fantasy
And make real our own.*

I was getting more difficult to work with, aggravated by the
pressure of doing political work. Amy suggested I see a therapist. I
snapped at her that I didn't need a therapist. I needed the bottomless pit
of work to be completed and the money to complete it with. The next
day I secretly went out to find a therapist. I tried several but I could talk
circles around them. Finally, I found a woman who was a black Jew.
She was older than I, a straight feminist with a very clear head about
lesbianism, and she didn't let me outtalk her. The hardest part of the
work was learning to get angry. Every time I tried, I would start to cry.
My rage could always be undermined by grief. She tried to get me to
act "as if" I were angry, reminding me that I was an actress. But I
couldn't. I had lost parts because I didn't know how to get angry.

One day she took me to one of her weekly sessions made up of
other therapists. No one talked. They just stood in a circle and took
turns getting furious. They had phone books you could rip up and a
rolled piece of carpet that you could hit with a rubber pipe. I stood and
watched. After each person was done, she/he seemed so relieved.
Sometimes it ended in tears, but mostly it ended in silence or laughter.
No one talked about it, they just did it. I got more and more scared as
my turn came. I went into the circle and did my best to pound on the
piece of carpet. I was mild compared with those who had gone before.
I guess I had never really allowed myself to be "mad." It had not been
one of my family's forms of expression. If someone got upset, she/he
took a long walk out on the mountain. In the safety of strangers, I took
a step toward a new emotion.

Meg and I did a concert at Harvard. We had a solution now for
working together. We would do two shows, one for women only and
one for a mixed audience. But some young law students decided to
make a case and a grade for themselves, and they sued the producers
for discrimination . . . and won. Although the women-only show was
sold out, the judge said fifty tickets had to go on sale to the general
public. Men who were friends of women's music and women's right to
gather together stood in line, bought the tickets, and gave them to

women. I think only one man came to the show, and he came with a reporter. The case was picked up by UPI. I got asked about "reverse discrimination" for years. Sad how that bothered people so much more than the fact that there were no women in the Senate.

After a concert that Meg and I did in the Midwest, a group of men came backstage. They told me they had been supporters of my work for years and advocates of women's rights, but they felt bad about this concert. I pulled out the set list and pointed out that I had sung and said absolutely nothing critical of men in the whole show. In fact, I had not mentioned men at all. Then I reminded them of the songs I had sung at a previous concert a few years before. There had been several feminist songs critical of men. I suggested they were hurt not because they felt criticized but rather because they had been completely ig- nored. I asked if they thought they could celebrate women without being the center of attention. I watched their faces as this idea settled in. They went away, but months later I got a letter from them explain- ing that they had discussed this a lot in their men's group. They thanked me for my music and for the opportunity it had presented them to understand feminism and sexism. I wished I could have flown them to Boston to meet with the Harvard boys.

Olivia decided to move to the San Francisco Bay Area, to Berkeley. I asked Meg to leave them, to stay with me. I offered to support her. I even suggested we leave the country for a while and get out of the women's-music rat race. But she decided to go with them. We carried on long-distance as best we could. A sweet song came out of it. I sent Meg a lyric on a napkin: "Won't you write a melody for me, pretty woman. I need a little song in the middle of the day. Won't you write a melody, just a simple melody to rock me in your arms, so far away." She sent it back on tape to a lovely melody.

During one of my visits home in Ukiah, my mother showed me a letter that had arrived from the East Coast. It had been preceded by several others, all full of love and romance. This latest arrival was a proposal of marriage and included an empty book, which the suitor described as the photo album we could fill up together, starting with the wedding and honeymoon photos and then going on from there. Mom said she wasn't sure she should continue to help me with my fan mail. "It is one thing," she said, "to help you respond to your adoring and supportive fans or even your critics. In fact, they may even enjoy getting a letter back from your mother when you are unavailable to respond. But it is another thing for me to read and respond to marriage proposals.''

We agreed that she would forward all lesbian love letters and marriage proposals to me. She would have forwarded any heterosexual love letters and marriage proposals to me as well, but I never got any!

I didn't know how to answer love letters any better than she did. But I did understand the phenomenon. I had been entranced with actors or musicians before; I just didn't write them letters. I kept my obsessions to myself, which I feel is where they should be kept, unless, of course, one wants to share them with a therapist. I enjoyed the fan mail. But there was a difference between loving the music and coming on to the musician. On the other hand, if straight women wrote love letters to Paul Newman, why shouldn't lesbians write love letters to me? I had never been a famous lesbian before. It took some getting used to.

My folks were ready to turn Redwood over. It had become a much bigger enterprise than we had originally imagined. I suppose that if it had simply expanded, they would have stayed on a while more. But we all felt that I needed to make a decision about the future. Was Redwood going to be a peace-and-justice company or a lesbian feminist company? If the latter, Mom felt I should get lesbian feminists to run the company. I liked our little family business. My folks were doing a great job. I didn't feel secure about them leaving. They knew more about running a record company than I did now.

Back in L.A., by candlelight over Irish coffees, Amy Horowitz and I found ourselves talking about the need for an organization that could pick up where the individual artist left off. So many invitations and requests came to me that I couldn't accept. Wouldn't it be great to have a feminist booking agent, so that if a request came in for me that I couldn't do, it could be channeled to another artist? We wanted to share resources and we wanted to promote cross-cultural understanding. If Redwood was going to grow, we needed to record other people besides me. I would need help. I didn't want to decide between peace and justice and feminism. I didn't see how the world could function without blending those perspectives.

Amy began laying the groundwork for a nonprofit arts organization to do multiracial coalition work. She decided to move to Washington, D.C., where she could work more closely with such artists as Bernice Reagon. I paid her four hundred dollars a month for six months to start up Roadwork. The transition was exciting but hard on us as we carried on this work three thousand miles apart before computers or fax machines were part of daily life. In California, I began the work of expanding Redwood Records. I thumbed through my address book. Whom had I met over the years who would want to do this potentially thankless job, make absolutely no money, and move to California? There were Joanie and Jo-Lynne, but they owned a woman's bookstore in Kansas City, the second largest in the country. I was sure they couldn't come. There were Trudy Fulton and Marsha Cummings, who did women's music work in Minneapolis. They might be up for a change. There was that wonderful woman I had met at the NAM conference in Iowa, the redhead, Torie Osborn. Yes, there might be some possibilities. I'd start by calling Trudy and Marsha.

With truly brave and adventurous spirits, Trudy and Marsha agreed and soon they moved to California. Mom and Dad bought a house in downtown Ukiah and turned the family house over to Redwood. Ukiah was a wonderful place to work, surrounded by hills and redwoods. A live stream ran by the house. There was a pool and a vegetable garden. It was hot in the summer and cold and damp in the winter. If and when we needed to touch base with the city, we were only a two-and-a-half-hour drive from San Francisco. Torie Osborn would join the new Redwood team later in the year and soon I would move back to Ukiah. Meanwhile, I ran the expansion from L.A.

Things did not go as smoothly as I had planned. I didn't want to be a boss. I wanted us to do this work together, for everyone to own their jobs. I started to feel they couldn't own their jobs if they didn't own the business, but they couldn't afford to buy into it and they weren't sure they would want to even if they could. They hadn't been with the company long enough for them to inherit it in exchange for service.

Torie and I came from middle-class backgrounds, Trudy and Marsha from working-class. Torie and I were friends. Trudy and Marsha were lovers. Torie and I were used to having self-motivated jobs. Trudy and Marsha had come from the nine-to-five world, where it was them against the company.

In the midst of realizing the problems caused by our differences, we recorded an album with Sweet Honey. The timing was terrible, and it was my error in judgment. I wanted to record Sweet Honey. The album budget of twenty thousand dollars would not leave much money for the cost of transition, but I was impatient. Trudy and Marsha were just becoming acclimated to Redwood. Torie hadn't even arrived yet.

I should have either recorded Sweet Honey first and then expanded Redwood or expanded Redwood and then recorded Sweet Honey. To do both at the same time put an unmanageable strain on me and my finances. On top of that, by its very nature, this work would force us to confront our racism, which is not something one tosses in on the side!

Cross-cultural feminist coalition work was courageous. I knew very few artists who were doing it on such a grand scale as I had been, which made it hard to find role models and advisers. I was in a state of despair that I was not learning this work any faster and I seemed to keep making the same mistakes, mainly falling into the assumption that people from different backgrounds share a common experience. It was in relationship to this very point that we hit a snag.

The nature of the conflict was, on Redwood's part, white ignorance of Black history, culture, and struggle, coupled with the frustration and anger felt by white working-class lesbians as they too struggled to survive in a hostile world. The specifics of the conflict focused on a particular song that Sweet Honey recorded for the album Redwood was to release. The song was called "All Praise Is Due to Love," which spoke about "He," referring to God.

Trudy and Marsha preferred not to record a song that perpetuated Christianity and a male God. In their lives, Christianity had been used against working-class people, saying if you suffer now you will get yours in heaven . . . a convenient way for the powers that be to keep their wealth and to control the work force. Guilt was a major weapon used to keep women down. The violent attack by the patriarchy had killed millions of women in the Middle Ages, burning them at the stake (fires often kindled by throwing gay men into the fire and using them as faggots/fuel). Pagan culture had been destroyed, pagan holidays ripped off and replaced, an example being Christmas, which apparently is not really Jesus' birthday but strategically placed near the celebration of the winter solstice. . . . So, it was important to these newly fueled radical lesbian feminists that they not put out a record that celebrated Christianity or Him.

Sweet Honey in the Rock, on the other hand, explained the role of the church in the lives of Black people, in the survival of the Black community, and in the struggle for liberation. Black people had been torn away from their homeland, had not been allowed to organize on the plantations or to learn to read. They had seen their families ripped apart, tortured, and murdered. They were instructed to become Chris-

tians and to give up their beautiful African ways. Black people refor-
mulated Christianity, pulling out that which was relevant to them,
peeling off the stories that spoke of the liberation of the Jews in the Old
Testament, and refashioning the traditions so that they were as much
African as European. At the height of their struggle for survival, Black
people gave birth to a true Afro-American religion. And while the
slave owners may have thought the slaves were simply singing those
nice Bible stories, the spirituals were quickly becoming a part of the
underground railroad. The church was at the heart of the Black-
liberation struggle and an outpost for change.

Later, I came to understand that white abolitionists had also
worked for social change through their faith. My own mother had
received some of her political education through the *Catholic Worker*.
Segments of the church, in both the United States and in Latin America, became central in putting forth liberation theology; leading literacy
campaigns; calling for human and civil rights; organizing the families
of the disappeared; confronting the horrors of racism, poverty, and
war. It is not surprising that many human/civil rights leaders rose from
their ministry, whether it be Dorothy Day, Martin Luther King, Jr.,
Jesse Jackson, Ernesto Cardenal, or Oscar Romero.

I grew up Protestant, attending services so I could sing in the
choir. To me, God was in the wind and in newborn calves. My parents'
main interest in Christianity was that Jesus had been a revolutionary in
his time.

There was another issue lurking in these debates between Redwood Records and Sweet Honey in the Rock and that was who owns
and controls art? Does the person who puts up the money have any
right to input? What is the role of the producer, of the record company, of the financier? For me, the issue of God was not as big a
deal as the fact that I didn't like the song or the performance of the
song and thought it weakened the album. I'd gone into the project
with no strings attached, but I found myself wanting some control.
I also wanted Trudy and Marsha to feel they had some influence at
Redwood, even though they were new. That the ones with the
money and the criticism were white and the artists were Black, complicated the issue. If there had been a political Black record company, such artists as Sweet Honey could have documented their
music on their own terms without having to put up with a lot of
white folks once again trying to ''own'' it. I should have completely
understood that, given that I had separated from male-owned record

companies so I could control my own music. The entertainment industry had exploited Black music for years, getting rich while the artists seldom gained any wealth or power from their work until Motown emerged. I felt physically ill that I had found myself in a microcosm of the very system I deplored. After having flown to D.C. to argue against the song, I backed off.

The album, *B'lieve I'll Run On . . . See What the End's Gonna Be,* was released by Redwood Records. It is a powerful record. "All Praise Is Due to Love" remained on the album and as I listen back now, it amazes me that this song triggered such a debate. Out of a desire to support my new co-workers and to defend lesbian feminism, I articulated a point of view on behalf of Redwood that was valid but narrow. I sided with my white friends out of security and familiarity more than belief. I moved too fast. I did not trust that time would take me where I needed to go. I did not hold tight to my essential belief that coalition isn't about "taking sides." Instead, I pushed for resolve when resolve would only drive a stake through our collaboration. I wish I had had the wisdom to support my co-workers' self-esteem and their struggle against homophobia without allowing it to endanger a coalition that is essential to the success of feminism. I had not yet learned that there is no way to fix a thousand years in a day.

The gap that grew between Sweet Honey in the Rock and Redwood Records broke my heart. I didn't care about the records, or the money. I cared about the trust lost. I grieved for many years to come. Sweet Honey did not agree to do their next album with Redwood. I watched Amy sweat and strain as she studied and practiced coalition in D.C. I watched her white friends distance themselves from her in this effort, yet she carried on, choosing clarity over peer approval.

Someone came to my defense back in 1977: " . . . but what about Sweet Honey's part in this? No conflict is ever one-sided." Of course not. But their part is their part and my part is my part. I will take care of my part.

I went to work on my racism actively and aggressively, which in large part meant scrutinizing cultural misunderstanding. I was going to get beyond my racism if it killed me . . . it *was* killing me. Racism was altering my ability to think clearly, it was affecting my creativity, it was determining my friendships, it was narrowing my vision, it was denying me full personhood. In time, I found two teachers: Jewish feminist Ricky Sherover Marcuse, who was one of the forces behind a practice called Unlearning Racism, and Black activist Jim Dunn, who worked with an organization in New Orleans called HUMAN. These fine teachers helped me to forgive myself for not having escaped that which burdens all children, the learning of prejudice. I went back over every encounter with other cultures I could remember: in music, in film, in jokes, in language, in real life. I celebrated that which I had instinctively valued and defended. I meticulously undid that behavior which uncharacteristically hurt me or anyone else, for it is not my nature to destroy intentionally. I learned to sit quiet, to not always know what to do. I began to notice what freedoms of expression and movement I took for granted, avenues that were not open to people of color. And I fought to rid myself of assumptions about how people think, what people want, and where people come from. It was like learning to walk again. Both Jim and Ricky died of cancer in the winter of 1988/89, a great loss. But they were pioneers and their work is carried on in me and all of their "students."

Ricky once told me a story about a woman who had grown up in a liberal family, and in her childhood, her parents taught her not to notice color, which, in search of a way to break the chain of racism, had been the school of thought at the time. This was before the civil rights movement and before Black power. So this child was sitting in the classroom of her Quaker school, and although there were no Black children, there was, uncommon for white schools, a Black teacher. The teacher asked the children to draw the classroom. The child did but when she got to the teacher she was confused. What color should she make the teacher if she was not supposed to notice she was Black? Not knowing whom to ask for help, she erased the teacher from the picture. I began to cry, deep, old tears. Yes, this is how it was for progressive white children. Unable to accept racism and yet with no help to learn how to combat it, we created an intellectual activism coupled with painful Northern-style segregation, a brutal combination. This story helped me recognize the avoidance that comes from terror and ignorance. I might still feel confused, but from now on I would ask for help.

Over ten years later, Sweet Honey in the Rock (a national treasure), Amy Horowitz, and I still work together in this world. We respect one another as artists and political activists. And I remember hearing Bernice Johnson Reagon say that if coalition feels easy, then you aren't doing coalition work!

My parents phased out of Redwood as the new women arrived. It was a mistake for them to leave. They provided necessary perspectives and skills that were lost with their departure. I was not "capitalized" and had three full-time salaries to pay. In keeping with my support of the developing feminist culture, I made a decision to throw Redwood's weight in support of the growing Women's Music Distribution Network, a move that alienated the other alternative distributors with whom I had worked for years. Straight friends and fans were backing away from my outspoken identification with lesbianism. So with the wind coming from the front, we became a lesbian feminist record company. Given the odds, we didn't stand a chance.

But I was damn sure we were going to try. One evening we took out a deck of tarot cards and decided to ask some questions about our new work together. Some of us believed in the tarot cards, some saw them as a diverting form of entertainment. The cards came out full of doom and disaster. We were feeling so good about our collaboration, however, that we couldn't believe the cards and figured we must have laid them out wrong. We threw them again. Still doom. We wondered what we were doing wrong. We consulted the book carefully. It never occurred to us that the cards were right. We were heading for disaster.

I called a breakfast meeting at the local coffee shop in Ukiah to ask each of them what they would like their jobs to be at Redwood. One wanted to focus on culture and community organizing. Another wanted to improve her engineering skills. Another wanted something else. I was stunned. *Nobody* wanted to run a record company. Two of them wanted to create a workers' policy that included full health insurance, vacations, and raises. I couldn't understand where they thought the money was going to come from. They had always worked straight jobs and had never been bosses; they didn't understand the nature of a small privately owned business. The shopkeeper of the local corner store doesn't get vacation pay. I said that if they wanted to own the business, an idea I was encouraging, they would have to behave like owners, not workers. It was not possible to be assured of anything when owning a small business in a capitalist country dominated by big corporations, especially a small business that was putting out music by lesbians, black activists, and anti-imperialists. This was not what one would call a secure risk!

If it weren't for the fact that our music was completely changing the lives of thousands of women and their friends and families, we might not have had the stamina to go on. There wasn't enough money. The women's movement, like society at large, was riddled with addictions and internalized oppression. Although most of us wanted more

141

people to hear the music, some were willing to make more or different compromises than others, which led to hours of debate. There were power struggles among the labels and more conflicts between the labels and the distributors as WILD (Women's Independent Labels and Distributors) was formed. But still, we shared a common excitement for the power of culture and the beauty of this bold music that touched us so deeply. Distributors were walking into major record stores with feminist and lesbian feminist music and getting our records into the bins, often under the heading of "Women's Music." We were creating a genre. Dozens of concert producers were sprouting up all over the world, presenting feminist artists in a feminist context. There were between three and five hundred different albums and singles documenting this new wave of feminist creativity. Ladyslipper, a nonprofit label in North Carolina, started a mail-order catalog dedicated to the achievements of women in music; it has grown to include more than four thousand titles. And there were the women who listened to our music, who had to work up the courage to walk into a record store, pick out an album of lesbian songs, walk to the counter, and proudly buy a record that was not covered in a brown paper bag.

But amid all this herstory in the making, I missed Meg. I missed Amy. I was relieved to have my struggles with them out of sight for a while, but I got lonely for their love. A few days before I was to meet Meg and her mama in Lynchburg, Virginia, for Christmas, I made love all afternoon with a bass player, a woman I had been flirting with for some time. I hadn't made love to any other woman but Meg. I was not disappointed. We loaded my suitcase and Christmas gifts into her car and raced through the December storm to the airport. Her car broke down a block away from the terminal. I kissed her in the rain and left her to deal with her car. I was still crazy about Meg and couldn't wait to see her. I didn't know this would be my last Christmas with Meg.

9
SOMETHING ABOUT THE WOMEN

IT HAD BEEN A WHILE SINCE I HAD MADE AN ALBUM. I HAD THE songs, and with the new crew on at Redwood it seemed time to record. I decided to do an all-women album, from musician to graphic artist, arranger to engineer. The only man involved was Jeff, as a co-writer of a few songs. One reason for this choice was peer pressure. There was a call out for women to hire women, the argument being that if we didn't hire each other, who would? It was easy for me to hire men. I knew a lot of talented, experienced men. They had been given the opportunities to get good. It was harder to find women with experience. Where were the women engineers, the women drummers, the women bass players, the women arrangers? The next trick was trusting them if they did know what they were doing, and training them if they didn't. I decided to bring all women onto the Redwood staff, and we had made the complicated move to the women's distribution network. So this seemed like a good time to record a women-made record.

My audience had loved *A Live Album*. It captured the excitement of a live concert experience; people could take it home after they saw a show. My main contact with the audience was through live performance—I didn't get much airtime on radio. It would also be cheaper to make a live album than a studio recording, and I had just invested all my money in the Sweet Honey album.

Marsha found a space at the San Francisco Conservatory of Music and invited Joan Lowe to engineer. I asked Meg if she would arrange the songs with me. I would produce and sing with J. T. Thomas on piano, Barbara Cobb on bass, and Meg on guitar. We rehearsed at Redwood, but it was rough on my guests. They weren't used to 110-degree weather.

143

The songs came together nicely. Meg was good at deciphering my outbursts often expressed in terms of feelings, concepts, and colors. However, because I owned the business, I knew how little money there was to work with. It kept me from being the prima donna I might have liked to have been!

The concert weekend came. We were all ready. Trudy, Torie, and Marsha had done a good job of preparation. But I was exhausted. I started to lose my voice and feel sick. I went to an acupuncturist. I don't know if she triggered the wrong place or if I was going to get sick no matter what. But I got worse. I went to the show, sang a few songs, and then had to say to the audience, "I'm sorry. I can't do this. Let's everyone relax and have a good time. My friends up here will do some music for you and I'll sing a few songs, but the album is off." I was devastated but smiled graciously and tried to keep the evening light.

We salvaged two songs from the live recording—"Riverboat," which we doctored up a bit later in the studio, and the audience singing along on "Something About the Women." The rest was scratched. In a never-give-up-if-it-kills-you frame of mind, we decided to take what was left of the budget and go into the studio. Ironically, it was the exact reverse of what had happened with *A Live Album,* which had started out to be a studio recording run amuck and ended up being live.

Once in the studio, I felt we needed drums on a few songs, so Linda Tillery joined us and Rhiannon did some great background vocals with Meg and me. For economy, we worked at a studio that was far from home. I spent too many hours getting to and from the studio when I should have been planning, practicing, or sleeping.

Joan, the engineer, really tried to please me, but when one is patching it together, it is hard to be pleased. And there were too many cooks making the soup. I tried to work collectively, taking everyone's opinions seriously, which is fun but makes doing a record a bit difficult.

Finishing the recording did not mean the record was done. There was the cover. I hired a photographer from the women's community. She had a good reputation, partly because she photographed lesbian erotica, which I had seen and thought was magnificent. I should have realized, however, that just because someone can sing a torch song doesn't mean she can do country and western! I wanted a wholesome picture of me in the fields as they were just turning to a dry, shimmering beige, with the green oak trees in the background. She couldn't seem to see what I wanted her to see. Torie came with me. We shot and shot in the sun all day. At one point she said, "Why don't you take your sweater off and let me shoot you shirtless. The women who love your music would love to see those creamy white shoulders." I laughed at her, but I was so hot and tired, I took my shirt off. After about thirty seconds I knew that was enough of that. The sun went down and we went home.

When the slides were ready, I took the old family projector into the walk-in closet and viewed the day's work. Nothing stood out to me. We were up against a stiff deadline. I went outside and hugged one of the redwood trees. There was something about the rough of the bark on my cheek that helped me when I was sad. I took a deep breath and said to my tree, "I'm going into that closet and I am making a decision. It is just a picture! The music is what is important. So, get very calm and very pragmatic and pick a picture." I did, and that is the cover of *Imagine My Surprise.* It's my Doris Day look!

Now when I think of *Imagine My Surprise,* I hear only the voices of women who come to me after concerts and write me letters telling me how that album has been so vital to them. It has held their hands and caressed their cheeks just as my redwood did for me. It has helped people come out and healed the wounds that come from being in the closet so long. This makes the problems we had making it fade in comparison.

The Redwood gals had some fun up in Ukiah. There was a working-class bar that used to be a rough-and-tumble kind of place. All of a sudden, I discovered it was owned by two women who were lesbians in the old traditional roles. Sandy wore dark men's clothes and a ducktail haircut slicked back on the sides. She poured the drinks. Her lover wore sexy dresses, a lot of makeup, and a bleached-blond hairdo. She was the hostess and waited tables. It was not a gay bar but a country-western watering hole.

On weekends, a live band played, the musicians a mixture of Indian, white, and Chicano, men and women, gay and straight. It was one hell of a band. I don't think most of the folks noticed, but we sure did. Once Sandy and her lover discovered I was Holly Near, they were thrilled and had the band dedicate "My Way" to me. They sang it with all their hearts. Sandy looked on just glowing from ear to ear, so pleased to be able to give me something back.

Later that night, I decided I wanted to learn to play pool. I went up to this guy who was playing and asked him to teach me. Before the lesson began, two other folks showed up and wanted to play doubles. My "teacher" grinned and said, "This is a good way to learn," and we started a game. I went into a trance, focusing on this game with deep, fiery energy. My teacher would sometimes stand nearby and quietly offer his perspective. His advice seemed to go from his voice directly into my game. I played unbelievably well. We kept winning. I understood that look I had seen in Paul Newman's eye.

There was an outcry of rage when Supervisor Harvey Milk and Mayor George Moscone were murdered by Dan White in San Francisco, November 1978. I heard the news in Ukiah over the radio. Torie and I immediately got in the car and drove through the rain to the city. We couldn't talk: It was just too sad. I felt the tears coming down my face and started to hum a melody to keep myself from sinking. Soon there were words. On Castro Street we brought our rage, our candles, and our voices together. Soon we were singing, "We are a gentle angry people and we are singing, singing for our lives." Several years later, I stood watching the Lesbian and Gay Pride March in San Francisco. I have always loved the sound of a marching band but hated the military context. I got to my feet, as some people do for the national anthem. It was the San Francisco Gay Freedom Day Marching Band. I laughed and cried. Like a military band, it instilled pride and courage and inspired heroic behavior. But it did not call us to war. It invited us to love and to live. You would have so enjoyed this day, Harvey. We miss you.

My sister Timothy came onstage and changed the face of my work in an instant. She had been working with the National Theater of the Deaf as a bilingual actress. One day she came to me and said, "Hol, would you like to see your songs?" I was deeply moved as she introduced me to a visually poetic language that had meant nothing to me before. This, along with seeing the work of NTD, encouraged me to learn more about deaf culture, which in turn led me to understand more about accessibility and disability.

While traveling throughout California with the Women on Wheels tour in 1976, Tim joined me for a song that Jeff Langley and I had written about her, "You've Got Me Flying."

146

Something About the Women

You've got me flying, I'm flying
You inspired a sister song
All the pain you're feeling
I will share with you, see you through
You've got me flying, I'm flying
You inspired a sister song
Never knew how good you'd feel my friend to me
You are family

You would run and dance across the field and hay
I would hide behind to see where you would go to play
You were being Isadora
I was being you
Did I know that I'd grow to say?

(Chorus)

I believed the world would lay before you
All the passions—all the gypsy secrets that you knew
I would wear the rose and cape
When you were not at home
Did I know that I'd grow to say?
You've got me flying, I'm flying

Timothy signed the first major performance of a song that night on the Women on Wheels tour, her long arms and hands dancing through the air, and people not only heard and felt the music that night, they saw it. Women often mistakenly thought that feminism was about woman in one's own image. The more feminism opened up in the world, the more clear it became that "woman" is a creature of extraordinary diversity and that feminism must reflect the world—and all the women who live in it with their families, children, friends, and enemies.

In Boston, I met Susan Freundlich. She was an audiologist who had many deaf friends. One of them asked about a record on Susan's turntable, wondering, "What is it on that record that makes you so happy?" Susan signed the songs to her. It was Cris Williamson's *The Changer and the Changed*.

147

At the Boston Women's Music Festival in 1976, Susan worked with the organizers to have the performances signed. She was too shy to do it herself and recruited someone else. The interpreter stood on a chair placed on the floor below the stage in front of the deaf women and, although untrained at signing music, she did her best to convey the lyrics.

From Timothy's solo performance to this very basic heartfelt attempt blossomed an art form based on the ever-developing knowledge of linguistics of American Sign Language. We did not know what we were doing, and most deaf people were not yet part of a deaf-pride movement, so they were grateful for whatever was done for them. Soon, however, deaf people would not be willing to settle for tokenism. Challenged by their newfound self-respect, we learned how to meet some of their demands. As a result of Susan's and my willingness to take criticism and spend time and money, we finally made the form fairly professional and acceptable. Like any coalition work, it was frightening and exhausting. Mistrust and misunderstanding among those who care is more devastating than the insensitivity of those who do not.

Susan was a hard-working artist. She spent hours working out translations for each of my songs. There were so many complicating issues. I had to learn that not all deaf people use ASL—some use signed English; that there are different regional forms, like slang; that sign language is not universal but each country has its own; that sign language, even in such English-speaking countries as Australia and the United States, is not always the same. I had to learn that deaf people often have their own very active and busy societies; that simply because we signed a show didn't mean they would automatically come. For some deaf people, the idea of going to a concert, even if it was signed, was like rubbing salt on an open wound. I learned that many deaf children had been forced to take music lessons! I learned that there was a battle in the world of deaf education over sign-language versus forcing deaf children to learn to speak. Some schools punished students for using their hands, trying to break them of the habit of signing and make speech their only form of communication. I subscribed to the school of thought that believed ASL should be the first language, and a spoken language the second.

Knowing how important the lyrics to folk and pop music had been to our own development, Timothy, Susan, and I wanted to make them accessible to our new friends. Susan helped to facilitate a film called

148

See What I Say, which was nominated for an Academy Award in the short documentary category and featured a song from one of my concerts. We got the whole audience signing and singing together.

> *One woman weaves a message singing the sounds of silence*
> *Another wheels her chair to the center of the stage*
> *Changing minds and attitudes with eyes that hear and hands that*
> *   see . . .*
> *Oh, there's something about the women in my life.*

Amy Horowitz and I were driving down the East Coast from D.C. to Chapel Hill, taking advantage of that wonderful feeling of uninterrupted time that happens in cars, when ideas are born, songs get written, conversations take wing, and solutions appear. Amy had done powerful things with her company, Roadwork. She booked and managed Sweet Honey in the Rock. She continued to book me and before she was done, she would have booked thirty artists on two hundred tours. We had been through the mill with each other more than once but, damn, we were good friends.

We stopped at an open-air theater where the audience could look down to the stage and out to sea. As we sat in the top row, we could hear the concerts we hoped to bring forth. We were tingling with possibilities. I walked down to the stage and began to sing to Amy, to the trees, to the sea.

Back in the car, we started brainstorming about a national anti-nuke tour, a tour that would bring people together around the basic issue of survival, pointing out both the dangers of nuclear power and the insanity of nuclear weapons. No one had ever done a national anti-nuke tour before. The issue was only minimally "popular," but we felt it was a feminist issue as well as a global one. We could invite community organizations to set up in the lobby to address local issues. Local, national, and international concerns could be linked. This was great. When Amy and I were on a roll, we fed each other's creativity and courage.

Needing a bit of vocal rest—I was to sing a concert that night—we turned on the radio and retreated into our own thoughts, which, knowing Amy and me, were as parallel as the white lines on the highway. A newsbreak interrupted a song to tell us that there had been an accident in the nuclear power plant at Three Mile Island. Yes, well . . .

A few days later, I called Joanie Shoemaker and Jo-Lynne Worley in Kansas City to see if I could meet with them on my way home. They had produced concerts for me, distributed my records, and ran their bookstore. I liked them—good businesswomen; great with detail; professional, pragmatic, spiritual, good senses of humor and politics. Jo-Lynne had degrees in marine biology and psychology. Joanie had a degree in religion and had been a social worker. Their interests in culture and community had led them to develop the second largest women's bookstore in the country. They met my plane. I knew they were busy but I was brutal. For three days I stayed at their house, grabbing their every free moment during the day and keeping them up late into the night until they agreed to co-produce a national anti-nuke tour with me. Before I left, they were talking about taking a leave of absence so they could work out of my California office. I had a huge grin inside. Mission accomplished. Amy agreed to come to California to book the tour.

Meanwhile, the Redwood team was crumbling under our own weight. I had run out of solutions to a never-ending stream of problems. I got tired of being called *the* problem, so I decided to remove myself to see what would surface. I gave them Redwood. We had one last meeting. I brought in an ally so that I wouldn't feel it was them against me. But my ally got so insulted by the way the "they" treated the "me" that she walked out, which didn't do me any good. So I left them with Redwood and tried to get on with my life. Maybe they could make it work as a collective. I didn't want to be in a collective. I wanted either to own it or co-own it with partners, preferably the latter. I was hurt, furious, and worn out. I'm sure I said something pleasant, like, "If you think you can run this fucking record company without me, then run it!"

Within a matter of weeks, the company, in debt and complete disarray, landed back in my lap—minus partners and staff except for Torie, who needed a job and was unwilling to give up on the vision. But we soon found ourselves screaming, which hurt us both because we loved each other. I fired her. I'm not even sure I had the right to fire her. Who knew who was working for whom at this point? Torie was and still is a visionary and a good organizer. She is now the director of the Los Angeles Gay and Lesbian Community Center. Fortunately, we survived the storm. We are great friends.

*   *   *

150

Something About the Women

Meg moved into her own apartment. Ginny and I started to get along better. Meg was sober now. But I had always known Meg with her dependency. It had been a major part of our relationship. Now that she was in a program, she was changing. That part was great, but it meant that I had to change too. I went to some Al-Anon meetings to learn how to do that. I was never much of a group person. Maybe Meg was disappointed that I didn't stay with Al-Anon. But, then, she always wanted me to do what she was doing, eat what she was eating, think what she was thinking, and watch the TV shows she wanted to watch. I guess it was a good sign for me that I didn't go to Al-Anon just for her sake.

One day I picked her up at the airport. She was returning from a tour. The moment she got into the car I knew something had happened in New York City. I drove in silence, waiting for her to tell me. We made small talk and then, after a long silence, she said, "Holly?" and I said, "I know." We both wondered how I knew, but I did. Meg had had an affair. I was scared.

I remembered that my affair had not made me love Meg less. I asked her if it had been fun. I tried to be supportive since I knew it was a rather courageous thing for her to have done. But something turned around that night. I think we both realized we were coming to the end. But we didn't want to let go of a love that for three and a half years had been so strong. Damn, we loved each other so. Then Meg called it. I hated that she said it first. I guess I cried for a few months. There was a lot to cry about . . . so much passion, so much love, so much pleasure all wrapped up in one relationship. We were dear friends and great lovers right up to the last night we spent together. And then, of course, there was the music. I will always love Meg and wish her the greatest happiness. When I think of Meg, I still think of her hands—on the guitar, cutting mushrooms, playing volleyball with her fingers wrapped, holding her kittens, touching my body.

10
PARTNERS

JOANIE AND JO-LYNNE MOVED TO UKIAH IN THE LATE SPRING OF 1979. We commuted to San Francisco for meetings and resources. Redwood acquired a ghastly little hole-in-the-wall just down the street from The Artemis, a women's restaurant and cultural center. We hated the hole so much that we held most meetings at the restaurant. The anti-nuke tour was growing fast, so we hired a wonderful assistant named Roberta Goodman, a tall, handsome woman very committed to political and antiracist work. We made a good team. I was still crying a lot over Meg, missing her terribly. And I was scared. I had never been a single lesbian before. Addicted to stress, I now realized I was what the AA world called co-dependent. But I was also crying with the relief of being out of the circle of conflict. Redwood was on the back burner. Olivia was no longer my in-law. And I had new friends—political, kind, efficient, and ready to work.

Torie alerted me that she had done a bit of matchmaking and the next day I got a call from Nancy Vogl. We went out, but I was quite uncomfortable. It made me wonder if I was really a lesbian or if I had simply fallen in love with Meg. I liked Nancy. She had co-founded the Berkeley Women's Music Collective, one of the early Bay Area women's bands. I went back home to Ukiah, where Joanie and Jo-Lynne and I continued to build the anti-nuke tour, worked in the vegetable garden, and got to know one another.

In a few days I would fly to Michigan for the women's music festival. Joanie and Jo-Lynne, whom I now affectionately called J2, were going to drive straight through with a friend, but in the middle of our meeting the friend called to cancel. That meant the two of them would have to drive all the way without a third driver for relief. They would never make it on time. I offered to drive with them instead of fly, but since I needed to be in Michigan early, it meant—we counted—we would have to leave in three hours!

We went into high gear, first calling Roberta in San Francisco and asking her if she could come to Ukiah to follow through on the deadlines J2 had intended to meet. If she left San Francisco right away, she could get to Ukiah before we left for Michigan. Synchronizing our work, we got everything done. Roberta arrived, we exchanged papers, reports, graphic designs, promotional photos, and hugs, and, as if in a relay race, climbed into the Toyota camper and left Roberta standing on the doorstep shaking her head in disbelief.

We drove hard, stopping only for meals and gas, taking turns riding in the back where we had made a little bed. At one point we stopped and tried to sleep, but I lay with my eyes wide open, listening to the trucks roar by, so I got back behind the wheel. I seemed to have an inexhaustible amount of energy. I couldn't figure out why I was so wired. Then, of course! I had a crush. I'd been too busy to notice the presence of a powerful drug flowing through my body. Not only was the women's music festival in Michigan, Nancy was in Michigan.

We arrived at the site five minutes before my sound check. The place was buzzing with energy as thousands of women gathered. Strong bodies were hanging lights, laying sound cable, tuning pianos, and working over stage diagrams. I stood at center stage, stretching my tired spine, letting the sun bake out the stiffness of driving, and enjoying the excitement that was generated by my presence. I looked out over the valley. Then I spotted a Hawaiian shirt, broad shoulders, and magnificent suntanned arms. Feeling my eyes, she turned and looked right at me. A spark went through my body. I didn't think I needed to cry anymore.

The annual women's music network meeting took place at the festival; it included record labels, distributors, concert promoters, and sometimes artists and managers. I reported to the group that I was folding Redwood Records. There had been too much conflict and I had never intended Redwood to be an albatross. I would find some other company to distribute my records. People were startled. Ginny came up to me and asked if I was okay. She knew Meg and I had broken up, and now here I was folding Redwood. I think I just smiled and said I was doing fine. To my surprise, I was.

That afternoon, in her steamy tent, Nancy kissed me. That did it.

How someone kisses is very important, and if that works, then it is worth seeing what might happen next.

Outside, Nancy got her first dose of what it is like to be with me. It took us forty minutes to walk the same distance others covered in ten. People kept stopping me to talk. I watched to see if Nancy could take it. She seemed to be doing fine. In fact, she even seemed proud of me. I liked that. And I couldn't stop looking at her . . . I wanted so to find out how we touched.

Later that day I met with Joanie and Jo-Lynne. I wanted to know how they felt the distributors had handled the news about Redwood. Somewhere in the conversation I asked them if they thought I had done the right thing, then added jokingly, or did they want to run the company? There was a long pause. In that moment, I began the most important union of my life, second only to my family. Joanie and Jo-Lynne would help me build a political and cultural base from which I could do my work. We would throw our lives together into the storm. We would be critical but not judgmental, present but not dominant, expectant but not demanding, essential but not exclusionary. I would laugh for them when they could not. They would cry for me when I could not. And yet, we did not try to replace emotions for one another that eventually we would each need to be willing to feel. Summer 1979. I turned thirty.

We tested the new partnership on the anti-nuke tour, discovering a team energy. We combined music, politics, spirituality, love, and hard work all in a grand dance. We linked the dangers of nuclear power and nuclear weapons. We made connections between love of child, love of lover, and love of planet. Joined by pianist J. T. Thomas and sign-language artist Susan Freundlich, I crossed the country singing to thousands of people who wanted freedom from the nightmare of nuclear war and environmental disaster. So we decided to take the next step. It was time for J2 to cut their teeth in record production. We hired June Millington as the musical producer. June had been a member of Fanny, the first serious women's rock band in the music industry. Leslie Ann Jones was the engineer, Adrienne Torf was on keyboards, Carrie Barton was on bass, Cam Davis was on drums, and Mary Watkins arranged and conducted the strings. The material was strong and compassionate, the love songs sexy. I look back on these records in wonder. While successful mainstream artists were working with million-dollar budgets, we were lucky if we had thirty to forty thousand and the artwork and the promotion had to be squeezed out from those same dollars. Yet we were listened to and reviewed without regard for the discrepancy in conditions, and I must say, I think we did really well.

There was a lot of sexual energy flying around this project. I was happy to be in love. Nancy was on the road, so I had nowhere to take it home. "Fire in the Rain" indeed! I kept wanting to open a window, which is not possible in a soundproof studio. Nancy would call in from the road, but often just when I was about to do a vocal. I was torn because the clock was ticking (studio time is expensive!), but I needed just to hear her voice for a minute, to hear her tell me she loved me. I confided to her that I found myself flirting with Leslie. I had set up my own little world in the vocal booth, designed so that I couldn't be seen. I don't like to be watched while I'm recording. The lights were soft and candles burned; a favorite mug with hot water, apple cider vinegar, and honey steamed; a humidifier sprayed cool mist into the air; and love notes from J2 hung on the walls. Then I would hear Leslie's voice over the headphones: "Shall we give this a try?" or, "I need you to do that again, Miss Near," or, "If you keep singing like that, I'm just going to have to fall in love with you!" Her gentle encouragement was like a soft kiss on the neck. Nancy, bless her modern heart, told me to do what I needed to do to take care of myself while she was gone, adding, "As long as I'm still the one you love!" But I told her Leslie was in a relationship, and it wasn't likely anything would happen.

As the last day came around, we celebrated with a bottle of champagne. The tracks sounded good except for one song, "Working Woman," which just didn't belong on the record. My partners had done well. We had not blown the budget out of the water. My voice sounded strong. I looked at Leslie, her feet up on the console, her eyes closed, listening. I was putting the candles in my bag when a hand took mine and led me to a hidden room up the stairs and down the hall. Champagne and the successful completion of a project had apparently altered someone's previous sensibilities. We slipped onto the floor and in a matter of moments offered each other well-deserved finishing touches.

The National Preparatory Committee of the youth festival to be held in Cuba met on Saturday, June 24, 1978, and voted 28-to-2 to exclude me from the cultural delegation because of my lesbianism. Although a few lesbians were going on the delegation from the United

States, many believed that they were tokens and that I was excluded because of the publicity I would get. I actually could not have gone to the festival because of conflicting commitments, but I had applied during the first round of applications before I knew that and had not heard back from anyone. So I was surprised to hear that a vote had been taken on my participation. The committee comprised representatives of several progressive groups, but I understand that it was dominated by the U.S. Communist party. I wrote a letter of protest to the committee.

The National Lawyers Guild was embarrassed to discover that its representative in the committee had abstained from voting. They sent me an official apology and asked me to appear at their next annual conference to sing and to receive an apology from all the members. I did appear and they were wonderful. I also spoke to Cuban singer Sara Gonzales about being excluded. She said that it was a U.S. committee decision and had not come down as a Cuban edict. She invited me to come to Cuba anytime and assured me that I would be most welcome. I knew she would welcome me, but I didn't think that would necessarily go for the country at large. But then, what country does enthusiastically embrace its homosexual population?

I went to Cuba a few years later, guest of the Ministry of Culture. What a beautiful island! My first surprise was how green it was and then, once the plane landed, how black it was. Somehow, because it was a Spanish-speaking country, I had forgotten that black people were central to Cuba's history and culture. It was Carnival and the streets were filled with music and dancing. I went to hear Castro speak. It was like a history, economics, and fine arts lesson all in one, so different from the rather boring and rhetorical speeches I had grown accustomed to hearing from our own presidents. I did several concerts and at the encouragement of the famed author and filmmaker, Jesus Diez, a documentary was made about my work and shown the following year at the international film festival. I loved Cuba. Yes, of course it has problems. So does the United States. I long for the day when the United States ends the embargo so we can work to solve the problems together.

Hardly any of my audience was in the theater since no promotion had been done. The show sold out by word of mouth and the place was full of Deadheads. The first half of the show featured an array of local

156

S.F. artists. During intermission, I could feel the impatience of the audience. It was an anti-nuke benefit but they wanted to hear their guys. When I walked on stage, two thirds of the audience was in the lobby and as far as I could tell, didn't plan on coming back in until the Dead came on. "My band," Adrienne Torf, Carrie Barton, and Vicki Randle, dived into a high-energy set. By the third song, the audience had returned to the hall and we had them with us. I hate to feel the need to "prove" myself, but I was pleased to hear that Bill Graham had come to the wings to see who had done the impossible.

There was another challenge before me. I had been invited to visit *Sesame Street*. My sister Timothy was on *Sesame Street* a lot and there was a buzz in the air because her little sister was coming. Big Bird was excited. He didn't have a sister and wanted to know what it meant. Timothy and I performed "You've Got Me Flying" so that he could understand sisters and sisterhood. But Oscar the Grouch had another plan. He talked me into singing the irrigation song, "Water Come Down," and then drenched me with a bucket of water after I finished, singing out in his own scruffy voice, "The water come down, water come down . . . the water sure does come down!"

As I became more aware of the drug and alcohol problems in the world, and because a drug bust would be an easy setup if anyone ever wanted to "interrupt" my political/cultural work, I decided to put it officially in my contract that there were to be no drugs or marijuana in the dressing room, backstage, in any of the cars used for transportation, in any of the housing or hotel rooms where I was to stay, or at any of the parties thrown in my honor. We called for "chemically free space." Often when we did benefits or community events in a town, folks would generously offer their homes for me and my group to stay at. This saved costly hotel expenses. We arrived at one woman's home a little early and found her doing last-minute cleaning. She had her arms full of containers from under the kitchen sink. She apologized and said, "I'm sorry, I was just told it is in your contract that you need chemically free space." Bless her heart, she was literally taking all the chemicals out of her house.

Joanie, Jo-Lynne, Nancy, and I decided to go to Mexico. We all needed a break from our nonstop work. We enrolled in a Spanish school in Cuernavaca—the overachievers' idea of a vacation. Nancy and I had been having some hard times. She wanted me to make a commitment to our relationship. After two and a half years together I couldn't do it. I could say "I love you and I am here now." But I couldn't seem to wrap my tongue around the word *tomorrow*. I thought that maybe if we had a little fun, today would become more important than tomorrow.

Instead, I slept with my Spanish teacher, an act that even now I only marginally understand. I hadn't been with a man in years. I know there was a rebel in me, the same rebel that led me to be a singer rather than a cheerleader, a progressive rather than a liberal, a feminist rather than a lady. But seducing a young man in my sweetheart's face was unacceptable behavior. Nancy was patient and tried to understand, but I was being a total jerk.

Nancy went with Joanie and Jo-Lynne to Oaxaca in a rented car. I went off with some of the students to spend New Year's at a beach south of Acapulco. When we arrived at the beach we set up a tent and claimed the hammocks that were already swinging in the breeze. The fish was fresh, the beer cold, the toasts romantic.

In the morning I swam in the ocean and ate fresh fish, fried eggs, and beans for breakfast, prepared on an open fire. The days went on like this. On New Year's Day hundreds of townspeople swarmed to the beach. The women swam in their dresses. The air was full of sound, from rock and folklorico to the laughter of happy people playing. Turkeys and ducks wandered around the beach, vacuum cleaners for dropped bits of food. Pelicans flew over and dived for fish. The hammocks were full. Turkey eggs and beer were the delicacies of the day. Hot. Humid. And then a child drowned. She was only six. We mourned for the parents who would have to live with this day for the rest of their lives.

I met Ricardo. He was young and self-assured, egotistical, cocky, a chess champion in Mexico. On New Year's Eve, after lots of alcohol and laughter, I invited him to walk on the beach. A half-mile down, in the dark, in the sand, we made love. There was a part of my life that was not at all dignified, a grade B movie, tacky and lustful. We tried to repeat ourselves but it was not worth doing twice. Happy New Year.

My relationship with Nancy was probably one of only two really sane relationships I had ever had, Arthur being the other. Did I need something jarring and unpleasant to get me to move away from the kindness and comfort of this love so that I could move on in my life . . . a life that does not seem to be about coupling or settling.

But why men again? Why now? Was it because the transition from Arthur to Meg had been so quick and devoid of process? Was I really a heterosexual all along who fell in love with radical lesbian feminism? Did I simply fall in love with some wonderful women and it had nothing to do with sexual preference? Yet, what about the passion, the romance, the sex? What about making love at dawn and sleeping again so peacefully, knowing that my life was complete in her arms? I talked to my folks about it. They didn't let out a parental sigh of relief at the possibility that I might be straight, after all. Their eyes were sad and worried, and Mom said, "Hol, your life is so full and complex. This will be hard. But you have always followed your instincts, your heart. You can't stop doing that now." Dad sat in his chair. I sat at his feet and hugged his knees. He said, "Who knows, Holly, if one has taken the right path? But how can you know? There is no way of knowing what was down the other path. More or less happiness?"

That weekend, my father died. Nancy and I began the long process of breaking up. I left on a tour. Nancy moved on and fell into a love that lasted. Although I have loved and been loved in the years that followed, I have not been in a long-term relationship since, which as I write now was more than eight years ago. I've never lived with a lover, although I find I'll do the strangest things for love. Someone once said to me, "If you give your heart to the world, it is hard to give your heart to an individual. There just isn't enough heart to go around." Maybe. Maybe not. I did notice, however, that when I began to have sexual relationships with men again, I began to gain weight and the diet cycle returned. If I learned one thing, it was that men are fattening!

Timothy, Laurel, and I decided to do a ten-year reunion of The Near Sisters. We had sung together for several months way back then, and for a while considered a career together as a family trio. But Laurel went on to dance, Timothy went on to direct, and I continued singing. For the reunion, we wanted to integrate our specialties. We performed the piece at Zellerbach Hall in Berkeley and at Royce Hall/UCLA. Although it was a work-in-progress, we were good. Timothy directed the show and did a fabulous sketch of her own about Sadie Hawkins, reminding me why I had wanted to grow up to be like her. I knew Laurel was a powerful dancer, but in this work she revealed her talents as an actress, writer, and comic. I was so inspired by my sisters' talents. Although we each went on with our own work, we have not put the script away. For some reason, I believe we will come back to it.

My whole family is creative, which has been a vital part of my work. My mother is a writer, my father had a beautiful voice, my sisters seem to have endless sources of talent, and my brother, although he has chosen a nonperforming career and prefers to stay out of the spotlight, is my favorite dancing partner.

In the summer of 1982, I recorded a new album. A lot of the same folks who worked on *Fire in the Rain* returned—Ady, Carrie, Cam. We were easy with each other now. Evie Sands and Leslie Ann Jones produced, Ray Obiedo played rhythm guitar, and I invited Robben Ford, an old high school buddy, to play lead on two songs. And then there was Afrikan Dreamland, a reggae band from Nashville that I had met at a disarmament conference. They arrived with drums, percussion, keyboards, and flutes. These were pleasant days. I would swim naked in the early morning sun before anyone had risen. I'd then bring fresh fruit and herb tea out in the sun. Mustafa, Darrol, and Ashid would bring out the drums, Mustafa placing a drum ritualistically before me. I had been invited. My hands touched the skin. I felt the pulse in my fingers, hot like when I rest my hands on someone's temples to take away a headache. Mustafa played the rhythm I was to play. When I had it, he moved to his own. As Ashid and Darrol began to play, I heard differently than I had ever heard before.

I returned to Cuernavaca the following year, the way a thief returns to the scene of the crime. But I couldn't concentrate on the Spanish classes and I was not interested in the young schoolteacher. I tried to write songs, but I couldn't write about what was on my mind— confused and forbidden thoughts that would not be acceptable to my audience, which counts on me to be clear. I didn't feel clear. The songs I wrote documented desperation and offered no insights. I threw them away.

I hadn't done much traveling alone. I packed a shoulder bag and got on a plane to Oaxaca. A simple room in a quiet hotel became my home, a block away from the noise and bustle of the town square. Indians came into town each day to eke out a living by selling their wares to the tourists. I saw the poverty and the disruption of their culture. My eyes lingered on their brown skin, creased like relief maps

160

of their people's long and magnificent story. I went to mass and knelt praying with the old women who begged God to offer them a better life after death. I was glad I could not understand the words of the mass so that I could make up my own sense of the ritual. I walked through the market, examining meat parts that even this farm girl couldn't identify. Sidestepping gigolos, I stood in the *zócalo* after the rain and listened to a Sunday concert. I sat in a sidewalk café sipping strong coffee and listening to an old fellow tell a young North American student about the days when he worked for the CIA. Finally, some Californians joined me. I enjoyed their company until they figured out who I was, then I moved on to have dinner alone in an outdoor restaurant, serenaded by roving folklorico trios. I went to bed and slept calmly all night.

The next morning I was up early and went out into the square, where the streets were full of people marching and chanting. Twenty thousand schoolteachers from all over the southern region were protesting the federal police killings of several progressive rural teachers. I stood on the sidelines full of questions but trying to remember the laws about international visitors and demonstrations. I had heard horror stories of North Americans stuck in prison in Mexico City for being involved in the student revolts of 1968. I had no desire to spend time in a Mexican jail. So I stayed behind the ropes and watched like an innocent tourist.

Still, I wanted to know what was going on. I saw a kind-looking man in his thirties caring for five children, some very dark and some very blond. He was explaining the march to the children. Perhaps he would explain it to me. It turned out that he was a lawyer and father to some of the blonder children. He invited me to join them for ice cream and afterward to his house. I looked forward curiously to meeting the mother of these blond children, since he was quite dark. But instead I met his brother, his brother's girlfriend, who was European, and his sister, who was the mother of the darker children. Apparently, his wife was North American and had left him with the children and returned home to the United States after realizing she was a lesbian. Out of twenty thousand people at the march, this is the man I chose to meet! He seemed relieved to have someone to talk to about this. I told him I was lesbian . . . well, I am except when I'm not. He asked if I was bisexual. I said I didn't feel like a bisexual. I felt like a lesbian when I was with a woman and a lesbian making love to a man when I was with a man.

161

We went out to see the ruins and the famous two-thousand-year-old tule trees that have grown to heights of 140 feet. A peasant funeral passed by. The eldest son was weeping, carried along by his friends. Other family members were moaning and wailing. Three old men marched, playing trumpets that had long ago lost their bright original tone but conveyed an ancient cry that I will never forget. The women carried long-stemmed flowers to the church. I let myself cry. For me, it was Russell's funeral, the one we never really had. I remembered a dream that had come to me a few months before Dad's death:

Indians and farm workers in white peasant clothes were sitting in a circle on a large raft in the middle of a huge lake. They sat quietly in meditation. Then, all at once, they stood and lifted their arms to the sky as if they were letting go of doves. I knew that Dad was dead. I looked across the raft to see my mother. As I rounded the circle to go to her, she would move in the other direction, so that I was always across from her but could never reach her. Then I dived deep into the lake until I reached the center of the earth. There I found my father standing with his sister-in-law Jean. She was holding my record under her arm. He asked me where I was going. I said to L.A. He wanted to come with me. I said lovingly, "Oh, Dad, you're dead. You can't come with me. I have enough problems in this world without being accused of hanging out with a ghost." He laughed and said okay, but told me to travel safely.

My new friend bought me a carved bowl, a black elephant, and some fresh coconut as gifts for my tears. Then I went home to California.

Ronnie Gilbert and I were talking once about autobiographies. She said she mistrusted the writer who says everyone was great and everything was wonderful. But I understand it now, Ronnie, it is easy for me to remember how great it was and is to work with you. It is harder to remember the rough times. However, I will try to say something bad about you and me as an autobiographical exercise. First, indulge me as I celebrate the magnificence of this collaboration.

Tucked away in one of my journals, I found a list of at least one hundred names of women singers to whom I wanted to dedicate my second album. It included Miriam Makeba and Odetta, Judy Henske and Cynthia Gooding, Edith Piaf and Leontyne Price, Julie Andrews and Mahalia Jackson, Yma Sumac and Judy Garland, Patsy Cline and Joni James, Ella Fitzgerald and Morgana King, Janis Joplin and Peggy

Lee, Aretha Franklin and Marta Schlamme. And Ronnie Gilbert. I had a wonderful time making the list, but it became unmanageable as I became obsessed with the prospect of leaving anybody out! I listened to the tapes of my album, preparing the sequence of songs. I heard myself belting out at the top of my voice, and delicately reaching deep inside for the sorrow that can be expressed only by no sound. I heard myself balancing precariously between personal reflection and political outcry. I heard the audience cheer out of identification. And although I didn't know anything about her, except that she had sung with the Weavers; I didn't even know if she was still alive! I jotted down on scratch paper, ". . . to Ronnie Gilbert, who knew how to sing and what to sing about."

As she later told the story, her daughter Lisa called her on the phone and asked, "Mom, do you know a singer named Holly Near?" She didn't. "Well, she's dedicated an album to you." Ronnie was aggravated at first—who is this woman who has put my name on her album without asking me? Ronnie put off listening to the record. She didn't much like what the folk world of the sixties had produced and preferred the company of theater people. She decided to clean house while she listened, so as to ease the boredom she had already decided she would feel.

Several hours later, the house untouched by broom and mop, Ronnie had laughed and cried and played the songs again and again. Something felt different about this music, she told me later.

Soon after, she came to visit me in Ukiah, en route to Canada where she was living with and working in a theater company. Ronnie spent the day with me and my folks. How lovely it was to meet her. I tempted fate as I sat at the piano and pulled out a few old folk songs. She hummed along but really didn't sing. I didn't push it. As she left, I told her about a women's music festival that she would drive past as she headed north. She did stop.

We became pals. Then a Weavers reunion concert and film were in the works, *Wasn't That a Time*. The Weavers didn't want it to be a nostalgia piece but rather a reflection of the circle unbroken, bringing forward "the children of the Weavers" who sing now and, in turn, have influenced the Weavers: people like Arlo Guthrie, Peter, Paul, and Mary; and me. Ronnie introduced two of my songs to the group, and although there was some resistance to the strong woman-identification of the songs, Ronnie convinced her three brothers (Lee Hays, Pete Seeger, and Fred Hellerman) to back her on

163

"Oh, there's something about the women in my life . . ." I was thrilled she chose to sing my songs. They also sang "Hay Una Mujer Desaparecida." The filmmaker wanted to interview some of the Weavers' "kids." So I flew to New York to talk with Ronnie for the cameras. We sat up in her loft, talking about music and times and ideas. I began to sing "Hay Una Mujer," she began to sing—we began to sing. *We* began.

Did we know we had begun? I don't think so. Not quite yet. It took a few more casual encounters to recognize a form our music could take. After an event in New York City put on by Performers and Artists Against Nuclear War, where we sang a few songs a cappella spontaneously and unrehearsed, people came up to us on the street as we strolled home. "When are you two going to do a concert? We're waiting!" That night when I got to my New York home (my good friend Kathy Goldman's apartment, affectionately called Redwood East), Kathy and another pal, Jessie Cagan, echoed the sentiment. "When are you and Ronnie going to do a concert together?" For the first time I really let my mind contemplate the question.

That summer I got to sing with the Weavers at the Clearwater Folk Festival. Such a thrill it was! Later that year, Lee Hays died. He was one of a kind. We had just lost one of our finest feisty political humorists. The Vancouver Folk Festival dedicated the weekend to Lee, and the promoter, Gary Cristall, asked me if I thought Ronnie would come. She did. We sang some more unrehearsed folk songs. The next thing I remember is Ronnie and me sitting with Jeff Langley in his New York apartment with stacks of music and tapes, singing. We sang song after song, finding keys, experimenting with harmonies and arrangements. We told stories about what this song or the other had meant in our lives. And we laughed, so much wonderful laughter. I loved this woman. It seemed to me she did not hold anything back. In fact, I felt years of pent-up music pour forth. It was not an accident that we asked Jeff to work with us. He is one of the best when it comes to working with women singers.

I had wondered if Ronnie could really sing—it had been a long time since she had sung more than a song here or there. But my fears were put to rest. She was a powerhouse still, and her theatrical sensibilities gave me the room I'd seldom felt I had with other singers. I could sing big and hard with this woman, and she refused to be bowled over. We were reduced to tears or hysterical laughter from time to time, but we were never down for the count.

Partners

We took the show to our critics—my sister and director, Timothy, and Ronnie's friend and director, Joe Chaiken—who helped us to see what we could not see alone. Then we headed for Chicago for the first concert of what would be one of many tours and several albums together. The concert halls filled with people crossing generational, cultural, and life-style boundaries. Parents brought children to introduce them to Ronnie Gilbert. Children brought parents to introduce them to Holly Near. Four generations of women came together. Red-diaper babies sat next to upwardly mobile liberals (sometimes they were one and the same). We were in the midst of a unique, unforgettable coming together of past, present, and future.

Ronnie and I were both tough, opinionated, creative, and insecure. She, having spent recent years in a collective process in theater, was not used to being a soloist and running her own show. Although I certainly could not have done any of the things I'd done without help, I had worked essentially alone all my life, and was not used to being part of a duo. We struggled with ourselves and each other to make room in our stubborn natures for this collaboration.

Ronnie was coming into this adventure as if she had been in a time capsule. The last time she had done a singing tour was with the Weavers in 1963. They had gathered in a semicircle around a single microphone to sing. In the prefeminist era, Ronnie had trusted the men around her to take care of everything. Now she had to learn to do sound checks, become accustomed to onstage speaker monitors, and tell sound people what she liked and didn't like—which requires *learning* what one likes and doesn't like and finding a language to explain it. She had to learn about money and negotiating contracts. She had to decide what she needed before a show, what she required in her dressing room. She had to learn about putting together a set list, and translating her theatrical experience into the musical dynamics of sound and emotion in order to bring the audience to its feet by the end of the night. Since I had stretched my lessons out over the previous twenty years, I was initially unaware of how much there was to learn. I was a strong ally for Ronnie, but at times I was a protective and patronizing drag. It's just that I wanted the world for her and I wanted her for the world. Night after night audiences honored her for the music she had contributed to their lives at the top of her lungs in 1949, the year I was born, and singing on with the Weavers through 1963. Now the music was even stronger and wider because of the civil rights movement, the peace movement, and the women's movement. The audience stood night after night not because an old lady had come back and offered a nostalgic evening but because a great entertainer had done a fabulous show and lifted them up to where they belonged. Even people who saw us sing together only for a moment in *Wasn't That a Time* felt something extraordinary.

We recorded the concert for four nights at the Great American Music Hall in San Francisco. Jeanne and Tom Bradshaw co-owned the club and offered the kind of support we needed to make this project special. Although we had done the show in large halls like Avery Fisher in New York City, the intimacy of the club allowed a more relaxed and personal atmosphere. The last of the four shows was videotaped by an independent company in hopes of selling it to PBS or a cable network. I was exhausted before we even began. The last day was a marathon, spent with the video crew lining up shots, deciding on makeup and wardrobe, and running out at the last minute for different clothes, which really weren't an improvement.

I was down to empty just when I needed to feel full. I sat in my dressing room and tried to find some hidden source of energy. I couldn't find any. So I decided to warm up a little, stretch and vocalize a bit. I opened my mouth to sing a few light "lue, lue, lues." There was no sound. I rolled my head to loosen my neck and tried again. No sound. I stretched my jaw and swallowed. Silence again, except for the sound of air trying to pass around a mountain that had settled in my throat. The next minute I was on my knees, weeping. My shoulders rocked in slow motion and I could hear a tiny voice inside me saying, "Okay, you win. I give up. I'm not as strong as I have pretended to be all my life. I have my limits. I've pushed this too far. I've tried to do too much."

This was not the first time I had collapsed. Each time, however, I'd successfully put it out of my mind so that I could carry on without changing my life. I'd forget it happened and experienced each collapse as if it were the first. I could hear the little voice say, "I will not sing if you don't take care of me, I will rebel. I will fail you, for you are failing me." I got up off my knees, looked in the mirror, and said, "There is absolutely nothing you can do about this, Holly. If you have no voice, you have no voice. You will simply have to warn Ronnie that this may be her San Francisco solo debut."

I cooled my face with a wet cloth and went out to find Ronnie and my manager, Jo-Lynne. My news did not please them but there was nothing they could do, either. Jeanne announced the five-minute call and we stood silently in the wings. I told Jo-Lynne I was having trouble breathing and thought I was going to faint. She said, "Just keep coming to the wings during Ronnie's solos and I'll help you." The lights went out, I heard our names, I heard the crowd break into cheers. I remember Ronnie squeezing my hand. The roles had been reversed. She, who had been so confused and nervous at the beginning of our tour, and I, so confident, had just traded places. She walked onstage strong, solid, and full of energy. I followed, barely in my body, truly wondering what was going to happen.

We began to sing. I expected nothing more than silence from me. Instead, there was a voice. It was not a voice I recognized. It felt strange and sounded foreign, but it was a sound. Song after song, we traveled through the show—video cameras rolling, audio tape running, and the audience at its best— Ronnie and I clowning and laughing in one song and then breaking our own hearts in another. When she soloed, I moved to the side to drink a magic potion of brewer's yeast, orange juice, and other earthly wonders that Jo-Lynne had concocted. But it was not earthly remedies that got me through the night. I was guided by angels who pulled the notes out of me and instructed me to get out of the way so that they could do their work.

Days later, when we listened to the four different shows in search of the best cuts for the album, we surprisingly took many from that Sunday night show. We sounded great. We looked ridiculous—too made-up, too color-coordinated, too coiffed; none of our disorderliness, none of the wrinkles in Ronnie's clothes or my face, none of the renegade hair falling in my eyes, none of the beads of sweat on Ronnie's naturally perfect skin. Maybe someday it will be aired and enough time will have passed so that I won't care how we looked.

Not long after the taping we did another sold-out show, this time at the Geary Theater without the pressure of recording. We did a great job and followed it with a party at the Great American Music Hall. I felt tremendously relieved that it was over. I let off steam by dancing hard and drinking too many "Lusty Bitches." Then I went downstairs to the bathroom and threw up dinner. I threw up months of stress and panic, I threw up grief I didn't even know was there, I threw up men, I threw up music, I threw up women, I threw up money, I threw up sex, I threw up my father's death, I threw up guilt and hopelessness. I threw up my body. I turned myself inside out. I dry-heaved, groaned, gasped, and cried. Susan, Joanie, Jo-Lynne, Tess, and Jeanne tried to calm me. But by the time I surfaced, the party was over and everyone except the bartender and my caretakers were gone. Susan drove me home and helped me through the night.

The album was released with great fanfare and was a big success. It was a celebration of many reunions—a reunion of generations, a reunion of Jeff and Holly working together again. The beat was determined to go on. The album was called *Lifeline*.

Instead of basking in the success, I grew restless and more easily annoyed. As Ronnie gained confidence and no longer walked on eggshells, she let more of her wonderfully snarky self show—in other words, she could be a royal pain in the ass. We still loved each other, but the honeymoon was over. Rumor was out that we were lovers. It did cross my mind (I find this big, white-haired powerhouse very sexy), but no, we were not lovers. We may not have been a couple, but we were definitely a pair!

I had wanted us to be successful, but I hadn't realized I would start to lose what precious little sense of self I had intact when we had started the project. I knew I was looking for something but I wasn't sure what or where to look. I headed off for a short tour of England with Jeff. We were to do several concerts with Inti-Illimani, a Chilean ensemble, in commemoration of the coup in Chile.

Ronnie went on to have a solo career, recording several albums, and I got myself into another collaboration. But this duo is still the duo of duos. Our work brings together worlds, times, and notes in a way that is completely ours. Our first record, *Lifeline,* was followed by a second, *Singing with You.* We still do concerts together. Audiences demand it, and each time I am amazed by who we are together. I enjoy watching Ronnie stride across the stage. There is a very particular way in which she sets her foot down and a painful tenderness when she puts her belting voice aside for a moment and a whisper comes forth. Ronnie, with her head thrown back, her voice hurled across the footlights—like the first time I saw her in San Francisco when I was only ten years old—is a woman who knows how to sing and what to sing about.

One night I went to see Susan Freundlich sign a Tom Paxton concert. I'd never seen her work from out front but always to my left onstage. She was great. So was Tom. That night, Susan and I sat in the hotel bar and time caught up with us. We had loved each other for years, we had worked close and hard, we had held each other when exhaustion and frustration took over, we had confided in each other about love and sex and fear, we had flirted wildly without hidden intention, we had struggled. Susan taught me a lot about anti-Semitism and helped me unlearn any vestiges of it hanging around inside me. As we sat peacefully together, we wondered out loud why we had never been lovers. Promising that we would not let the root of our friendship be altered, we spent the night together. We kept our promise about the root, but the leaves on the branches changed colors with the seasons. Sometimes we were passionately in love, sometimes we backed away to catch our breaths, sometimes we watched each other fall in and out of love with other people and we made room, noticing our jealousy but not being ruled by it. We work together still. Susan is the development director at Redwood now. And we steal five minutes from the day to walk around the block to talk about love and sex. Not so much about fear anymore. But we are able to look at the big world and the little moment at the same time, which is the perspective from which we go through life together.

Holly with her father, Russell, 1951

Holly as Peter Pan, 1960

Holly with high-school folk group The Freedom Singers, 1964

Holly with Don Johnson filming *The Magic Garden of Stanley Sweetheart*, 1969

PHOTO BY JOSH WEINER

Holly with the cast of F.T.A., 1971: *left to right,* Pamala Donegan, Donald Sutherland, Rita Martinson, Holly, Glen Chandler, Jane Fonda

PHOTO BY LESLIE AUSTIN

Holly with George Roy Hill, directing her in *Slaughterhouse Five*

Holly with her sisters, 1972: *left to right,* Timothy, Holly, and Laurel. This was the time of the first Near Sisters Show.

The Near Sisters' ten-year-reunion show: *left to right,* Timothy, Holly, and Laurel

Holly, 1974

Below, Rob Moitoza, Holly, Jeff Langley, and Julie Thompson on break at the recording studio, 1974

Performers in a concert benefiting the new Los Angeles Woman's Building: *left to right,* Liebe Grey, Lily Tomlin, Holly, Terri Carson, Cris Williamson, Tery Arnold, Margie Adam, Carol-Lynn Fillet, Meg Christian, Miriam Cutler, Miranda Garrison

Below left, Holly with Meg Christian, 1976; *right,* Holly at the first Michigan Women's Music Festival, 1976

PHOTO BY DIANA DAVIES

PHOTO BY LINDA WOLFE

Above, the musicians and production team that recorded *Fire in the Rain,* 1981. *Seated:* Mary Watkins, Adrienne Torf, Carrie Barton, Leslie Ann Jones, Jan Martinelli, Susan Gottlieb, Gail Brodkey. *Standing:* Carolyn Bowden, Bonnie Johnson, Joanie Shoemaker, Jo-Lynne Worley, Holly, June Millington, Bernice Brooks.

Left, Susan Freundlich, sign language artist/ interpreter, currently Redwood Cultural Work development director

PHOTO BY SUSAN WILSON

Above, the musicians of *Speed of Light*, 1981: *left to right*, Aashid Himons, Carrie Barton, Darrell Rose, Cam Davis, Adrienne Torf, Mustafa Abdul-Aleen, and Holly

Holly with The Weavers at the *Clearwater's* Great Hudson River Revival, 1983: *left to right*, Fred Hellerman, Lee Hayes, Ronnie Gilbert, Pete Seeger, and Holly

Holly with Ronnie Gilbert, 1983

Holly with Inti-Illimani on the Peace in the Americas Tour, 1984

Left, Holly with Rhiannon at the Redwood Festival, Greek Theatre, Berkeley, California, 1985

Below, Holly with Gus Newport, mayor of Berkeley, California, 1985

Left to right, Joanie Shoemaker, executive director of Redwood Cultural Work; Jeanne Bradshaw, producer/owner of the Great American Music Hall; Holly; and her manager, Jo-Lynne Worley, 1985

H.A.R.P. (Holly, Arlo Guthrie, Ronnie Gilbert, and Pete Seeger) at the Ohio State Fair, 1985

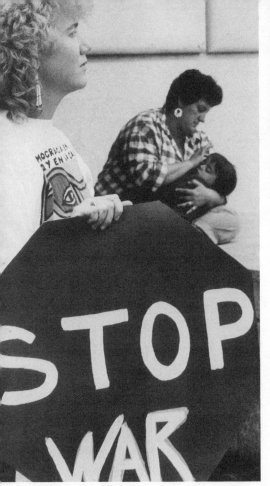

Anne Near

Holly at a demonstration for peace in Central America, 1986

Kenny Loggins and Holly "At the Ritz," a fund-raiser for Sojourn, a shelter for battered women

PHOTO BY RENÉE GAUMOND

The band from the *Don't Hold Back* concert tour, 1987: *left to right,* Bob Glaub, Julie Homi, Holly, John Bucchino, and Tris Imboden; *below,* film critic Dixie Whatley, Holly, and Andy Frances, music industry consultant

PHOTO BY J. A. RUBINO

Holly with Soviet journalist Vladimir Pozner, who, with Phil Donahue, was the recipient of the 1987 World Communications Medal at the Better World Society Second Annual Awards Dinner at the Waldorf-Astoria in New York; *below,* Casey Kasem, Ron Kovic, and Holly at a fund-raiser for Jesse Jackson, 1988

Holly in El Salvador at the festival "A Song for Peace with Sovereignty and Independence in El Salvador," 1988: *left to right,* Ubaka Hill and Beverly Grant from the group Human Condition, Holly, and Amparo Ochoa

San Jose Repertory Theatre's Production of *1940s Radio Hour,* 1988: *left to right,* Christa Germonson, Holly, and Jim Newman

Holly with Raul Julia at a fund-raiser for Children with AIDS, Carnegie Hall, 1989

PHOTO BY JOHN BUCCHINO

Below, Holly with John Bucchino, Vickie Randle, and Laura Nyro backstage at Riverfest Music Festival, St. Paul, Minnesota, 1989

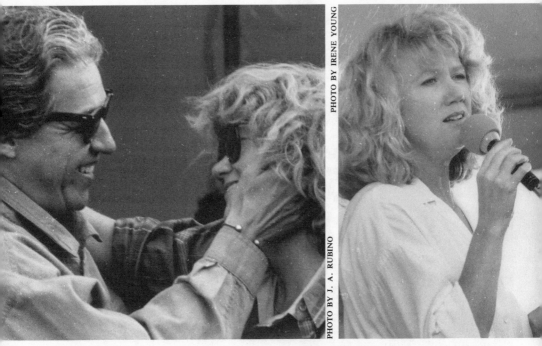

Nicaraguan singer and leader of Grupo Mancotal, Luis Enrique Mejia Godoy, and Holly, 1989; *right,* Holly, Redwood Cultural Work Festival, 1989

Holly with good friends Jill Eikenberry and Michael Tucker, 1989

Above, Holly and Stephen Powers, president of Chameleon Records Music Group, 1989

Above left, Holly with Argentinian singer Mercedes Sosa after their West Coast concert tour, 1989

Left, Holly and Bonnie Raitt, January 1990

11
GRACIAS A LA VIDA

Dear Joan,

I'm on the long flight home from Australia. Damn, I didn't realize that the CIA had used Australia's assistance for the coup in Chile. I think of you now, living in Santiago. I'd love to see your dance school, to meet your children and grandchildren.

I no longer think of you as Joan Jara, Victor's widow, but as Joan Jara, the dancer. You are also Joan, who was very much in love with Victor Jara—singer, director, writer, father, lover, husband—murdered by the junta as thousands were herded into the stadium.

When did I first fall in love with Chile, Joan? It began with a murder. It was in a meeting of antiwar activists on September 11, 1973. We were discussing strategies for ending the war in Indochina. Someone burst into the room and cried, "Allende's been shot!" I was startled by the passionate response all around me. Everyone cried out in despair. I didn't even know who Allende was, Joan. But I could see in the faces of those around me that they felt a great loss. I looked at a map to find Chile. Later, I bought a record of the martyred singer Victor Jara . . . your Victor, Joan.

Gradually, I involved myself in the solidarity movement. I did a benefit for Chile with Uruguay's exiled Daniel Viglietti, and North America's Phil Ochs. After the concert, Phil and Daniel drank late into the night. I sipped slowly, watching these two displaced men so full of passion and despair, that emotional dichotomy so central to their music.

One day, I looked at a list of names sent to me of women who had "disappeared." I spoke each name out loud, dozens of names. I went downstairs to ask my Cuban landlady (and mother of one of Cuba's

186

finest ballerinas), "How do you say 'there is a woman missing in Chile' in Spanish?" She said, "Hay una mujer desaparecida." I sat out on the front porch and began to sing out the names of the missing women.

In 1978, I sang at a Chile-solidarity event in Mexico. The audience didn't like me much. They wanted to hear the Latin-American musicians who'd come from all over the continent to sing . . . Sara Gonzales from Cuba, Chile's (and Violeta Parra's) children, Isabel and Angel Parra, and Inti-Illimani. I listened to a woman read a poem, the last by Victor, written in prison shortly before the prison guards broke his hands and killed him. The woman was you, Joan. I had tea with members of the Allende family. Chilean exiles took me to the Temple of the Sun and the Moon, where the gods planted a kiss that I never washed off.

It was cold and misty, the kind of early London morning I remember reading about in *Jane Eyre*. You came to the door, bundled up in a sweater. Your lovely house was cluttered and cozy. "I'm working on the part about Victor's death," you said. "I will be so relieved when it is done." And it is, Joan. *Victor** is a wonderful book. But that morning I could see the toll it was taking on you as you detailed the horror, the trip to the train station to identify the body, the escape from Chile with only your children and his last poem. I remember thinking, when this book is done, Joan, you can dance again. The years of serving as Victor's hands will be over and you can be the wings he fell in love with so many years ago . . .

Isabel Letellier, Isabel Allende, Coretta Scott King, Jackie Kennedy, Betty Shabazz, Lisbet Palme, Joan Jara, all widows of famous dead men, all living with someone who is bigger than life but not there at the table, not with the children, not in bed . . .

Later, I met Inti-Illimani in New Mexico, but it wasn't until Bochum that our paths truly crossed.

Bochum, Germany, 1983

I sat crouched on the sidelines of the stage and watched the over eighty thousand people gathered for the youth disarmament fest in Bochum, Germany. And more crowds were outside, begging to get in.

---

*Jonathan Cape Ltd., London, 1983; Tickor and Fields, New York, 1983.

Fire in the Rain . . . Singer in the Storm

Harry Belafonte spoke so pointedly, so representatively of the other America; Miriam Makeba sang, I had not heard her in years since her early records filled our farmhouse in Potter Valley, bringing Africa to a little white girl; a survivor of Auschwitz sang with a Palestinian folk group in a stadium in Germany; Inti-Illimani sang on the anniversary of the coup, and as the audience lifted their lighters in the air, the stadium was transformed into a candelabrum for peace, reclaiming "the stadium" that had been the site of mass murder and torture in Chile as Allende was shot and Pinochet became the executioner on behalf of U.S. foreign policy. And then NATO soldiers, dressed in various uniforms, entered the stadium in Bochum carrying a banner reading: NATO SOLDIERS OPPOSED TO NUCLEAR WAR. The crowd was on its feet, honoring these men who would be arrested when they left, for it is illegal to demonstrate in uniform, or at least to demonstrate for peace, since we know that a demonstration of weapon power is not only legal but required. A German woman walked onstage and sang in German, "Where Have All the Flowers Gone?" (The soldiers were arrested and later that year, in Dortmund, I met more soldiers who'd come to take the place of the ones who were put in the stockades after Bochum.)

Adrienne Torf (pianist), Carrie Barton (bassist), and I performed. The men in the sound crew were impressed by Ady and Carrie. I enjoyed watching these fine women musicians, quiet and humble as they set up the equipment, tolerating the patronizing remarks and the disinterest, and then those first notes. The whole attitude of the crew changed. It is tragic, this assumption of inability women musicians face while men get away with mediocrity all the time.

The following fall, I was invited to tour England and Scotland with Inti-Illimani and you. In Edinburgh, we sang "Gracias a la Vida" together for the first time. And on the train, we were all reading the newly published *Victor*. (We looked like a cartoon from the *New Yorker!*) Oh dear Joan, I am fascinated by the series of moments that make up our lives. How we turn and step and falter and leap. The times we say, "No, go away." The times we say, "Yes, I am willing."

The plane is landing in Hawaii. I have a concert here. Not a tourist event, but for local people, for activists, for students, and for people in the military if they decide to come. And on this island, so familiar with the disruption caused by foreign intervention, I will sing of Chile and think of you dancing.

Love, Holly

Gracias a la Vida

*　　*　　*

The beaches of Hawaii never looked so good to me as they did in December 1983. I had a concert to do at the University of Hawaii, but the following three days were designated R and R. The concert was great. A lot of women from the military dared to come even though they had to stay in the closet. But I did all the coming out for them that night, singing sweet lesbian love songs. I remember talking to some women who had previously been stationed in San Diego. They said when new women arrived on the base who seemed "suspiciously independent," they would try to find ways to come out to them without jeopardizing their jobs if they had guessed wrong. So one would say, "Do you like music?" Another would say, "Ever hear of Holly Near?" And if they got a positive response, they would confirm their suspicions with "Ever hear of Meg Christian?" I love that story.

In Hawaii, I also did some fairly outspoken songs about militarism and supported the indigenous peoples' objections to occupation. I wondered how my army friends felt about that. But, then, for many of them, it was just a job with insurance benefits in a country with a high unemployment rate. Volunteer army, indeed!

The next day, my pals hit the beach. But I'm hopeless; I spent the day with Haunani-Kay Trask, getting an update on the work political progressives were doing on the islands. She showed me films and sent me back to my hotel with my arms full of books and literature. I did manage to put them in my suitcase and go to the beach with only sunscreen and one of those parasol-decorated rum drinks in hand. We toasted the miracle of overachievers taking a vacation!

I spent Christmas with my family and then, back at my house in Oakland, fell asleep before the New Year arrived, mumbling something to myself about George Orwell and 1984.

I jumped right into making a new album, which I called *Watch Out!*, named after a song I wrote with my co-producer, John McCutcheon, after Reagan invaded Grenada. The album featured the eclectic string band Trapezoid, with guest performances by Barbara Higbie and Rafael Manriquez. Like all my recording experiences, it felt hard. I could never *find* myself in a recording studio, the music always a step removed. As much as I was a singer and made a lot of records, my work didn't really seem to be about that. Joined by Redwood co-workers Joanie Shoemaker and Amy Bank, guitarist Jim Scott, my mother, Anne Near, and a film crew, I headed for Nicaragua.

189

We passed by the neighborhoods as we came in from the airport, neighborhoods of poor people who lived on the edge of the city. Our guide pointed out that these people were central to the revolutionary victory. A country is not reclaimed from the center of the city outward, but rather the reverse. Those who live on the outskirts are crucial in the final stages. Poverty without a people's government looks like hopelessness, but to see poverty in organized communities is to see relief-in-progress.

We got settled into our hotel, a conservative establishment with pictures of the pope in the lobby, where, in another hotel, one might see a picture of Father Cardenal, a new theology leader of the revolution, poet, and the minister of culture. When the pope visited Nicaragua, he refused to let this dearly loved priest join the others in kissing the ring. There seem to be two kinds of Catholics: those who want poor people to wait and get theirs in heaven, and those who want poor people to receive the grace of God on earth. Mom and I strolled through the garden toward the bus that would take us to our first meeting. I took a deep breath. There would be no rest for the next eleven days.

Seven peasant women walked into the room full of North American guests and sat shyly in wooden chairs, their hands like the earth by which they survived. Their eyes had seen more grief than mothers are meant to witness. "The birds have the sky, the fish have the sea, and we must have the land." For them, this was not a war about communism. It was about land, food, education, dignity, and life itself. They had formed an organization of peasant women called Mothers of Martyrs.

One said, "We walk in free streets, breathe free air. Life is hard, the war is hard, we suffer from shortages, but now that we are free from Somoza, we can have hope. We are learning to read, our children are immunized, there was not one case of polio last year. The government listens to our concerns and the land is being given back to the peasants. Why does Reagan want to destroy the first chance we have ever had?"

One by one they told stories of how their children died. "My sons died before the victory. I learned things from them and joined Sandino. My sons told me from prison we would win. I asked how can you know. Just wait and see, Mom. When they got out of prison and they went underground, I saw them every few months. Old woman, don't worry, we will win, you will see. In June 1979, they said, we are going to die, Mom, but those who live must defend the revolution. The living must defend this new life we are making. They were both killed by Somoza's troops one month before the victory.''

Another spoke: ''My babies are gone, but I defend what they fought for—health centers, land reform, schools. Is this what you are afraid of, Reagan? It was prohibited to be young under Somoza. Now we are all young and our children will not have died in vain. We the mothers will see that heads fly if anyone tries to stop us from breathing free air.''

I was curious that the mothers kept talking to Reagan, as if he were at the meeting . . . or perhaps it was their way of telling us: We are not blaming you who have come so far to meet us. It is your government that has gone so far to kill us.

''Four children fallen, the last in 1984. Every bone broken by the contras. You couldn't recognize him as a human. My daughter was electrocuted with wires. My husband brought her back in a body bag. Two others dead. But two live. Both are in the military.''

''My mother couldn't read. My daughters study medicine. This is the society we fight for. Is this what you are afraid of, Reagan? Now there are thousands of orphans. Reagan, you created a dangerous situation. Think of their rage. This you should be afraid of.''

I wrote in my notebook and passed it to my own mother. ''The U.S. must quit putting forth ideology as a rationale for raping the Third World.''

Joanie, Amy, Anne, and I sat with the other international guests looking out over the Plaza of the Revolution, which was filled with thousands of Nicaraguans carrying flags, shouting *consignas,* throwing each other up in the air, and catching each other in a human net. The country was commemorating the fiftieth anniversary of the birth of Sandino, the father of the revolution. Today, Daniel Ortega was going to announce the elections. Hundreds of people had participated in preparing the country for this long-awaited day. High school students had gone out into the countryside to teach the people to read and write. Law students had worked overtime to prepare the election codes. The political parties that were eligible to participate had debated and struggled (Socialists, Communists, social democrats, Christian democrats, two right-wing parties, and the Sandinistas). Thousands had died, including Sandino, in the process of bringing forth a new Nicaragua.

The young people seemed especially excited today, for they had been campaigning hard to see the voting age changed from eighteen to sixteen. Today the Sandinistas would announce their decision on this point as well. We sat with a new bilingual friend who generously translated throughout the day. The ceremony included the naming of the countries that were represented at the celebration. I found myself wishing there were a name for the peace-loving people of the United States that would somehow identify us as separate from the war-makers of our nation. On the other hand, Nicaraguans knew that North American peace activists were here in solidarity and they acknowledged our presence.

Two sixteen-year-olds spoke on behalf of lowering the voting age. Both had been severely disabled in the war. Then Commandant Ortega spoke. The elections were announced, the sixteen-year-olds were included, and the celebration was on.

That night, we went to Ortega's house for a party of international and Nicaraguan guests, which included such celebrities as Julie Christie and Carlos Mejia Godoy. There was food and dancing, and at our table, which was graced with Nicaraguans, Italians, and Swedes, we sang songs of liberation from each of our countries. One morning we went to the weekly demonstration put on each week by North Americans in front of the U.S. embassy. It had convened weekly to protest invasions ever since Reagan invaded Grenada.

We went to a jeans factory. The labels on the jeans read ''Revolution'' instead of ''Prime Cut.'' One worker told us, ''If the people say go to the front, I go. If the people say go to the factory, I go. I am ready to serve. Of course it would be better for our nation if the war was over and we could all go to the factory.''

I finished singing at the fifth event of the day. As we prepared to go back to the hotel, someone arrived and asked if we could come do one more. Our guide protested. ''Holly has been working all day!'' The other person argued the importance of the request. I didn't know if I should intervene. I took our host aside and told him I didn't mind. He looked surprised. ''Aren't you tired?'' ''Are you?'' I asked. He smiled. We agreed to go. We arrived at an open field where young men were slowly gathering, arriving in twos and fours from all parts of the city, carrying their packs. They were quickly being mobilized into the national defense. Word had come that two thousand contras were moving toward one of the borders. Some looked as though they were seventeen or eighteen. I was wrong. They were fifteen.

Our host set up the portable sound system and we stayed late into the night, serenading these children. Ramone, a powerful singer, chose his songs wisely. He knew what they needed to hear, for he too had been called up many times. I had sung for soldiers. There was nothing romantic about sending them off to war. I felt as if every one of their mothers were inside me as I began to sing.

The next morning I wrote notes that became one of the lectures I do at colleges, churches, and rallies:

> Regardless of what the Sandinistas do, the U.S. will not be satisfied because the U.S. doesn't want a democracy in Nicaragua. It wants a puppet government that will allow multinational corporations to set up business. Nicaragua welcomes business, but not if the visiting companies steal resources, underpay the work force, and undermine the duly elected government.
>
> Reagan screamed that the Sandinistas hadn't held elections. The U.S. took twelve years to announce elections when it was first formed and only white men with land were allowed to vote! But now there will be elections. The Sandinistas have sent representatives all over the world to study election systems. (One woman lawyer tried to come to the U.S. to do research but was denied her visa! And we claim we want to spread democracy?) The Sandinistas will invite international witnesses to guarantee that it is fair and legal, but if the Sandinistas win, Reagan will not accept the outcome, for surely the people will vote for Daniel Ortega.
>
> Then Reagan will decide to criticize Nicaragua for not having freedom of the press. The slanderous opposition press is backed by the CIA and usually allowed to publish. Only on occasion has it been shut down, which is not uncommon when a country is at war.
>
> The U.S. is judged guilty by the World Court for mining harbors off the coast of Nicaragua. The U.S. ignores the charge and dismisses the verdict.
>
> And people in Congress go along with this policy. They are so afraid of looking like they support Communists. I wish they would quit worrying about the Communists and start worrying about their own integrity. Think what our own country's black community or homeless population or school system could do with the millions we have given to the

contras. Anticommunism is costing us our country. It doesn't matter how big the defense budget is abroad if there is nothing left to defend at home.

The Omar Torrijos military base seldom had visitors and the soldiers rarely had time off. They were the most highly trained Sandinista forces, prepared to face the U.S. military, the CIA, and the contras. Yet I was invited to sing for them. As our hosts once again set up our portable generator-operated sound system, five hundred soldiers filled the benches in the makeshift outdoor theater. Victoria Grillo, the officer in charge of our visit, led them in crisp *consignas* to welcome us. Then I sang for forty minutes.

I told them about the Vietnam vets who were organizing in the States to oppose the war in El Salvador and Nicaragua. I told them of the women's groups and the students.

I looked at these bold faces turned soft by the sweet sounds of music. Did I dare linger too long on any one face?

"Will you sing one for me?" I asked. They laughed and turned to a man who was clearly their chosen troubadour. The singer rose and his friends took his gun, his camouflage jacket, and his hat decorated with medals. They lifted him up onto the stage in his plain white T-shirt and green army pants. Accepting the guitar from Jim Scott, he sang a love song. We sat quietly for a moment. The light was changing. I said, "Thank you for letting us sing with you. I hope peace comes soon between our countries. There is already peace between you and me." We applauded each other and they moved back to the task of defending their nation. I moved on to defending mine, for I do believe working for peace is an act of patriotism.

A few soldiers lingered to talk or just to watch. A note was handed up to me. I read it.

From where I sit I only see you in silhouette,
Your face and your hair the same color, the color of love.
To hear your voice like the voice of my people
I feel that the blood of our brothers flowers in you.
Continue as you are, in the path of dignity.
Mario Mongalo, Brigada de Artilleria

When I looked up, the messenger pointed to a young man standing shyly at a distance. I began to walk toward him when I was stopped by a young boy in my path. He was dressed in military fatigues. My first thought was that he was just playing soldier, dressed like his daddy. No. Meet Pedro Hernandes. The contras had attacked his home in Nueva Segovia. He played dead. When they left he was the only member of his family alive. He went into the mountains and found the Sandinistas. They told him that he was too young to be a soldier and that they must send him to an orphanage. But the child protested. The Sandinistas kept him on with them, became his uncles and brothers, taught him to read. Pedro taught them about the mountains where he lived. After three years of service, Pedro was thirteen.

"He wants you to give him something to remember you by," said one of his "uncles." Joanie handed me a medallion she'd been keeping for me and, as he stood at attention, so proud, like an Olympic runner receiving a medal, I put it around his neck. It read, "War is not healthy for children and other living things." Then I kissed him. He blushed like a thirteen-year-old and moved away.

There is the poet, still waiting. We shook hands. "Thank you for the poem," I said, not taking my hand away from his. "My bus is leaving." "Yes, I know." I couldn't leave. He kissed my hand.

As I walked to the bus, a hush fell over the camp. Sunset. The flag was being lowered. I stopped and stood silently with the others. Six birds flew across the sun as if they were replacing F-16 bombers. *Pedro,* I thought, *when I am ninety, you will be about sixty-five. Do you think you will be able to dance with an old woman in the moonlight when you are sixty-five?*

Redwood, under the new partnership, was doing well. We had taken on staff, new artists, and moved to a larger office space in Oakland. I liked working with J2. They seemed able to cope with my endless stream of ideas, were not overwhelmed by my enthusiasm, and were emphatic about budgets.

I was talking to a friend from New York City on the phone when there was an earthquake. I described the windows rattling and the vibration beneath my feet. But for me, the real earthquake had happened a few hours earlier when my back went into spasm again. I had been lazy about back exercises and behaved as if I were an athlete, not someone who had been through back surgery. My March tour began the next day. I called the Redwood office to confer with my partners. They suggested I take a staff person on the road to help. I didn't usually take a road person, but maybe in this case it would be a good idea.

195

Melissa Howden agreed to do the first half, and Cynthia Frenz did the second. My back hurt so badly that sometimes I felt I couldn't breathe for the pain. But I kept my spirits together until I hit Nova Scotia. Then I snapped. Alone in my bed, I curled up into a little ball and thought it would be much appreciated if I could get hit by a big Mack truck. Well, this was, after all, spring 1984!

The April sun was welcome in New York City. I put on my back brace and went to the airport to meet Inti-Illimani's flight. In the car, driving back to the city, we discovered a misunderstanding: I had sent them a tape of songs to learn so that they could accompany me on the tour. They assumed that my pianist was playing for me and that they were simply being invited to play additional backup arrangements. After our initial panic subsided, we threw ourselves into two intense days of rehearsal and pulled together an amazing show.

One night after dinner, Jorge started improvising on the piano in the living room. I could hear him from the kitchen. I slipped unnoticed into the corner to listen and then wrote a lyric and a melody to his chords. I moved next to him on the piano bench and began to sing to him. The song was complete from beginning to end. We sat quietly and cried.

> *When you speak the language of your life*
> *I do not know the story*
> *The words are only sounds*
> *And they leave my mind to wonder*
> *But when you soar through my heart with a melody*
> *I hear the dancing feet, I taste the salty tears*
> *I know the laughing child*
> *And the moment of the dream*

Jeanne Bradshaw and the staff of the Great American Music Hall co-produced with Joanie and Jo-Lynne and the staff of Redwood the Singing for Peace in the Americas tour. I liked Jeanne. Although I didn't see her much, she was one of those friends I imagined would be in my life always, so we weren't in a hurry. But I loved that she was going on this tour. I would be the beneficiary of her excellent work coordinating the logistics of the tour and her delightful friendship coordinating me! She rented a large bus for the East Coast part of the tour—one of those rock 'n' roll buses with a video player in the back, eleven little bunks, and a small kitchen. Usually no more than four or five people try to coexist in these buses. We were thirteen—nine men (eight Chileans and our driver, probably all straight, but who knows?) and five women (of Jewish, Italian, and northern European descent; two who were publicly straight but privately bisexual; one lesbian; and one who was publicly a lesbian but privately bisexual). Why does all this matter? Because when people are uncomfortable about each other's life-styles, it matters. When people can be exiled from their country for being outspoken Chileans or lose their children and jobs for being lesbians, it matters. We would spend the next three weeks together, not because we had to but because we chose to, because it mattered. This tour was another first. To our knowledge, there had never been a major collaboration between Latin American men and North American lesbian feminists.

Packing up after a show, we headed for the next town, watching the lights of each community race by our windows in the night. I was exhausted but I couldn't sleep. José and I stayed up late writing a song.

Out on the highway of flutes and fires,
A circle of gypsies and sparks.
Ancient forever, we head for tomorrow,
A circle of lights in the dark.
If the land is no longer our home and home is not where we are,
Then with love in our hearts,
We must go on and on and on and on . . .
The gypsy dances on!

Amy Bank, Redwood's first full-time employee, traveled with us as well. She was responsible for the grass-roots organizing, national networking, and political public relations. This was a large task given that our diverse audiences were being pushed to acknowledge each other. Some were learning of Chile for the first time, others were hearing songs about feminism and lesbianism for the first time. Some Chileans were critical: "Why are you singing with this gringa?" Some feminists were critical: "Why are you working with all these macho men?" We were intentionally stretching everyone's limits, starting with our own. Many felt a huge relief as parts of their lives were sung together. Amid all this, the music sounded great!

We indulged in the sublime and the ridiculous. One night, we all gathered in the "living room" at the back of the bus to watch *Godzilla* on TV. The movie was in Japanese with English subtitles and as best I could, I translated it into Spanish. This was multicultural work at its most fun! When in upstate New York, I arranged to visit the Onondaga Nation, including meeting with the tribal elders; a brief presentation at a grammar school; and a press conference with Dennis Banks, who was living on the nation in exile from North Dakota. I loved being a weaver, a quiltmaker. I was a student of the art of diversity, noticing where the colors blend and clash, working with the clay of our human conflict. Music outside of this context had no melody for my ears. We can take our differences to war or turn them into song, not a song that sounds like either of us alone, but a new song that is a coming together without either of us losing who we are. Sometimes I was filled with joy over the success of our collaboration. Sometimes I would go in my room alone and cry.

We landed at San Francisco airport. It was a great relief to be home, even if only for a few days. The music was ready. Now I just needed to put everything else out of my mind and concentrate on recording a live album. One of the Intis had the flu and his voice was weakened. On one song, a guitar was out of tune in the intro. I sang one of the Spanish songs, and although I felt it was going well, just before the end, as the song climaxed, I couldn't remember the words. We had to do it again. However, when we listened back, we were thrilled with the result and called it "Sing to Me the Dream."

At the end of the concert in L.A., as we joined together for the finale, I called out the verses from "Singing for Our Lives." When we got to the verse "We are gay and straight together," I noticed Inti had stopped singing. After the show, I told the road manager to change the transportation plans. Instead of riding in several cars, I wanted the whole band in the van, without anyone from the community. I needed to talk to them alone.

Driving along Highway 10 en route to Santa Monica, I confronted them: "I can't believe you aren't singing on that verse! I am putting my whole organization into strain mode for this peace tour. It is our understanding that this is a collaboration, a coalition, not a service that we are providing. Didn't you know who we are before you agreed to come? What do you think is your part in this coalition? In press conferences and from the stage, I speak of Chile. But you never mention the women's movement or the condition of women in Chile or the complex effects of exile on women and their children. Do you mention Redwood even once for every ten times I mention Inti? Do you speak of gay rights? Tonight, I look over and you are not even singing. Do you know how that makes me feel?''

Stunned by my anger, they responded slowly. Yes, they had known who we were and had decided very intentionally to do the collaboration because they felt we were the most organized and efficient group they had ever worked with in the solidarity community. They also felt they could learn from us. One said he was sorry he hadn't sung—he thought that verse was special to the gay and lesbian community and it would be inappropriate for him to sing on it but he would from now on.

I don't know if they changed their attitudes for the sake of the world or only their behavior for the sake of the tour and our friendship. It takes a very special man to really understand feminism and to make equality a priority. Such men are few and far between. Although some of my audience ''doesn't want to hear that Spanish music,'' the joyful truth is that a huge number of people who had had very little contact with Central and Latin Americans, have come into the solidarity circle as a result of this tour with Inti-Illimani. I believe feminism moved forward, and women's groups such as Altazor and Sabia have emerged.

We arrived in Iowa for a peace chautauqua, joining Sweet Honey, Pete Seeger, Susan Freundlich, Ronnie Gilbert, Trapezoid, John McCutcheon, and others. A tremendous storm was in progress. I had never seen such mud. A local shoestore sent a man to the hotel with rubber boots in all shapes and sizes. A horse-drawn wagon carried us to the stage. The brave audience huddled under tarps or danced nearly naked in the downpour. At the end of the day, we returned to the hotel. I stood on the balcony and looked down to the courtyard, where a jam session was carrying on. There were several people with whom I had been lovers all staying in the same hotel. We were all friends still. I felt very much alone. The Intis were going home soon. My back hurt. I was tired of wearing a brace. This had already been a remarkable year, but it was only April and I still had so much work to do with no rest in sight.

We moved on to Chicago and had a much-needed night off. We decided to go next door to a bar/disco. Only a few people were there so we took to the dance floor, which was surrounded by video screens. Ironically, my cousin Kevin Bacon appeared on the screens as Kenny Loggins's ''Footloose'' played. Inti laughed when I explained that he was my cousin. ''What else don't we know about you, dear Holly?'' they inquired.

Finally, we arrived at Kennedy airport. It was a quick farewell. There is no need to drag these things out. I would miss these brothers. We had done great work. We had raised fifty thousand dollars in humanitarian aid for Central and Latin American groups, made a beautiful record, lived together for a moment in time, and expressed our gratitude to the grandmother of *nueva canción,* the late Violeta Parra, who had written "Gracias a la Vida."

My partners and I and Jeanne Bradshaw lost money on the tour but, unwilling to dip into the aid money, we added it to a growing debt. It was becoming increasingly expensive to do this work, but how could we not do it? We had trouble raising money. People thought I was rich and capable of funding the work myself. I did fund it to the extent of my personal wealth, which amounted to what I earned. I would just have to tour more to pay the debt.

When I returned to California, there was a lovely letter waiting for me from one of the Intis.

I am going away from a waterfall. My eyes retain the cradling of the red and golden wave of your hair. I obey the rite. I divide myself in two parts; stepping on the air, flying to the opposite way of the universe and at the same time carried/towed by this ball of ground and water. I hope that my memory has written her cloud all words weaved, all glances; I wish may to touch them and achieve repeating in the throbbing the same sensation in the next time I have now very different feelings. I complain about this distance that separates me from your fountain, I'm happy these few days. I grow with that fertility, I fight against this large space, this separation. I take refuge to scrutinize the word "again." I stop my watch because I want to stay there. I love our sincerity, our thirst; I love the end of life. I love to look at you from my angle. I love your sweetness. I shall embrace you through the sea. I shall watch over the lightnings of your soul.

With love . . .

Now I had to try to come down gently. I hoped for it but there was no way to know when and if Inti would ever play in Chile again. But in 1988, Pinochet opened the doors of Chile in hopes of improving his image so that he could win the support of the people in a *sí/no* plebiscite. He lost the vote of confidence when a record number of people voted with a resounding NO! Pinochet did not step down. But while the doors were open, Inti-Illimani returned to Chile and did a concert in Santiago.

Out on the highway of death and madness
This plan of extinction must fall
Faithful forever to earth and to children
We answer a powerful call
If the land is our life
And life is where we are
Then let love come into our hearts
We must go on and on and on and on and on and on
The gypsy dances on!

12
PROCEED WITH CARE

IN 1976, I HAD SAT DOWN TO WRITE A LETTER TO MY PARENTS. DEAR Mom and Dad, there is something I want to tell you . . . no. Dear Mom and Dad, I know we have talked about this before. . . . No. Why was this hard? I had talked with them about everything, including lesbianism. They had read booklets on lesbian feminism put out by Diana Press. These were exceptional parents. Dear Mom and Dad, remember when I played that song for you by Meg Christian? . . . no. Dear Mom and Dad. No. Dear Anne and Russell . . . no . . . shit! Dear Mom and Dad.

How hard it is to come out! Somehow I told them I had fallen in love with a woman. I don't know how they felt about it when they read the letter, but whatever they needed to do they did alone, for the next time we spoke, there was love and support. Meg was invited home to visit and as far as they were concerned, she was family.

Then I slowly wrote friends and family to tell them I was in love with a woman. I wanted them to hear it from me and not from the rumor mill. Years later, my cousin told me that when she read my letter, she threw up. She laughs now with the wisdom of hindsight. I understood her reaction. When I was a little kid, I thought tongue kissing was ". . . so gross!" But soon, Dennis Peragrini and I slow-danced our way over to a big oak tree at a barn party and kissed each other long and deep. I thought it was the sweetest thing. That which is unfamiliar is often repulsive.

And now, seven years later, it was happening again. Word was out that I was seeing a man, or married, or had a slew of children, or was sleeping not only with a man but with men. The only part that was true was the latter. I was sleeping with men. I was also sleeping with

202

women. (Sleeping. What a funny way to talk about sex!) But in truth, I wasn't having many affairs or getting much sleep. I was working harder than I had ever worked in my life. I don't know where people thought I was finding the time to have all the fun they said I was having! However, I figured I was a grown-up now. I could decide when and with whom to make love without asking the permission of ten thousand dykes. Oh, but it isn't true. I was letting other people's judgment throw me into an identity crisis that I wasn't having. I doubt that any single time in my life has been more emotionally stressful.

When a longtime fan and supporter of women's music heard that I was sleeping with a man again, she threw up. And when I went into a restaurant with my friend Mustafa, I was aware that I had been recognized by a group of lesbians sitting at another table. Mustafa reached over and took my hand. I pulled my hand away. His eyes left mine as he looked around the room to see what had provoked my response. I panicked. What if he thought I had pulled away because he was black? I thought *I* was going to throw up! I laughed at the thought that sex apparently makes people sick.

I couldn't bear the idea of hurting lesbians, and I couldn't stand the thought of heterosexuals celebrating my relationship with a man as if somehow they had won, and I could not bear the possibility that people would think I was straight. But I was still "out" onstage. I sang lesbian songs in major concert halls and at Gay Pride Day. I still thought of myself as a lesbian, which was not altered by sleeping with men. I didn't give men that kind of power, nor did the sort of men I was with ask for it. So what, in fact, was going on here? I had long, hard talks with friends and stayed up many nights trying to think clearly.

It was hard to publicly discuss a problem or crisis within the lesbian community. We are so vulnerable to society's hostility, and I felt protective. I didn't know what to say. I had nothing conclusive to report. So I avoided public debate. But damn it, I was too interested in human beings to dismiss this anger and confusion, so within a close circle of friends, I struggled to understand why this hurt us all so.

I think lesbians were afraid they would lose me. When we have so few, it is hard to think of losing one. And although they were gaining new ones, they were already losing some of the longtime lesbian singers . . . if not to men, then to religions, to other careers, to other choices. I tried to fill one hand with names of outspoken lesbians who were as famous or more so than me, who spoke to a broad-based community. I could not come up with names. Well there are_____ and_____: We know they are lesbians but they don't publicly say so. And there is_____, who has said she is a lesbian but never comes to gay/lesbian marches or speaks out for human and civil rights or raises funds like I do. Then there is_____, who sings lesbian songs and goes to demonstrations for gay/lesbian rights but who doesn't say she is a lesbian. Then there are the big stars who go to gay/lesbian events, but they are all straight people there in solidarity. Of course, there are the wonderful outspoken gay and lesbian artists in the grass-roots movements who are out and on the line. Still, they aren't as well known as I am and have less access to large numbers of people. In a country of 250 million people, the importance of my role in the lesbian community hit me like a tragedy.

Some lesbians feared my choices might invalidate their own and they didn't have enough support as it was. Many had discovered their own lesbianism or had gotten the courage to come out from being at one of my concerts. They had grown into their bold selves with my music. In the fragile balance, my vacillation could rattle their newly found security.

Then there were the lesbians who said they didn't care if I was straight or not; they just didn't want to feel lied to. But I had no need to promote heterosexuality in some public announcement. Heterosexuality got more center-stage attention than most of us could stomach, starting with Top 40 radio. The career damage was done, the economic losses and exclusion already felt. Regardless of who was in my bed, it seemed more politically effective to be out as a lesbian in the world.

Mainly, I felt lesbians wanted to know I wasn't going to betray them. Was I going to pull a tennis-player-or-entertainer-takes-new-boyfriend-on-national-TV-talk-show-and-says-it-was-a-phase-and-a-big-mistake? No. I didn't want to disengage myself from lesbianism. I would try not to be defensive but simply let my life say, I am here as long as you'll have me.

The saddest part was the small but vocal boycotts: lesbians who wouldn't come to the concerts, wouldn't play my music on their lesbian radio programs, wouldn't buy my records. It felt cruel and destructive. It hurt me, it hurt Redwood, and, most of all, it hurt their communities, both emotionally and economically. It made we wonder if they weren't on the FBI payroll!

So now some straight folks wouldn't play my music because I was a lesbian, and some lesbians wouldn't play my music because I was straight. The absurdity of it began to be my friend. Still, the mainstay of my audience kept coming to hear me sing and to my great pleasure, was growing. People's fascinating diversity of experience contradicted the assumption that I was singing for the convinced, which I think is a funny concept anyway, for I always want to ask, convinced of what? (I can just hear a critic saying to a sexist/capitalist metal band, "Well, but aren't you singing to the convinced? Don't you really think you should be out there singing to Socialists and radical feminists, trying to lure them to your persuasion?")

Then the debate about bisexuality began. Well, aren't you a bisexual? No. I am too closely linked to the political perspectives of lesbian feminism. My lesbianism is not linked to sexual preference. For me, it is part of my world view, part of my passion for women and central in my objection to male domination. At the same time, I do not deny myself heterosexuality or my fascination with a certain kind of male energy. And due to the nature of my world view, I find I'm not good in narrow spaces. Life doesn't fit neatly into simple categories for me. The doors must always be open. If I close the doors, I won't be able to write or sing. This is not new. Look at my life. What if the doors had been closed when I was an actress in Hollywood? I never would have let in the peace and feminist movements. And what if the doors had been closed when she put her arms around me and I fell in love? And now, should I close those same doors?

I had been so "out," so willing to share my personal life, my lesbianism for the sake of social change. But I had no need to promote heterosexuality. I believed that gay and lesbian relationships could be creative forms through which to express love and a viable family alternative to the heterosexual nuclear family. I also valued privacy. And above all, as much as I was addicted to romance and passion, I believed my personal love should not be more important than my universal love. I was all too aware of what happens when any individual or separate community sees themselves as more important than the well-being of the world. The songs I sing are not all about me. They pass through me but they are not me. They are us. I wondered to what degree my personal behavior affected the movements of which I was a part. I struggled with how much I should obstruct my spontaneity with regard to its effect on others. I decided there is thin ice between responsibility and guilt, between arrogance and false humility.

I said once in an interview that sexual preference isn't really central for me like it is for some people. They took that to mean it doesn't matter. Being a lesbian does matter. Anyone who says, "Well, I don't care if he/she is gay, it's nobody's business" is the voice of heterosexual culture inviting gay people to be invisible. Well, heterosexuals don't keep it to themselves. They have proms and weddings and anniversaries, get breaks on insurance and health care. They are all over each other on billboards, in movies, and at football games. You bet it matters to them.

I worried about lesbians. How were we going to take this subculture created to defend ourselves from homophobia and sexism and let it burst forward into the world? Lesbians seemed to be everywhere, and they certainly played key roles in every progressive movement I'd ever been a part of. And the music. Our music had touched the lives of so many.

When I surfaced from my long and grueling self-interrogation, I concluded that I was one of the "foremothers" of this work and it mattered to me how we would proceed. I felt it would be a great error if we weakened internally over who I slept with or any other such individual choice. I learned that I needed to end my part in the codependency that might have developed between me and the lesbian community. We didn't owe each other political correctness. We owed ourselves meaningful lives. A sensation of relief swept over me. I would love women. I would love men. I would love myself. I would touch and be touched. I would be celibate (now there's an unpopular choice. People just can't believe a person can be happy on one's own). Regardless, hopefully I would continue to put forth my music to challenge, to heal, to entertain, to inspire, to empower. And I would proceed with care.

Many years later, to a woman who was still asking, "Well, are you or aren't you?," I tried to explain. "Maybe I relate to my sexuality differently than you do. Maybe lesbianism isn't my home the way it is for you. But that must not undo all we have done. If we are brave enough to be out, are we not brave enough to be different? Yes, I used to be very angry at men. I wanted them out of my life. I wanted so to get it right and I didn't think men could get it right. There is some truth to that, I fear, and it is why I continue to believe it is essential to the survival of the planet that men not be allowed to rule. However, I do not live well apart from society. It is more my nature to be inclusive even at great risk and women know all too well how risky it can be to relate to men."

Proceed with Care

Maybe I am trying to tell you about spiritual wandering, a kind of homelessness (different from that horrific condition brought on by Reaganomics). If one is a visionary, enchanted by the possibilities and repelled by the offenses, then is there a perfect home? I am always looking to discover how it might be if we knew today what we will know tomorrow. And so the song only pauses at the end of a refrain; it is never completed.

Am I a lesbian? If you like. Lesbianism seems so natural to me. But in the traditional sense? No, no, perhaps not. Mostly I feel the magnitude of being alive on this planet, the only one we know of that has our kind of folks on it. It is from this state of being constantly amazed that I come to my sexuality, my politics, my spirituality, my sense of humor, and my music.

"Doors" (May 1984)

I do not live alone.
I live in a house of many doors
Doors that slam shut in the howling wind
and blow open in a buttercup spring
Open doors, swinging doors
Doors made of glass, so easy to see through
So easy to break.
Hidden doors that I fall through accidentally
Trapdoors, secret doors that only I know
And I do not tell for surely someone would try to lock them
Closet doors are brazenly open
Murals that only look like doors
Painted on the wall by a woman who later disappeared
Behind prison doors so thick so as to protect us
From her screams—I will open this door
Tiny doors that have tingling musical melodies
When the door is left ajar
Doors left open so a little light
Falls on the sleeping child
Bedroom doors which I prefer to leave open
Yet what we prefer often causes others
To race around slamming doors with such a rage
Doors I have intentionally closed because I am afraid

I do not live alone
I live in a house with many doors
Doors that slam shut in the wind, blow open in spring
I live in the spring when I sing
Yet if the wind howls, I let the snow,
the floodwaters, the tornadoes
Break out of my soul—expanding my range
I sing notes I never knew were there
And an old friend calls out from the back row
"Honey, you're singing with all the doors open tonight."

13
1984

I WOKE UP AND COULDN'T REMEMBER WHERE I WAS. WHAT COUNTRY. What city. What bed? This year I had done 150 concerts. I looked at the walls, barely lit by a streetlight leaking through a curtain. I'm home. A dream had woken me up. It was a recurring dream. I would be in a wheelchair, recently disabled, sitting quietly on a front porch, reading or talking to children or humming a song my mother used to sing as a lullaby. . . . "I Left My Heart at the Stagedoor Canteen." I would always feel peaceful in this dream, moving a little slower, required to ask for a little help. I knew when I woke that if I were really disabled I would be working just as hard as now, only against greater obstacles, but the dream was symbolic of my longing for permission to sit still.

The doctor left me standing naked and went off to finish with another patient. It was a cold, rainy day in Paris, where we had some time off from my 1984 European tour between Denmark and Portugal. Somehow I'd gotten myself involved with a British rock musician. He wore a red ruby in his ear. We made love, and then shared a restless sleep on a soft, soggy mattress in a small French hotel. In the morning, with his minimal French, he helped me get to a chiropractor. There I was, shivering and so completely bent in all the wrong places that I could not stand up without leaning on a chair or a wall. Sweat beaded on my face. I had never felt such pain in all my life, even back in '73 when I'd had back surgery, or in April '84 in Nova Scotia. I had never gotten that close to wanting to end it all before. Scared me. I'd kept blaming it on 1984 and that vision I'd had that I would die at thirty-five. But the tour with Inti-Illimani in May 1984 had given me

209

hope, had refueled me. I'd adapted to my brace, and had been doing pretty well. Why did it snap again? Maybe it was the late nights jamming at the Toner Folk Festival with the Irish. Or maybe it was making love all night in Aarhus with a Dane. Or maybe it was the rainy ride through Germany to Paris with a Brit. Finally, the doctor came back into the room, and after what seemed like a minimal examination, he said I needed to rest and left.

I struggled to get my clothes on and went to meet up with my touring pals, Jeff Langley and Carrie Barton, for a songwriting session we had scheduled at a small studio. I needed my mother and wrote a song for her with Jeff.

Icicle blue, day sky blue
Blue almost silver blue eyes
Looking at me all my life
Blue skies, blue stones
Songs of blue sung late in the night
To a sleepless child
Mother, hold me, I remember now
It is through your blue eyes that I have learned how
To touch the red earth, to join the black night
To dance in the golden sun
That I see, through these eyes.

Back at the hotel I got progressively worse, not even able to get up to go out for dinner. I canceled the job in Portugal, stunned by my own decision. In the twenty-eight years I had been performing, I had only canceled two or three concerts. Carrie gave me some codeine and I dragged myself to the airport and onto a plane home. I found four empty seats, lay down, strapped myself in, and didn't move. When they served dinner, I pathetically reached up to the tray to try to feed myself, but the tray slipped and food spilled everywhere. I lay back and let the last nine months race before my eyes, and then tried to focus on the next four months to come. My life was a fire spreading out of control, a fire in the rain.

Lying in bed in Nova Scotia, in April with the cold March winds blowing outside the old wooden house, I had written a letter to my partners and friends, Joanie and Jo-Lynne: "I'm coming to the end of my rope. I'm giving up. I'm dying."

210

1984

I struggled off the plane into the warm September New York City night. 1984, indeed . . .

Live! In Concert. Holly Near, Arlo Guthrie, Ronnie Gilbert, Pete Seeger. We called it HARP, after our initials. Even as bad as I felt, I grinned at my good fortune. I loved singing with this group. I propped myself up on the couch with pillows so I could sing, and I must say, I felt quite the fool to be in such a weakened state next to Pete and Ronnie, who seemed so indestructible and full of energy. We had three days of rehearsal and then four concerts—in Minneapolis/St. Paul, Seattle, Berkeley, and L.A.—the last of which Redwood Records would record for posterity at the Universal Amphitheater. Ronnie and I have a musical-theater style and Pete and Arlo have a sort of anti-style, which is a style all its own. It was fun to watch us each move over a little to make room for the whole. I had been warned that Arlo and I might not get along. I think they thought his dry humor wouldn't mix well with my sincerity. On the contrary, we got along fine. He made me laugh. He also has a deep spiritual side that he offered me to help ease my pain. And dear Pete, the man with a million songs and stories and a banjo that have brought the world to its feet, millions of voices, singing out at the top of our lungs.

I had to squeeze in some visits to the doctor to see what was wrong with my back. The pain was shooting down my right leg. Walking down the street from the X-ray lab to the cane shop, I realized I didn't know if I could make it across the street. There was an old woman about to cross, and before realizing the irony of it, I said, "Could you help me across the street?" Without skipping a beat, the old woman put out her arm and guided me skillfully through the New York City chaos.

The cane shop was filled with an array of walking sticks, shiny black ones with gold tops just begging to be danced with, gray ones that were waiting for a matching ascot, gaudy gold ones that needed someone with a lot of pizzazz to pull off. I explained my need to the shopkeeper. She expressed her concern for my health and then asked what I would be wearing onstage. Perhaps she could help me find something that would match my gown. Funny, that had never occurred to me to buy something to match my clothes . . . or to wear a gown! I picked out a dark wooden cane that had a bit of natural gold streak—"to match my hair," I said to the shopkeeper, who seemed distressed with my masculine choice. I walked out of the shop with my new prop and there, facing me, was Carnegie Hall. I began to cry. What had happened to little Holly's dream of being a Broadway star?

I hailed a cab and went back to our friend Helen's house, where HARP was rehearsing. During a break Joanie and Jo-Lynne asked me what I wanted to do about the rest of the year. I had the upcoming voter-registration tour with Ronnie in October and the England tour planned for November. The doctor had told me to go immediately into hospital traction and get the pressure off the nerve, but I had no intention of missing this work with HARP. Nor did I want to cancel the work with Ronnie; I loved working with her, and I thought it would be very destructive if Reagan was reelected. Our tour would mean a lot. The producers in England begged me not to cancel. They were offering to drive me around in a van that had a bed in the back, provide beds backstage, carry me wherever and whenever, "but please don't cancel!" I agreed to go on with it all. I didn't want to let everyone down, and besides, we needed the money.

And what about me? I had not learned to ask that question yet.

The HARP concerts were great. I will never forget the nearly nine thousand faces gathered in the sun at the Greek Theatre in Berkeley. They radiated such bliss as different parts of their lives moved together onstage in familiar harmony. At the end of the concert, when we had done our encores and our time was up, the crowd wanted more. But the clock had just ticked into overtime. We didn't want to stick the co-producers, Redwood, and our friend Jeanne Bradshaw of the Great American Music Hall with that bill. We wrapped it up. Still, the audience cheered for us to return. When they saw we were not going to do more, they carried on in appropriate folk tradition. They started to sing themselves. We stood in the wings and enjoyed the best number of the afternoon, a perfect ending to a perfect day—nine thousand people singing "Goodnight Irene" as the sun went down. I knew then why I could never have canceled out of this tour.

As Ronnie and I began to prepare for our fall tour, we got word that our pianist had dropped out. We called Jeff. He couldn't do the tour because he was a professor at Juilliard School of Music and was writing an opera. We called Adrienne Torf. She couldn't do it because she was working on a musical-theater piece with June Jordan about the Klan. Ronnie remembered a tape Redwood had given her from a man named John Bucchino. We listened. We asked him to make a tape of a few of our songs, accompaniments taken off the live albums. We needed him to be able to play the songs the way we were accustomed to hearing them, for there would be little time for rehearsals. A tape arrived with note-for-note duplications. We asked him to fly up from Los Angeles and meet us at the San Francisco airport for breakfast just to see if we thought we could all get along. He seemed friendly enough although a little peculiar about food—he was on a strict macrobiotic diet. John was working as a waiter at a fancy restaurant in L.A. but said he could give notice. We made an agreement, then Ronnie and I flew off to Bryn Mawr College to be part of the documentary *Women of Summer,* about the working-class women who fifty years ago had turned Bryn Mawr on its ear each summer and changed their own lives. Ronnie and I sang for them at their reunion.

I didn't have much time to work with John. I arranged a four-hour rehearsal with him and hoped he was prepared. I do not like to rehearse, as my accompanists over the years will testify. We used only about two of the four hours set aside for my material. I had never seen anything like it. I found out later that John can barely read music, but he has such a highly trained ear that he retains anything he hears after one or two listenings.

We laughed a lot on this tour. The audiences were delightful and in the face of Reaganomics, needed a boost from the kinds of songs we sang—everything from Charlie King's great tribute to Sacco and Vanzetti to rowdy lesbian love songs like "Perfect Night" to Broadway hits like "Lucky to Be Me" by Comden, Green, and Bernstein. The concerts provided an environment for people to feel connected to morality, common sense, and love. In the long haul they set the agenda to which the right wing must endlessly react. I've always imagined that was why they were called reactionary—always put on the spot and having to react to people like us. I liked standing up there onstage with Ronnie and John. We were a bold bunch.

I filled out my absentee ballot and headed for England with John and bassist Carrie Barton. Frankie Armstrong, a powerful voice of social change in England, joined us for part of the tour. I tried to rest but England was cold and damp, which made my back feel worse. Determined not to be grumpy, I curled up with one of the road crew, who helped warm up the winter nights. Although I prided myself on discretion, I was tired and for the first time began not to care what people saw or thought. I'd tried so hard all my life to be "good." Well, enough of that!

In Leeds, we stayed with a woman who showed me a quilt of tenderly made patches sent to her from women in the United States who wanted to be part of the ongoing peace work in England, especially at Greenham Common, where the U.S. and British governments were deploying missiles. I sat quietly with her looking at the stitches that told a story of feminist sensibility and global sisterhood. I wrapped a piece of the quilt around me. There are many ways to be held.

In Scotland, we were sitting in a restaurant before the show having dinner. Some women came in, spotted me, and came over to say hello. They had recently been at Greenham Common. I asked them what songs they had been singing to keep the spirits up and the missiles down. They mentioned a few, then one woman said, "There is this one song we sing a lot . . . goes like this . . . 'We are a gentle angry people' . . . do you know that one?" I grinned. Yep, I know that one. I had written that song years ago. I loved that it had gone off around the world on its own.

On our day off, the tour group went out with our Scottish hosts. Edinburgh is one of my favorite cities, but I was not moving well, so I stayed in and made a huge tub of fish soup for when they returned . . . and thought about going home.

The final task of the year was mixing the HARP album. It was fourteen degrees below zero outside in St. Paul, Minnesota, but we were warm and happy inside—Joanie, Jo-Lynne, Leslie Ann Jones, and me. Christmas bells somehow seem appropriate only when it is cold. Each day we listened to the tape of Pete, Arlo, Ronnie, and me sing, tell stories, and joke around. As we put together the parts and the songs, we brought forth the past, the present, and the future. By night, J2 and I just hung out together. I loved this unique partnership. We were about to face some serious changes. My friends were worried about me. I was worried about us. I was worried about me. I could barely walk, on the verge of a nervous breakdown, but in the company of Cyndi Lauper, Geraldine Ferraro, and others, I had just been named "Woman of the Year" by *Ms.* magazine. I had made three albums, been in eleven countries, and had suffered a broken heart—all in one year. 1984 was finally over.

14
SIT WITH ME

Sit with me through the night
Tell me it's all right to fall apart with you
I'm so tired, I'm so scared,
I'm so sad about the world tonight
And sometimes, sometimes I feel
I can't defend myself, my love or my light
The thought of surviving, just makes me want to die
Come lay beside me, hold me while I cry

The first obstacle to my recovery I could not overcome alone. I turned to my partners, Joanie and Jo-Lynne. We had shared responsibility for Redwood, but we had built the company on my shoulders. J2 ran the company, booked and managed me. I continued to be the main artist on the label, the major source of economic income (80 percent), the most visible spokesperson, the A & R department, and the "director of vision." Now I was tired. My body was unwilling to carry on at this pace. I hated that I had burned out. It was a common error and I felt humiliated that I had done exactly what I had warned so many not to do. I needed to stop working. But who would take my place? Redwood might not survive if I stopped, and I might not survive if I kept going. We agonized among ourselves and consulted accountants, political advisers, therapists, and psychics. Yet, as has been true from the start with this unique partnership, we not only pulled through, we became closer and stronger as a result. But it would require huge personal and economic risks. We were going to expand the company while the main source of income retired. This would mean borrowing large sums of money, but we felt Redwood Records was an important cultural institution and it was our task to give it a chance. I'm glad I didn't know how hard it was going to be. I would have voted to fold!

I went kicking and screaming, but eventually I agreed to become a silent partner (we often laugh at this uncharacteristic title!), meaning I would not participate in the daily operations of Redwood. We would no longer make decisions by consensus. Joanie and Jo-Lynne would be responsible for directing the business. After twelve years, I had to let go. Joanie and Jo-Lynne had to figure out how to make the company stand on its own two feet. Could this company be economically feasible? No one in the business world thought so or they would be doing it. (Do you know any commercially successful record company that records lesbian singers and Nicaraguan dance bands?)

As "homework," which involved the delightful and terrifying new experience of actually being home, I wrote a list of everything I did in a day, in a year. Even I was shocked. It was the work of several people all jammed into twenty-seven-hour days and forty-two-day months. What did I want to do the most? Being an active record company executive was one of the first things I crossed off my list.

Joanie and Jo-Lynne found new artists to record or distribute. The music was good, but Redwood did not have the quarter of a million dollars to invest in promotion that the major record companies were putting behind such artists as Suzanne Vega. We had to remind ourselves that we could not make stars out of such deserving artists as Ferron and Inti-Illimani. We could not usually get mainstream airplay. We did not have the machine to ensure massive distribution. We would get calls from fans who said, "I have been in every record store in the city and I cannot find Holly's records." This news was distressing. We knew there were people out there who would buy our records if they could find them. But no matter how hard our network might work, often the major chains would not order from small independent distributors. On the other hand, we had encouraging success in major cities all over the United States, including New York, where our distributor and concert promoter, Virginia Giordano, not only got records into major stores but also eye-catching displays in the windows of Tower Records, and presented major concerts at Town Hall, Avery Fisher, and Carnegie Hall. Although television and magazines ignored us for the most part, newspaper critics were consistently present and usually complimentary. Media people commented on the high quality of our promotional materials. Bonnie Raitt and I became friends through our peace work and often appeared in benefit concerts to-

216

gether. She was always a strong supporter of women getting on with it. Redwood worked closely with Jackson Browne, who took strong positions on disarmament and Central America, often at the expense of his own career. He produced two albums by Nicaraguan artists, Guarda-barranco and Salvador Bustos, which Redwood distributed. Mainstream record executives began to notice that we could do with ten people and ten thousand dollars what took them one hundred people and one hundred thousand dollars.

But costs kept rising. Many of the artists we worked with could not tour as extensively as is necessary to sell an album or build a career. We could not afford to give them money for tour support. Often, the artists didn't even have management. Several lived in other countries and, in addition to political and economic problems at home, they had trouble getting visas and work permits for the United States for political reasons. Jo-Lynne and the Redwood staff took on the INS, organizing major campaigns, mobilizing support from progressive congresspeople. Sometimes this required as many as one hundred phone calls on behalf of a single artist. This was not income-producing work, but it is how the hours had to be spent. I imagine the INS knew this. They no doubt enjoyed wasting our time.

Concert attendance was down. This was true for the mainstream, too. Concert production costs and ticket prices were soaring, and the potential audience had less money to spend. The artists we had been working with were getting older, having to support parents or children or simply needing more income just to get by. Feminist concert promoters began to trim some of the things that we, as feminists, had worked so hard to achieve—such as child care at the concerts or sign-language interpretation for the hearing-impaired. We understood these cuts, for they were the same cuts we were making. We didn't like them and neither did some of our fans, but the economic realities of the Reagan era were hitting us hard. Some purists in the audience started to cry "Betrayal" or "Sell out" when feminist artists began to work in nightclubs or take jobs with commercial promoters. The performers were striving both for creative growth and for accessibility to the mainstream audience that might be able to support them. But political artists are thought of less as workers than as guardians of moral and cultural integrity. Usually it is hard to wear that honor or bear that responsibility and still pay the rent.

The Reagan administration had ceased funding of the arts as well as social services. We could not evaluate our situation apart from the context of hunger, disease, homelessness, drug problems, a deteriorating educational system, government scandals, low-income-housing shortages, and rising military budgets.

Redwood had to become more efficient and competitive in order to pay salaries and provide ever-more-costly health insurance coverage for its employees. The office had to be computerized. And we needed to move. We had been working on top of each other in a small Oakland office for too long. The landlord was not responsive to our needs. Drug wars were waged on our doorstep. We hadn't minded when it had just been the prostitutes. We had been a women's community there on MacArthur Boulevard, with Family Planning on one side of us, a women's accounting business and a women's herbal and acupuncture center behind us, and the women making a living on the street out in front. But when the guys showed up with drugs and guns, we started looking for a new home. And Jo-Lynne bought a fax machine.

Jo-Lynne and Joanie had their work cut out for them. Now I had to do mine. I worked with a kinesiologist-chiropractor and with healers. I tried acupuncture and massage and Alexander technique and yoga. I consulted a surgeon, a neurologist, and worked with a physical therapist. I let a lover into my life. I went on a stimulant-free diet, no sugar, alcohol, or caffeine. I spent a lot of time alone trying to get to know myself apart from my work. Through all this, I concluded that the problems in my lower back had done some permanent damage, and although I could improve my strength, develop a good preventative program, and retrieve some feeling, part of my right leg and foot would be numb for the rest of my life. I tried to see it as a reminder to take care every time I put my best foot forward.

The hardest task was learning to rest. I decided to rent a weekend of movies to help keep me home and still. I dived deep into each story without the distractions of a theater audience, without the interruption of having to leave the theater when each story was over. Without any inhibitions or restraints, I could laugh at parts that someone else might think somber, or sob openly when deeply moved, or rage out loud when insulted.

The room got smaller and smaller, darker and darker, as I climbed into the lives and minds of the characters, the actors, the writers, the directors, the camera artists. At first it was a glorious purge, an emotional indulgence, a total submersion. Then, as I stood outside myself for a moment, I saw that I was clinging to a cliff. Watching "her" from a distance, I could not seem to reach forward to help. I could not hold her and say, "Oh, darlin', what is happening here?"

Three days passed and "she" had not eaten, showered, changed clothes, or gone outside, but I could not bring her soup, or put a cool cloth to her face. I felt as if there were a gash tearing open her middle, getting wider and wider. This was pain that had been there so long it was hard to know if it was pain or some other sensation.

I looked at the videos she had been watching to find out what had slashed her open so viciously: *Frances, State of Siege, Le Bal, Yentl, Birdy, The French Lieutenant's Woman.*

I went to the curtains but I could not raise them. I went to the kitchen, but at the door I turned and went back to my room. I tried to sit in a chair and literally "pull" myself together, but my body was shrinking. A mantra repeated in my brain: "I want out, I want out, I want out, I want out."

Maybe the films had taken me to this place, but this was not their place, this was my place. This was a deep, lonely, frightening hole and I knew I would not get well until I could bring my own light to it, build my own staircase out of it. This was huge. This was unknown. This was mine.

I finally was able to call my therapist (a woman Joanie had helped me find to work with in January 1985. I had tested her to make sure she was up for the job. I watched her carefully to see what she knew about war, lesbianism, money, and music. I did not want to have to help her help me. I discovered she could not be trampled by my boldest self nor disappointed by my weakest one).

The rest of the year was spent working in and out of "the pit." All the creative energy that usually went into music, peace work, organizing, and love affairs I put directly into healing myself. I couldn't function well in social situations. I didn't know who I was anymore. Everything I did and said felt made-up. My defenses were down. My voice was in a state of suspension. It was no longer the old, familiar voice, and yet a new voice had not yet emerged. I was searching for the light I had so often offered my audience and neglected to offer myself. How frightening it was to leave space open without rushing to fill up every nook and cranny with familiar distractions. I learned to sit for hours without any plan and without being sure . . . of anything. There was no walking on water. I rowed every inch to get across the river.

The following are entries from my journal in the spring of 1985:

Learning to care for this body will raise my consciousness and give me wisdom, helping me to understand how to be a good teacher, leader, and artist. Each time I love myself I will gain humility. I have had to go very far away in order to come back. I think I remember Ho Chi Minh did that, too.

I, who have never prayed, must now pray. I do not need to pray to a Christian God. I can pray with the universe, for I have a great love for this planet and for this work. Making health a priority is not withdrawing, it is a recommitting. A little self-love can go a long way.

I feel like I am living with someone in an intimate relationship for the first time—me. I am even falling in love a bit and it brings me great pleasure. Now that I love her so, I will be more careful whom I let touch her, so that she does not have unwanted guests living in her peaceful gardens. When I need love, she will open her arms and create safe harbors. When I desire sex, she will open her thighs to loving tongues that do not bargain, negotiate, and lie for love. I will give her journeys to the sea, and nights under the stars, and time alone, time with trees, and together we will breathe.

There are times when children bring me sorrow, activists scare me, musicians annoy me, daily life discourages me. And I look in the mirror and say, "You may be talented but you don't think you are any good. You may be bright but you punish yourself for being imperfect. You may think you have too much but you think you don't deserve anything. You may think you are able-bodied but you can hardly walk. Dear sweet woman, sit down." I take off my coat and shoes that I had put on thinking I was going somewhere and return to the chair by the window.

Often thoughts are given to me with the sole purpose of giving them away.

I have been working with my voice teacher, Faith Winthrop, to find my voice. She has helped me to rediscover that if I were to point at my voice, I would not be pointing at my throat but rather at my eyes and cheeks and lips and jaw and shoulders and chest and arms and trunk and thighs and feet. This morning I sang a note. I could hear my heartbeat in the note.

I sit among old and new trees, morning sunlight sparkling on the page, squirrels catching my attention as they grab limbs with their little feet, church bells clanging out old hymns in the distance, spring birds in a mad chase for procreation, the Mexican neighbors making music up the street, a bee and I coexisting. I am learning to be complete unto myself and appreciate that which surrounds me without needing to be it. Like any art, the creation of self is both natural and seemingly impossible. It requires training as well as magic.

The mind is a magnificent thing. And yet only in recent years have I learned that I must have control of the windows and doors so that not all things are allowed to enter and not all things may be allowed to escape or be shared. As an artist, this has presented some problems for me since I always felt that relentlessly collecting ideas and sensations was necessary if I was to be prepared when it was time for a song.

But I needed to receive it and impart it with greater care and discretion. There were still mindless jabs from shameless critics, but I did not question my very existence. I still became breathless at the thought that the Guatemalan Indians may become extinct along with the condor if capitalist expansion continues to kill anything that is in its way, but I paused to catch my breath rather than leave myself gasping in despair—for I can better help when I am breathing calmly and thinking clearly.

In dressing rooms backstage—which are sometimes adorned with pictures of Leontyne Price on the wall and other times simply with a broom and a glass of flowers to help brighten up rather dreary surroundings—I sit for a moment in the chair, my feet resting flat on the floor, my eyes closed, imagining the hundreds of tiny golden braids not only rising from my open mind but reaching out from all over my body, antennae that have been alive and alert for thousands of years and serving me well. Then I begin to reel them in slowly, wrapping them lovingly around each other until a glorious rope has been wound.

One end of the rope becomes a belt surrounding my middle. Sometimes I even loop it up and around one shoulder and then back down across my heart like a serape. I send the other end of the rope down through the base of my spine to the center of the earth. The farther down it goes, the hotter it becomes, until it unites with the red, hot, molten sun that burns inside this whirling planet. I throw a splash of cold water and, with an eruption of steam, the unification is given the strength of permanence. Then I move back up my body, clearing a passageway through the bottom of my feet, up my legs and thighs and sex, opening up the channels from my belly to the tip of my head so that all that I am about to learn can sail forth free of doubt. And finally, I release three delicate gold braids from the rope so that they might reach out the top of my head into the heavens, eager to receive.

Then I am ready to sing. Sometimes I do only a small part of the meditation, maybe only for ten seconds while standing in the wings with John. But my body remembers the whole meditation and is filled with grace.

My voice is my instrument. I cannot put it away in a case. It is not in the throat, from where it appears to come. It is in my feet and how they touch the floor, in my legs and how they lift and sink with the rhythm of the song. It is in my hips and belly and lower back, where the air drops deep inside me, often creating the sensation of sex, where personal power hides or exalts. It is in my upper back, locked in if I am tense, released when I am not afraid. It is in my lungs, so strong and willing, and in my heart. It is in my arms unencumbered by a guitar or a horn. My mouth and tongue and cheekbones are the sound box, the amplifier, the resonator, but they must resist the temptation to interfere. And when I am willing, all sound is available to me . . . and I find my voice.

What does one want to say with one's voice, not so much in words as intention? What will be the spirit of the sound? And then consider the words. What do I mean by words? Is it the same thing that people hear? There is no way to protect the listener from misunderstanding any more than I can protect myself from believing one thing today and modifying that belief a moment later. I do not want to be protected from evolution. I hunger for it.

I sat down at the piano and began to write. Although I had gone kicking and screaming, I was getting well. I went back out to the world to work.

*　　*　　*

Sit with Me

In 1986, Timothy and I went on a vacation in Mexico. Our first stop was Oaxaca. We stayed at the same little hotel I had stayed in before. It felt wonderful to be with Timothy. I enjoyed being tour guide, and watching the stress and strain of work wash away from my sister's face. I called the lawyer I had met on my previous trip to see if he and his family would like to join us for dinner. We agreed to meet in the square.

Timothy and I got there early and waited in a sidewalk café. Two young men asked if they could join us. We said for a moment, yes, but told them we were waiting for friends. They said they were students and asked a lot of questions about the United States and, interestingly, about the women's-liberation movement. At first I was surprised, then I felt that something funny was going on. Soon we realized that they were hustlers and had discovered that the "women's lib" question helped them to find out if their prey was sexually liberated, i.e., might want to have an affair, might be willing to pay for it.

When my friends arrived, they recognized the boys and wanted nothing to do with them. One of them took off. The other counted heads and realized we were two men and three women. The hustler decided Timothy was the "available" woman. Curious to see how these guys actually got to the point of negotiating, Timothy let him tag along for a while. But he didn't last long in our company and eventually went off to find a more profitable way to spend the night.

Tim and I went on to a southwestern town called Puerto Escondido, in a plane that ran only by the grace of God as far as Tim was concerned. She hates flying. We contemplated driving but were warned that there were bandits in the mountains along that particular highway to the coast. I think they are not bandits but left-wing guerrillas. So Timothy boarded this plane and we flew so low that the mountains were on either side of the plane.

Puerto Escondido was wonderful. We wandered along the beaches and up into the town, where we chatted with women hanging out the day's laundry. We found a fisherman who would take us out in his boat. He caught a fish and handed me the line to reel it in. I didn't really want to yank a fish out of these peaceful waters. Nor did I want to insult him. But we delivered the fish to the cook at our hotel and she, slightly annoyed by the whole thing, fried it up with garlic. We watched the sun set from the dining table and ate our fish.

Timothy, brave soul, got back on that airplane so we could catch a flight out of Oaxaca. When we boarded the flight to Mexico City, we found seats next to a young man who was holding the tiniest baby. I quickly realized the baby was very sick and was having trouble breathing. I asked the man if I could help. He explained that he didn't know what was wrong. The baby wouldn't take food and would only cry and cry. He had left his wife and family early that morning and had walked for several hours to the bus, carrying the child in his arms. Then there was the long bus ride to Oaxaca, and now this flight to Mexico City, where his sister was waiting to take the baby to a special children's hospital. I took the baby and tried to quiet her little cries. I rocked her and Tim sang soothing lullaby sounds. We both sent our strongest uninterrupted energy to this baby. Soon the baby stopped crying. Holding her close, I tried to put the bottle where a breast would be. She began to take some milk. The father watched and wept. The poor man was so exhausted and worried.

When the baby finally slept, I turned my attention to him. He apologized for his tears. I encouraged him to cry. "It will be good for the baby. You will be able to better care for your daughter after you cry." He put his head in his hands and sobbed. At the airport, we saw that his sister was there and hugged him and the baby good-bye. After they left, Tim and I stood silently for a while, feeling a little lost. We would never know if this little girl survived. We decided she would always be alive for us.

15
IN THE FACE OF LOVE

I STOOD IN THE WINGS OF THE GREEK THEATRE IN BERKELEY, CAL-
ifornia, and watched with pride the Third Annual Redwood Records
Music Festival. Redwood, in co-production with the Great American
Music Hall, had started by presenting Ronnie Gilbert and me in the
Greek Theatre, followed by HARP with Pete, Ronnie, Arlo, and me
the next year, and now, in 1986, a full-day fest with seven hours of
magnificent music from artists whom Redwood distributed: Sweet
Honey in the Rock, Ferron, Inti-Illimani, Ronnie Gilbert, Arlo Guthrie, Linda Tillery, Judy Small, and myself with John Bucchino; special
guest appearances by Krissy Keefer and Rhiannon; sign language interpreters Susan Freundlich, Lynnette Taylor, and Shirley Childress
Johnson; and a special welcome by Mayor Gus Newport.

Redwood was in good shape. I was in good shape. Strong political music was in good shape. I looked over at my partners, so grateful
they were in my life. I wouldn't see them for a while. I was about
ready to go out on the road again.

I fell into the cold, tightly stretched sheets of a hotel bed, my skin
still tingling with the music. John and I had done a good first show, but
I needed to develop "the touring muscle" again. To think I used to do
this all year long. Unlike many artists who take hours to unwind after
a show, I am blessed with the ability to fall asleep immediately.

The alarm went off at 5:30 A.M. The morning paper found outside
my hotel room was not reassuring. The world has always been rife with
violence and atrocities. Some might say nothing has ever changed
substantially. From that premise they conclude, "Why bother?" For
me, the answer is that "bothering" is as much a part of the human

225

experience as violence. There have always been people who cared about the quality of life, whether it is Jesus, whose life and work have been exploited to abuse the very people he cared for, or whether it is the bag lady down the street who always remembers to feed the birds with a part of what little food she has found for herself. And even if nirvana were put forth on a silver platter, this would be the first day of struggle to keep it. I "bother" now, not out of guilt but rather because "bothering" improves the quality of my life, challenges my mind, pushes my creativity, and provides me with dignity. And now when I hear people say, "You are such a bother," it brings new meaning to what used to be an insult.

I was sitting in the dressing room, preparing for my concert. The Texas audience was hungry. An Amnesty International representative came backstage and asked me if I'd make an announcement regarding an execution taking place that night: "The state of Texas will kill Thomas 'Andy' Barefoot by lethal injection in Huntsville, seventy miles north of Houston. A car pool is being formed to go to the place of the execution right after the end of this concert. If you would like to join the nonviolent candlelight vigil . . ."

I ached inside as I read her carefully written note. The words of my song Ping-Ponged in my brain.

"Foolish Notion"
Why do we kill people who are killing people
To show that killing people is wrong
What a foolish notion
That war is called devotion
When the greatest warriors are the ones who stand for peace

Death row is growing longer
The problems stay the same
The poor ones get thrown in prison
While warden what's-his-name
Is feeling justified
But when will he be tried
For never asking

Songs are too real sometimes. The woman who handed me the note apologized that she couldn't stay for the concert. She was going out to spend the night with his family. How does she do this work?

The mirrors in the dressing room form an infinity picture. One teapot inside another teapot inside another teapot. When does the steam explode? When does the water run out? When does the pot turn a fiery red?

"Now, may we have a moment of silence for officer Carl Levin, the murder victim, and for Thomas 'Andy' Barefoot."

After the show I did an interview with a man visiting from India who was doing a book on progressive Americans.

Subject: Texas woman
Focus: abolishing the death penalty and working with
   prisoners
Heart: full
Courage: strong
Title: *Progressive American*

In 1983, I was invited to Belgium by the Women's International League for Peace and Freedom to protest NATO's seemingly endless obsession with nuclear weapons. I like this organization of "gray hairs." They are tough, energetic, and tired of messing around with arrogance and destruction. They like having young whippersnappers like me around. We are physical assurance that their work will not end when they are gone. I marched down the streets of Brussels arm in arm with a lovely actress/peace-friend, Julie Christie. Thousands of women and men from dozens of countries had gathered, singing and calling out in all our languages.

The day before the march, I sang at the women's peace conference. Right before I was to go on, some women from the Greenham Common Peace Encampment proposed to the conference that a delegation of women lead off the march since it was a women's march for peace. It sounded reasonable to me, but an instant after it was said, tension shot through the hall like the bullet we had come to protest. Someone stood up in a fury and said she would not participate in a march that was separatist, that she had traveled a long way to this march with her husband and found the proposal horrendous. Another woman tried to calm her and said that no one had said she had to march without her husband. Only that the first delegation be women. Well, then everyone wanted to talk and did, all at the same time.

A woman from Greenham Common came to where I was standing

and said they had not meant to trigger such a conflict. They were so used to the idea of women doing things together that it had not occurred to them the proposal would delineate such a war zone. She asked if there was anything I could do to calm people down.

Sometimes I think people shouldn't be calmed down, that it's good for everything to fall apart because when once put back together, the new union is wiser. But I agreed to say something after my first song.

"How can groups of people who feel differently work together? Coalition work may be the hardest thing any of us will ever do. What about the issue of women leading the march? Let's not try for agreement. Let's try for understanding.

"First I want to talk about the perspective of those women who would like to walk hand in hand with the men in their lives. We are not taking sides, remember? We are practicing coalition. We are trying to appreciate each other. If we can't do that, we can't successfully work together.

"There are women who, throughout their lives, have fought fascism with their comrades in Europe and in the U.S.A., and we are proud and honored by how many older women there are in this organization. They have survived sectarianism and red-baiting and grand juries. They have worked with their husbands in the labor movement, in the civil rights movement, in the peace movement, and now invite their husbands to work with them in the women's movement. And at a march as important as the one tomorrow, who of us would not want our loved one standing next to us?

"Now I want to talk about those who want to have women lead the march tomorrow. It is hard to have one's woman-ness constantly put on the back burner as being less important than our other identities.

"Salvadorans often lead demonstrations to protest U.S. intervention. It would be appropriate for black civil rights leaders to lead a civil rights march. In another situation, perhaps the children should lead, or Native Americans. So why not women? The women who made the announcement only wanted to say this is how we feel about women who work for peace and is this not a good time to honor and celebrate.

"I value both of these perspectives. However, this is a coalition gathered to protest military madness. So I think we must not argue at this moment. Tomorrow, you will each decide where you stand and there will be no one policing your conclusion."

Then I sang "Unity."

228

In the Face of Love

Doesn't always mean agreement
Doesn't ever mean the same . . .
You don't have to rob me
Of the pride that I've just found
There's enough love and dignity
To go all the way around

Later that day, some of the women who had wanted to lead the march thanked me for trying to cool things out, but there was a look of sadness in their eyes. I recognized the matriarchy of long ago looking at me through these windstung faces. Other women, who had opposed the idea, came up to me and thanked me, saying, "I can't believe those separatists wanted to take over the march. But you handled it beautifully. The perfect diplomat." Oh dear, they had missed the point. And the sad look I had seen in the feminists' eyes came into my own.

I enjoyed being the mayor's wife for a few days, probably as much as he enjoyed being the singer's discreet lover from time to time in whatever city our paths crossed. Neither of us would tolerate these roles long term, but no one was asking.

Gus was in Italy working with city administrators . . . mayor talk. I had flown in to meet him. We never explained our relationship to our hosts and no one was rude enough to ask. Some called me Mrs. Newport and referred to "my husband" with great admiration and respect. I was amused to see how a politician's wife is treated. When introduced as a singer, I was welcomed with curiosity. But when perceived as the mayor's wife, I was immediately attributed power. And if they wanted something from the mayor, they decided that I could best facilitate their request. "Would the mayor be willing to . . . ?" "What time will the mayor be rising?" They never consulted me about foreign policy but I regularly offered my opinion, to Gus's great delight. The mayor would lean back in the overstuffed chair, put his feet up and enjoy "his wife." He was tired of deciding what "the mayor was willing to do."

The Italians, from the middle of the road to the left, wined and dined us, to perfection. It was fun to be hosted by the Communist party without McCarthy's children jumping out from dark and dusty corners, screaming irrationally. I swam in the Mediterranean at sunset, and we walked through the streets of Perugia, a partial moon lighting our way. It was just as I had imagined Italy to be.

229

Our last night ended too soon as a car arrived for me at dawn and took me away to the airport in Rome. I had a music festival to catch in Portugal. Gus stood in front of the hotel and watched me go, the sensation of his warm body on mine. Leaving. I am always leaving.

Lisbon is a great city. My back troubles in Paris had forced me to cancel my participation in the festival in 1984. But they had asked me again.

This festival was the largest cultural gathering of the year. Millions of people passed through the gates to eat and to party, to hear international and contemporary music as well as enjoy traditional Portuguese artists. There were sporting events, fine arts exhibits, and an international village filled with display booths of political organizations and solidarity groups from all over the world.

I was not performing the first night, so I wandered into the crowd and observed the stage from different areas to get a sense of how I would be perceived when I was performing. The space was so big it made me lonely. I went to one of the smaller stages and listened to old Portuguese love songs over a warm beer.

The next day, the vice-president of the Communist party came to meet me. He apologized for my difficult slot in the program. I was scheduled between Dimensión Costeña, a Nicaraguan dance band from the Atlantic coast and a U.S. group, The Band. "We know it is hard for a solo artist to follow a band but we wanted your world-view politics and we understand you are capable of miracles."

A bit overwhelmed by the assignment, I looked around for someone to fall in love with instantly so I could be temporarily distracted. But I wasn't in the mood. I went off alone to the international village to see if I could learn something about someone who was from somewhere.

Then night came. The Nicaraguan band was great, bringing the music of Bluefields, Nicaragua, to Lisbon. The crowd was dancing. I stood in the wings and tried to find air. When I heard my name I walked onstage. I was prepared for cries of "Rock 'n' roll!" I had not been prepared for whistles. Challenged rather than insulted, I decided that before my set was over, these whistlers would become singers, identifying rather than objectifying. I did what I often do when the crowd is too high to take them any higher, I sang a root, "Mountain Song," slow and extended, and then began the journey of rising together. It took three songs to get the audience to stop fighting me with rowdy energy. But when they finally gave themselves over, they were great. One hundred thousand people out in the moonlight. Unable to communicate in Portuguese, I spoke and sang back and forth from English to Spanish, hoping that somewhere in there, my new friends would grasp the essence of my work. By the last song, they were all standing with their lighters aglow in the dark, singing with me. "We are a gentle angry people, and we are singing, singing for our lives."

Joanie, Jo-Lynne, Susan Freundlich, and I decided it was time to evaluate our work of signing concerts. Hundreds of deaf people had experienced a progressive-feminist concert and world-view information was conveyed. Simultaneously, hearing people had been profoundly affected, discovering a language they had never known, meeting a culture they had never considered—one result being that literally hundreds joined sign-language classes, leading many into the field of deaf services.

Church people, political organizers, and artists started using interpreters more regularly. Timothy had worked with dance companies, teaching them to integrate sign into their work. She had directed several plays using deaf actors in traditionally hearing roles, pushing through all the inconveniences to make it work. We also felt a rush of pride when *Children of a Lesser God* was such a big hit and when Broadway shows in general started offering special ASL-interpreted performances for the deaf community. Inspired by the deaf activists who had been our teachers, we witnessed the effect of our accumulative work. Deaf pride was changing the nation's attitudes and we had been serious allies. The day the students went on strike at Gallaudet, demanding a deaf president, I felt full of pride. "Yes," I said out loud. "Yes!"

But what should we do now? For eight or nine years, my concerts had been predominantly signed concerts. We had organized them on a nationwide level with Susan traveling with me for major tours. But with the research, front work, outreach, resource materials, phone bills, and paying the interpreters' travel expenses and a minimal per-concert fee, I couldn't keep it going at the cost of $100,000 a year. And besides, there needed to be more local participation in order for the work to be effective. It was not good long-term strategy for this work to rest on a few shoulders.

My hope is that networks can be created between local concert promoters and the deaf community so that artists who are particularly popular with the deaf can be interpreted. I continue to include information in my contracts about accessibility and ASL, suggesting that promoters work with local groups. I do not travel with an interpreter, nor is one mandatory. However, initiated locally, many of my concerts are signed.

Susan and I still work together. Only now, with five years of fund-raising experience under her belt, she is the development director of Redwood Cultural Work. Occasionally she returns to the stage to sign a performance and it all comes back to me. Susan is definitely part of the band.

I am in Nicaragua for a second time, not as an invading soldier but as a friend, a singer, a peacemaker. There is a war going on in this summer of 1986, but life doesn't stop. So what should I sing at the party tonight? What song is appropriate in the wake of death in Beirut, Capetown, Esteli, Seoul, Belfast? I will follow the Nicaraguan tradition. First, we mourn the loss, then we celebrate the living. I found my pen and began to write in the margin of the newspaper. The headlines announced another contra attack against a civilian bus.

At sound check, I sang my new song off the newspaper margin. Grupo Mancotal joined me. The percussionist found the dirge rhythm and created the space in which all the other players could fill out the song. I watched these young men. It is hard enough to keep it together as a touring musician, what with leaving lovers and family, living in hotels, working under difficult conditions for low pay, eating in truck stops, sleeping alone or with strangers, trying to stay clear of alcohol and drugs, or not staying clear. But these guys have to add war to that list, war and the cruel economic sanctions that the United States has placed on their struggling country, making it hard to get cooking oil and penicillin, much less highly prized designer jeans, Michael Jackson albums, or guitar strings. They rehearsed in a tiny room filled to the ceiling with equipment. I cringed when I first saw it. This was not a work space, this was a match box. The mike stands were held together by tape, the horns were hardly playable. When I heard Harold blow sound out of a sax that should have been put to rest long ago, I vowed to find him a horn when I got back to the States.

The guests arrived. Before starting the dance music, we paused to acknowledge those who had been killed and wounded in the contra attack. My friend Amy Bank, who had fallen in love with Nicaragua on our first trip, had returned to work in a Spanish school for North

In the Face of Love

Americans. She translated the words to my new song and we offered it as a prayer.

"Nicaragua Night"
We are dancing in the moonlight, in a Nicaragua night
For the mothers of the soldiers, we bring our spirits here
We call on midnight's mentor to mourn the murder done
For the mothers of the soldiers, spirits now be here

In the heat we learn your language
In the night we learn your songs
Voices call across the canyon in search of echoes
Bloody pictures point the finger
     at the devil's brand of terror
And the wailing will begin soft and low

There is passion in remembering
There is fire in the heart
On the mountain grows a tree that roots the fury
The river moves the story, it's a troubadour's revenge
As the tortoise slips beneath the sea
     the hare begins to worry

In Detroit a child is crying
On Big Mountain a people die
But in Washington the palace lamps are burning
The hand that bought the ambush has tried to buy my soul
But like you I won't sell out and I will never surrender

And we'll keep dancing
In the moonlight
Hold our children through the night
For the mothers of the soldiers, we bring our spirits here
We call on midnight's mentor to mourn the murder done
     (all over the world)
For the mothers of the soldiers, spirits now be here

Then we danced all night under a full moon. Amy and I pulled out all the steps we had learned together in the States. We were hot! Legs and arms flying. Then I danced with the band's percussionist, Chico,

233

with whom it was all in the hips, pelvis, feet, and eyes. Then I danced with the children, and here with them, it was all in the heart.

Then I talked into the night with a group of young people who were dealing with the issues of coming out in Nicaragua. They were privately working on creating a model for sex education, AIDS awareness, and antihomophobia work.

The next morning, Amy and I flew to Bluefields in a two-engine plane. We couldn't talk over the noise, so we gazed out the window at the fields below and imagined what was going on down there. The Atlantic coast has a different history than central and western Nicaragua. There were no major roads between the two parts of the country. The trip can only be made by boat or plane. Somoza had little interest in the eastern region, so the coastal people didn't feel the grip of his regime. U.S. missionaries brought schools, roads, and hospitals to the area, but they did not create an economic infrastructure. When they left, they left very little.

Nicaragua's Atlantic coast is a different world—the sea, the trees, the air, the foliage. We feel a Caribbean country. We hitched a ride into town in a military Jeep. We were greeted at the Hotel Bluefields by the manager, a young Creole woman named Nydia and by representatives from the radio station. I was eager to meet with them. They had the complex task of fairly serving the diversity of the Atlantic coast area, where there are at least six different languages, four indigenous, plus Creole and Spanish.

Amy and I unpacked just enough to find clean, cooler shirts and then went out for a walk. The houses here were mostly made of wood, unlike Managua, where houses are made of stone and concrete.

Amy paused and smiled at me. "What?" "Hear that?" It was my voice on the radio, in one of the houses we were passing by, singing "Once or Twice." I had heard that they liked country music here. I felt pleased to be so welcomed.

Our schedule allowed us to stay only two days in Bluefields, not nearly enough time to see anything except the town. We met with officials, mostly protocol, then went to find the Zinica rehearsal. This is a group of older black men who before the revolution had been the town drunks and keepers of the old shanty songs. Now, they are officially recognized cultural workers and paid to preserve their traditions. That night we had a lobster dinner in a restaurant filled with baseball players in town for a game and with Bulgarian construction workers who were building a port, their services donated to Nicaragua by the Bulgarian government.

Our second night, we met Nydia and her boyfriend for a drink. They brought along the former mayor of Bluefields, who was in his late twenties, and a man who worked for the Ministry of Culture. As we sat in the moonlight at a café by the water, someone said, "I got a tone out of it." I liked that. In the song of life, a special moment is a tone.

On our way home, our host suddenly pulled the car over and said, "It's a party! Let's go!" Amy and I grew shy about going into the party uninvited. He assured us there wouldn't be any problem, so we followed him in. The house was absolutely dark. The only light came from the kitchen in the back. But the room was full of music and people dancing—black people in the black night. The ex-mayor disappeared into the dance. Our other host tried to entertain us, but he was in his tour-guide mode and kept rattling off statistics about the cultural movement. We didn't really need to *talk* about the cultural movement at the moment. We were *in* it!

The party was for the hometown baseball team. Nicaraguans love baseball and have a national league. A man came over to get a drink at the table and started up a conversation with me. He spoke English, but I got lost in his rich Creole accent. When I asked him to repeat what he had said, he laughed and, taking my hand, led me onto the dance floor.

The fact that I was in a party of Creoles in Bluefields was no more or less remarkable than that I was at a party of baseball stars. The only baseball star I know is Johnny Bench. (Not so bad if you're only going to know one!)

Amy and the ex-mayor stopped by to see if I wanted a ride home. I decided to stay and dance. The right fielder assured them he would see me home. After a while, the room was so crowded that there was not much dancing going on, just steamy bodies rubbing in time with each other. We went outside to the porch, where the moon offered light and the sea, a breeze. We walked down the dirt street toward my hotel. He stopped and touched the bark of a tree with his fingers, quietly, contemplatively. "Stay with me," he said. "What?" This time I was not asking him to repeat because of his accent. I was creating time to think. "Spend the night with me." I explained to him that it had been a long time since I had gone to bed with a stranger. "I used to," I said, "but it leaves me feeling empty and sorry in the morning." But even as I spoke, I didn't feel as if I needed anything from him, so there was no reason to feel empty or sorry if I got nothing more in bed than I was getting from watching him touch the tree bark.

We walked on until we came to the street that turned to the hotel. I was a guest in this country; I had no idea what was culturally acceptable behavior here, and I didn't know why none of that mattered to me at the moment. I stopped and said, "I don't want to be empty and sorry in the morning." "No," he said, and we walked on, along an alley and up some winding steps, where two old women sat in a doorway. I panicked. It never occurred to me that I would have to meet his family. He did not introduce me, but instead handed the old women some money. Neither of them looked at me. One rose slowly and walked down the hallway. She paused in front of a door, then turned and disappeared.

Inside the room was a double bed with a clean white sheet, no blankets, a single light bulb glaring overhead. Of course. There are housing shortages in Nicaragua. No one lives alone. How could I possibly have thought we were going to his house? I had been to one of these rent-by-the-hour places in Cuba. It is a reasonable solution to the housing shortage, a place where parents can get away from kids and grandparents, where lovers can go if they aren't married. I am constantly amazed. Well, good. That's the way it should be. We had a lovely time except for one moment when he showed his male heritage of misinformation and arrogance by responding to my inquiry about birth control, saying, "Women don't get pregnant unless they want to." In my earlier days, I would have gotten angry. Tonight I laughed, and a greeting card by Nicole Hollander came to mind: "Can I be a feminist and still like men?" "Sure, just like you can be a vegetarian and still like fried chicken."

I like wet heat. It makes my body glisten and my hair curl. I like lying in bed with a lover, neither of us wanting to touch the other for a moment. I like the feeling of slowing down because there is no possible way to go fast. The dawn came before sleep. I had to go back to the hotel. It felt awful to put on clothes. A swim in the sea would have been better.

I watched him primp in the slice of mirror hanging on the wall. Recalling the Chinese soccer team I'd seen in the hotel when I was in Hanoi, I laughed to see my suspicions reconfirmed. Yes, a jock's a jock no matter where he's from. As I grew impatient, he moved even more slowly, so I went out the door, past the old women who were asleep on the porch, and into the new day. He caught up to me, unaccustomed to a woman who won't wait, and saw me to my hotel, as he had promised the ex-mayor the night before. I slipped quietly inside and slept. I felt empty but not sorry.

Mary Ellsberg walked into the hotel. I was so surprised to see her. She was a grown woman, no more the fifteen-year-old girl I had known in L.A. who had almost been kicked out of school for inviting me to an assembly to sing and speak about feminism and the Vietnam War in the early seventies. Mary was a mother now, married to a Nicaraguan, and in charge of a major health care project throughout the Atlantic-coast region. Mary told us disturbing stories about her work. When a boat goes up the river, the contras often stop it, hold up the men, and rape the women and young girls. The men try to offer money to get the women back. The contras say, "We don't want money, we get that from the U.S. We want women." Eventually the women are freed. The contras are targeting health care workers. One woman, a midwife and a leader in health care, was killed when the contras fired round after round of ammunition into her house. She was with her children, some of whom were also killed. The ones who survived lay still all night in the blood of their family, afraid to move. They were found later. One of the children was no longer able to talk.

When we said good-bye to Mary, I didn't know that I would see her soon. On her U.S. speaking tour, Mary was joined at one event by her father, Dan Ellsberg, and some old friends—Dr. Benjamin Spock, Mary Morgan, Patricia Ellsberg, and me.

The mayor of Bluefields, a Black preacher, offered to drive us to the airstrip. He left us there to wait for our departure, which in Blue-fields can mean hours or days. If the plane breaks down or needs a tire, the only spare parts are in another city. Our wait turned out to be about seven hours. As we flew back to Managua, I found myself looking at Amy, resting her head against the vibrating window. I had first met her when she was in high school. She and a few friends faithfully came to concerts at the Ash Grove in L.A. and the Icehouse in Pasadena. They even grew bold enough to start offering criticism when they felt I wasn't singing enough political songs! I liked these young, bright, radical Jewish women. Many years later, Amy applied for the first full-time position offered at Redwood Records after we moved to Oakland. She got the job and became a lifelong friend.

I had come to Nicaragua specifically to see Amy and to do some work with Nicaragua's finest singer, Luis Enrique Godoy and his band, Grupo Mancotal. We wanted to work out a set of music so we could perform together at international music/peace festivals as a statement of friendship between our people in a time of war.

I almost didn't get into the country at all, but that wasn't the war's fault. I hadn't realized that my passport was too close to its expiration date. Airport security stopped my entrance. I couldn't believe that I was going to have to get back on the airplane and return to Mexico to apply for a passport extension at the U.S. embassy. I knew President Ortega and his wife, Rosario Murillo, but I didn't have their home phone and it was Sunday. Luis and his band were in the mountains performing for the coffee workers. Amy didn't have a phone. Damn! Someone in the lobby heard of my predicament. Her sister was a friend of Commandant Borge, the minister of the interior. She agreed to make a call on my behalf. The phone rang next to the guard station where I was standing. The guard picked the phone up and then handed it to me. The voice at the other end said, *"Compañera* Holly?" *"Sí,"* I responded. "Commandante Borge would like to speak to you." I was too relieved at the moment to grasp completely the magnitude of my good fortune. Borge gave me clearance to enter the country. But would I please come directly from the airport to see him? Of course I would.

Amy and Greg (the guitarist in Grupo Mancotal) had just arrived to greet me at the airport. We headed for Borge's house. Seeing him, it suddenly hit me more completely that I was in the presence of the only living founder of the FMLN. This was one of the great minds and unconquerable spirits that had led this country to revolution. He had been imprisoned and tortured. When Borge toured the prisons after the revolution, he found his torturer in jail, the roles reversed. But instead of torturing him, Borge said, "My personal revenge will be that from your prison cell, you will watch children learn to read, you will see flowers grow." Borge smiled at me. "I hear you are a great singer." I smiled back. He said, "You and your friends come to the ministry's house by the lake tomorrow. You can come swimming with me. You like to swim?" I lied and nodded. "Good, then perhaps you will sing us a song." I accepted on behalf of us all and said, "It would be a great honor to sing a song for you."

Once in the car, we all sighed with relief. From the brink of disaster had come a grand opportunity. The next day we found a party going on at the lake house. Poets and writers gathered who were visiting from around Latin America for a literature conference. Borge again invited me to join him for a swim. Out of protocol, I did so, but only for the first few strokes. He wore fins and soon was halfway across the lake. Earlier, I had wondered at the lack of security around him. But as Borge headed for the water, a young swimmer appeared to my right. A man with a walkie-talkie cradled in his arm strolled down the beach to my left. Out in the lake, as if from nowhere, a rowboat with three young men in swimsuits, looking as if they were just out for a good time, rowed across the lake about twenty feet from Borge. It was an amazing sight compared with the blatant twelve-men-in-black-suits security that surrounds the high leaders of the United States. It was evident that the subtle web of security was not protecting him from the people, but rather from the ever-present possibility of an assassination attack.

After the swim, we lunched in an open-air restaurant and danced to a live band. Then the poets and writers and musicians sat together with Borge and talked about art. To our surprise, the discussion turned to the topic of homosexuality. I stayed quiet, curious to see what would be said. The Nicaraguans (all of whom I believe were heterosexual) were shining. Borge watched, listened, and nodded in agreement with the more humanitarian point of view. Someone would say, "I think it is okay if people are gay but they shouldn't be allowed to be teachers, they might make their students gay." A young Nicaraguan replied, "If a heterosexual man comes on to a girl in school, it doesn't make her into a prostitute. It is simply inappropriate behavior on the part of the teacher. It is the same with gay teachers. Any sexual advance to a student is inappropriate." Another said, "It isn't natural." Again, the Nicaraguans spoke up. "Love is very natural." Yes.

The plane landed in Managua and brought me back to real time. Amy went back to work at the school. I went to spend some time with Luis. We sat in an outdoor bar as the day began to cool, talking about the hardships of cultural work when artists are not only forging a path, but laying down each brick before taking the next step forward. Our careers shared some of the same responsibilities. He was the head of Enigrac, the only record company in Nicaragua. He seemed eager to hear how I was trying to separate myself from the work of Redwood Records so as not to lose myself as an artist to the daily demanding pragmatic work of running a company. We talked about songwriting, about trying to stay healthy on the road, about the joys and horrors of being a role model and a revolutionary artist, about the economic conditions. On tour in the United States, a group of organizers wanted to take the band on a field trip to an organic farm. One of the players politely declined, "We live on an organic farm. Could you please take us to a mall?"

Ten days later, I left Luis and Grupo Mancotal. I left Amy and Greg. I left the brave gay men and lesbians who were breaking new ground. I left the health care workers who were such a threat to Reagan's policy of destabilization that he was having them murdered. I returned home to write, borrowing the images from all who had opened their lives to the visiting poet.

"In the Face of Love"

Silver hair falling over me
So soft, so fine, I hold my breath
And I feel you moving up like a sunrise
        over my body
Inside we remember birth
Outside we are facing death
In the face, in the face, in the face of love
In the face, in the face, in the face of love

Silver hair falling over me
So brave, so strong, I find your eyes
And I feel you moving down like a sunset
        over my body
Inside we are making love
Outside another dies
At the front, at the front, at the front for love
At the front, at the front, at the front for love

The guns are waiting in the mountains
Kids playing quiet in the dust
It's time
And if I make it back to you
My sunrise, my sunset, my earthquake, my soft
        and fine silver hair

And I feel you moving up like a sunrise
        over my body
Inside we remember birth

240

In the Face of Love

Outside we are facing death
In the face, in the face, in the face of love

I drove past familiar trees and gardens, winding up the hill to
Cedric and Mary Belfrage's house. They had come to Cuernavaca to
settle after being exiled from the United States in part because of
Cedric's outspoken position supporting the Rosenbergs in the New
York paper he co-founded called *The Guardian*. I paid the taxi and
went through the high walls that surround the larger homes in Mexico.
Mary hugged me hard; Cedric more gently. He was recovering from a
stroke and was quite fragile. But he looked wonderful and was back to
translating Galeano's books. I had become one of their wandering
daughters in the world. The gardens were lovely; the library bursting
with books calling me to distant lands and curious minds; the dining
room filled by a big round wooden table that easily sat a dozen guests.
That table always felt like a symbol of the friendship Cedric and Mary
offered to refugees, some like me, some literally having escaped from
their own countries, like Ana Clara. Ana had escaped from Uruguay.
We sat quietly in the living room. I knew she wanted to tell me about
her country. I was ready to listen. Her little daughter played quietly,
never leaving her mother's side. I wondered how often this child had
heard what we were about to hear. What does she think? How old do
you have to be to know that your mother is alive only by chance? Ana
talked about home, work, politics, and music. She did not speak much
about herself. She wanted to talk about Chicha.

"Chicha has been at the women's prison, Penal de Punte de
Rieles, for about eight years. Her crime? It is hard to point to one crime
when a person is part of resisting fascism. One's very life is a crime.
Chicha was editor of a magazine. She was arrested in October 1975.
There were massive arrests of alleged members of the Uruguayan
Communist party.

"Chicha was held in a prison called El Infierno [meaning 'hell'].
El Infierno is a warehouse made over into a torture chamber. The
prisoners are kept on the ground floor. They are forced to wear hoods
so they cannot see. Often they are not allowed clothing. They are nude.
Each person has a number. When your number is called, you must
walk up the stairs to the mezzanine, the torture area, where you are
hung nude by your arms, which are tied behind your back, or you are
hung by your hair. No one below knows who is being tortured. There
are no names. There is no night or day. Loud music is played to drown

out the screams . . . music! . . . twisted into a brutal psychological weapon.

"Sometimes a doctor in a white coat stands by—an accomplice—who notifies the torturer when to stop before the prisoner dies. He is trained to know how far torture can go before it kills. Lighted cigarettes and matches are used to burn people like Chicha . . . applied to sensitive parts of the body. Limbs stretched away from the body. Hands crushed in iron frames. Electrodes attached to fingers, to the head, to the genitals. Then you are sent back downstairs to recover. The next number is called. This goes on and on.

"Chicha was held there for six months before being sent to another prison, the Punta de Rieles prison for women, where she is presently serving her sentence. We are told Chicha sang all the time. Against the orders of the guard, she would sing. She sang to identify herself. She sang to break down the psychological warfare, as well as to sustain her courage during torture. She sang to make contact with other prisoners. She sang to fight alienation and insanity. She began to get the women organized. They did clandestine art, pulling threads out of what little clothing was available. They did an embroidery on a potato sack, which was then smuggled out of prison. The women were forced to wear hoods, so they had to sit very straight and look down in order to see their message: *'Despues de la tormenta siempre sale el sol'* ('After the torture the sun always comes out').

"The women talked together about their guilty feelings for having chosen revolution and struggle, knowing how it affects their children."

Ana Clara cried out, grabbing her own child. "The best of our people!" Ana Clara did not speak much of her own life. I knew from Mary that she had been a teacher at the secondary and university levels. With help from the Belfrages and others, she and her family escaped.

Mary recalled the time she went to pick up Ana's three-year-old at day care in Cuernavaca. The child had a little friend who was crying because her mother had not come yet. Ana's daughter said to her, "Maybe your mother has been arrested." Such is the experience of children who have survived fascism.

It takes a willingness to know more truth than we bargained for . . . the only limitations come from thinking there are some things we cannot bear.

Ana Clara returned to Uruguay when conditions improved, but

economics forced her to return to Mexico. She recently found out she has multiple sclerosis.

The Great Peace Marchers decorated L.A.'s Griffith Park with their beautiful colored tents. I could feel the excitement as twelve hundred brave people said good-bye to friends and family and began to meet those with whom they would walk across this huge country. I would fly across the country many times before the marchers arrived in D.C. and would often look down and think of them in the desert, in the snow, at community meetings talking about peace. But tonight I would teach them the song I wrote especially for them. It was getting dark as we gathered on a hillside together. As I began to conduct the parts, a few campers got out their flashlights to focus light on my hands. And a beautiful choir of voices rose from the black night.

My friends David Mixner and Torie Osborn, who along with hundreds had worked so hard to make this march/dream come true, sat with their families and lovers enjoying the sensation of being amazed. Jill Davey, who had been my road manager, would make the walk. A new friend, Liz Marek, would also make the walk, but her work for peace, feminism, and lesbian/gay rights would be cut short. Liz died on the Pan Am Flight 103 that went down in Scotland in 1988.

But on this night we sang together:

We will have peace . . .
And as daring as it may seem, it is not an empty dream
To walk in a powerful path
Neither the first nor the last great peace march . . .

Reagan ordered the bombing of Libya, killing a single small child. I had planned to go to a Giants game, but I just couldn't face thousands of people standing to sing about bombs bursting in air. I went to a candlelight vigil instead. I felt so sad that night. Then I saw my brother in the crowd. That helped.

. . . Forever, for love and for life on the great peace march

16
WE'RE NOT ALONE

I WANTED TO MAKE A "POP" ALBUM. *FIRE IN THE RAIN* AND *SPEED OF LIGHT* both had a pop feel; four folkish albums had been added to the collection since then, three of them live. I was ready to return to a more-produced studio format, and I wanted to make a fun love-song record that my fans could play while stuck on the freeway; that people who dismiss political music might listen to by way of introduction and then discover some of my other, more outspoken recordings; that radio DJs could fit more easily into their pop format. I entrusted the project to Steve Wood, recommended to me by Kenny Loggins. Steve was Kenny's right-hand music man and keyboard player. I rented a room in Laguna Beach, close to where Steve and his family lived. The fun part was working with some of the best: drummer Tris Imbodine, bassist Bob Glaub, sound engineer Terry Nelson, and singers Linda Tillery, Bonnie Raitt, and Kenny Loggins. The hard part was trying to do a "commercially viable" record on a tiny budget. Redwood spent about $50,000 on *Don't Hold Back* while Elektra spent about $250,000 on Tracy Chapman's record. The record industry also spent huge amounts of money on promotion, often over a quarter of a million dollars, which at the time was one fourth of Redwood's total annual budget!

The record was not supposed to be "political," but, in fact, I think love songs are political. The artist chooses to perpetuate certain myths . . . an evening of twenty-five I-can't-live-without-you-baby heterosexual love songs is political! For the sake of making the record accessible to a broad audience, I decided not to use pronouns. But as I began to write, I rediscovered how complex is the task of expressing love without falling into conventional traps. I wrote songs of friendship, sex, passion, despair, rage, aloneness, independence, obsession . . . a fantasy, a long-term relationship, a one-night stand, a breakup, a new beginning. The album intentionally ends with a moment of clarity in "Plain and Simple Love."

"Plain and Simple Love"
No fancy fantasy, no magic mystery
No wide-eyed wonder, just a plain and simple love
You see me just the way I am, I know you as you are
We're living down on earth, just a plain and simple love . . .
No frantic façade, no lies at the start
No great expectations, just a plain and simple love
Oh the years of pretending to please and impress
Left such a scar of loneliness too mighty to confess . . .

However, the song I like best on the record is the sensual antiwar love song that Steve and I created from the poem I had written after my last trip to Nicaragua, "In the Face of Love."

The letters I received about this album confirmed my goal of reaching new people, and from the conversations I had with DJs, I believed that if Redwood had been part of the music-industry machine, this record might have charted. We didn't have the money to compete, and of course I'm not a new, young rock 'n' roll singer, either! At the same time, *Don't Hold Back* brought on a wave of criticism. Some of the mainstream press that had for so long accused me of being too political now accused me of selling out for a commercial career. My audience bought the headlines. Ticket sales to my concerts dropped and the record was slow to sell. In the first year, we sold only thirty thousand. One woman approached me after a concert. "Why is everyone saying you have sold out? This was one of the most inspirational and politically challenging concerts I have ever heard you offer. Anyone who listens carefully to the words on your new album will *feel* you in them. I hear your politics in your love just as I have always felt your love in your politics." Her words touched me and came at a time when I needed to be reassured. It was scary that even with my track record and my body of work, I could become suspect so quickly.

I had made this journey from airport to festival many times and in many states of mind. The Vancouver, Winnipeg, Edmonton, and Mariposa festivals in Canada; women's music festivals in Copenhagen and

Amsterdam; the Cambridge Folk Festival in England; Tonder and Aarhus folk fests in Denmark; the Communist party music festival in
Portugal; the Nueva Canción peace festivals in El Salvador, Ecuador,
Costa Rica, and Mexico; the anti-nuke festivals in West Germany and
Japan; the women's festivals in Georgia, California, Michigan, Washington, D.C., Indiana, and Illinois; and the folk or jazz fests in Con-
necticut, Maine, Rhode Island, Ohio, Massachusetts, Colorado,
Pennsylvania, and Iowa. I had performed at the Ten-year Anniversary
of the Michigan Women's Music Festival, but I was back again for
year eleven.

The luggage area of the airport was full of musicians and campers, all looking like dykes, if not in fact. A woman carrying an amplifier or a backpack has a charmingly queer look about her, regardless
of whom she sleeps with. Tracy Strann, my road manager, found our
bags and we made our way out to the car that was waiting to take us
to the festival site. I was pleased by the clockwork organization that
had developed after all these years.

My "festival friend" met us on arrival. To my delight, Adrian
Hood had been assigned to help me. She is Alix Dobkin's "little girl,"
and I have known her sweet face for years. Alix is a lesbian music
pioneer, ever loved for her first bold dyke album put forth in 1974,
Lavender Jane Loves Women. Adrian, graceful, articulate, and wise
for her years, has grown up on these festivals and now she is seeing to
it that the tradition of her foremothers continues. I enjoyed putting the
logistics of my life in her hands for the next few days. Immediately,
Adrian and Tracy hit if off, as Jews, as caretakers, as music lovers, and
as two of the very few heterosexual women in attendance. They were
easily enjoying the women-only environment and the lesbian energy,
rather than fearing and resisting it as so many straight people do.

Women had gathered weeks in advance to make ready the campsite, laying carpets through the fields and forests so that women in
wheelchairs could get around the vast spread; pitching tents and building kitchens; bringing in grand pianos, sound, and lights; creating
spaces for child care, AA meetings, workshops, jam sessions, show-
ers, games, massage, and emotional support for those overwhelmed by
the experience of spending the week with thousands of women. This
was space designed to create room for revelation: round bellies, tat-
toos, mastectomies, muscles, artificial limbs, scars, body hair, burns,
voluptuous thighs, and skin of every shade from iridescent white to

pitch black. We also brought our violence, our self-hatred, our mis-information, and our confusion.

The performers gathered in the backstage area. Women from all over the country, and from other countries, hung out together or not-so-together, depending on who was in love with whom, who had a new record, who was broke, who was angry at her manager, who was invited to be in which collaborations. But mostly I hear waves of laughter coming from one table, where Kate Clinton and Ferron are discussing world affairs. Or I see/hear Betsy Rose and Deidre McCalla building bridges with their soothing good sense and gutsy voices. Or there is the circle of drums where Edwina Lee Tyler, Nydia "Liberty" Mata, and Carolyn Brandy are connecting earth and sky. Or the familiar throaty voices of Therese Edell and Maxine Feldman. Or there are the notes zooming like shooting stars from the vocal equivalent of a Stradivarius—Rhiannon. (When she and I sang Cris Williamson's "Waterfall" for the Ten-year Anniversary, I felt part of one of the most sensual lesbian performances in the herstory of women's music. Fortunately, it had been recorded for posterity.)

This year, the crew had built a ramp that went out like a Miss America runway into the audience. At sound check I was challenged by a teasing production crew to make full use of it. In fact, they said they had built it with me in mind. That night, it rained off and on and the ramp was slippery, but I moved toward it throughout my set, my foot touching it slightly in passing as I crossed the stage, like a coy flirtation. I enjoyed hearing the excitement level grow in the first few rows as they thought I was about to walk out into the crowd. As I came to the end of my set, the crew told me later that they began to wonder how I could have passed up the opportunity. But no, I was just holding out for high drama. I invited Toshie Reagon, Alix Dobkin, Betsy Lippitt, and Lorraine Segato onto the stage to sing backup on my last number, and we started to have some kind of fun on my song "Crushed." Just when the singers were really locked in, I hit the ramp and the crowd went wild. I danced and shook my ass like a regular rock 'n' roller. So much so that even Toshie Reagon, twenty years my junior and heavily into rock, told me I had definitely shattered a few stereotypes she had had about me being elder-generation folk. But for my encore I returned, and thousands of women stood to join me in "Singing for Our Lives."

Maybe it was the music or the night or the woman. I hold all three responsible for looking their best as I suggested I spend the night in her tent. Don't think me bold, I wouldn't have asked if I wasn't pretty sure she would say yes. My "festival friend," about to go off with her pals, inquired, "Is there anything else you need before you turn in?" I shook my head and bade her good night. The storm raged outside the tent, but inside we were warm and wet. No, can't think of anything else I need.

The Southern Women's Music and Comedy Festival is important since there are fewer opportunities for women in the South to hear women's music live or to gather in feminist and lesbian environments. Robin Tyler and friends produce it. Robin is a lesbian comedian, out and outspoken for longer than most of us. In 1986, I accepted her invitation to sing. I would do my set a cappella.

I invited Melissa Howden to go with me as friend/road manager. She had been my road manager before, had worked with Redwood, and was an easy traveling companion. Mel and I were met at the airport by a young woman who disclosed that she was very nervous about meeting me, but when she had asked Robin what she should say to me, Robin had said, "Oh, don't worry. Just ask her about Central America and she'll do all the talking!" Melissa and I howled, and for the duration of the trip we assured our driver we would talk only about makeup, underwear, and sex!

The festival site was lovely, with a swimming lake and a covered theater space. It was smaller and environmentally more manageable than Michigan. I arrived just in time to hear the last few songs of the performer before me. I was curious as to what the next generation was producing. At first I thought, *Oh, no, another girl with a guitar.* But she was tearing them up. She ended with a Janis Joplin classic and did it no discredit. Her name was Melissa Etheridge.

When I walked onstage, the women stood and applauded for the longest time. I felt so honored, like an elder. I had been singing to some of these dear hearts for fifteen years; others had been "raised" on my music. Their timing was perfect. They may not have known I had hit bottom and was on the rise again, but I needed to feel honored, so I gratefully received their love and appreciation. Not even forty yet, I felt wonderfully old. The audience quieted, my feet locked into the ground, the top of my head opened, and the music took over. I sang and preached and called on the greatness of each woman whose path had brought her to this moment:

We're Not Alone

"Mountain Song"
I have dreamed on this mountain
Since first I was my mother's daughter
And you can't just take my dreams away
Not with me watching
You may drive a big machine
But I was born a great big woman
And you can't just take my dreams away
This old mountain raised my many daughters
Some died young, some are still living
And if you come here for to take our mountain
Well we ain't come here to give it
I have dreamed on this mountain
Since first I was my mother's daughter
And you can't just take my dreams away

My foot kept slow time on the stage floor and I began to song-talk: ". . . this is a story about an old woman, sixty-eight years old. She had tried every legal way to get the company to stop strip-mining her land. But now they came, the heavy equipment facing her heavy heart. She stood on the mountain and said, 'If you are going to take my mountain, you'll have to take me first.' She sat down in front of the scoops and refused to move. Now, the sad part of this story is that on Thanksgiving Day, 1965, the sheriffs lifted that woman up by her ankles and her wrists and they carried her off the mountain. But the great part of the story, and the part that inspired this young woman to write a song, is that she did not go willingly. The next day, about one hundred of her kin descended upon the jail with their hog rifles and demanded her release.

"I have dreamed on this mountain
Since first I was my mother's daughter
And you can't just take my dreams away"

I can feel the call of the mountain deep in my lungs. ". . . And a young woman heard the 'Mountain Song' and took it in her back pocket to the other side of the world where she stopped at the foot of the Himalayas. There she met the Chipko women, who are struggling to save the trees that surround their old villages. Companies are coming in and cutting down the trees to make tennis rackets, causing the land to slide down on top of the villages, destroying the ancient traditions and an ecology that had been balanced for centuries. The men are mostly gone to the cities now, trying to make money to send home to their families. So the women decided to face the machines that are cutting down their trees.

"They do not have knowledge of the law. They do not have weapons. They only have themselves as they wrap their bodies around the trees to keep the saws from cutting through. By their courage and persistence, they got a stay on the cutting for ten years. Chipko women means hugging women.

"One night, they welcome the stranger who has arrived at the foot of the mountain, for she comes to learn. She comes carrying seeds for planting, much like that which grows on their land, only she says this plant has more nutrition. It is called broccoli. She also brings sewing needles.

"They gather in a circle to sing songs, songs that tell of their ancestors who, in the 1700s, first moved to save the trees. Three hundred women were slaughtered before the king called off his soldiers. They sing songs of today as well, of Chipko courage. Then they ask the young stranger with the white skin to sing a song. She sings,

" *'I have dreamed on this mountain*
And you can't just take my trees *away.'*

"She tells them of the women in the Appalachian mountains so far away who stand strong to save their mother earth. The Chipko women are amazed. They do not know of this place called the United States. They raise their voices and send mighty prayers and love to the women across the seven seas.

"The young woman returned and sought out the songwriter to tell her of the Chipko women. The songwriter was amazed. She had never heard of the women across the seven seas and she raised her voice and sent mighty prayers and love . . . the courage, the struggle, then the song, the back pocket, hearts traveling on the wind, from circle to circle, kitchen to kitchen. Now, when the singer calls out the song, she remembers the Chipko and she has developed a fondness for broccoli.

"You can't just take my dreams away
No, you can't just take my dreams away"

250

When I left the stage, the audience would not allow the moment to end. I returned again and again. Then I walked into the arms of my old friend Mel, standing in the wings.

Melissa once said to me that we needed more words for friends, just as the Eskimos have many words for snow. What is the word for a friend who shares a holistic and revolutionary perspective on the world; who is simultaneously humbled and empowered by music and dance, film, and art; who has seen my weakest moment and my strongest self only to love me more; who has been or is or could be a lover and yet it doesn't define the friendship; who strives for a coming together of all that is woman including the part of us that is man; and who stands in the wings ready to hold her friend, the singer? What is the word for that friendship?

Later that night we danced. We walked in the moonlight to the artist accommodations. A huge salmon mousse was brought to the table. Food. Women. Music. Humor. Healthy political sparring. I put my feet up and savored the women's movement.

Sisterfire was the only urban multicultural women's music festival. It grew under the direction of Amy Horowitz with artists like Sweet Honey in the Rock and myself as its mainstay of support. Appropriately, it took place just outside Washington, D.C., a major black city and the center of national political activity. This was the festival that looked around the corner in the tradition of Bernice Reagon's song "B'lieve I'll Run On . . . See What the End's Gonna Be!" Such artists performed at Sisterfire as Buffy Sainte-Marie, Elizabeth Cotton, Alice Walker, the Moving Star Hall Singers from the Georgia Sea Islands, and musicians from other countries—Nicaragua, the U.S.S.R., Australia, and Canada. Sisterfire moved me like no other festival. Yet I knew it felt the strain of coalition as some black women thought the festival was a white organization and some white women thought the festival concerned itself excessively with multicultural issues. Lack of money always put pressure on the dream. But it was racism and misdirected separatism that was the straw that broke . . . two women refused to let two men into their crafts booth. They then accused them of being violent. When the organizers of the festival did not automatically accept the accusations against the men, the women organized a vicious campaign against Sisterfire at the festival and later in the national women's press, saying Sisterfire allowed violence against women to take place at their festival.

The men accused were black gay men who were longtime supporters of the festival. The festival security coordinator, who had arrived at the crafts booth as the tension was beginning to build, said she saw no violence from the men. She did say that she saw one of the women, in her rage and frustration, raise her hand, and then one of the men lifted his arm to defend himself from a potential blow from the woman. From that moment sprang forth a reaction that quickly spread through the whole marketplace, and soon the two women had organized a gathering that reeked of a white Southern lynch mob out to get a black man for having disturbed a white woman. Obviously, I don't support violence against women, but I wanted nothing to do with women who perpetuated racism while in search of self-defense.

Ysaye Barnwell of Sweet Honey and I went onstage to restate the purpose of Sisterfire, to remind people that this was multicultural, open to the public, and welcomed men and women of all cultural backgrounds and ideologies, just as we would have defended women-only space at Michigan had it been threatened. But this was not one such space. Coalition work is fragile work and required our most developed and creative selves.

The damage had been done, however, and the angry minority mounted a successful boycott of the next year's festival. This put even more of a strain on the economics and the organizers. Sisterfire tried one more year to put on a small concert as a fund-raiser for the festival. It was poorly attended and they lost money. Later on we found out that these two women had come knowing the nature of the festival, but insisted on intentionally violating the spirit of the festival in order to promote their own brand of separatism.

Let us be warned that racism and sexism have obstructed the forward motion of humanity again and again . . . weakening the abolition and suffrage movements, undermining the civil rights and peace movements, and devastating the women's movement. Beware of those who invite you to be less than you are. Stay close to those who dare to be more than we ever imagined.

Sisterfire!

Playing the Royal Albert Hall gave me a chuckle. Having been raised in the country, I was impressed more by the wind that could lift tin roofing off the barn and send it flying, a true example of danger in the air, than to be overwhelmed by a concert hall. However, once there, I became sufficiently moved when I realized that the Beatles,

252

Princess Di, and the world's finest show horses had all appeared in this hall. I wondered what category I fell into.

Then Mercedes Sosa began to sing. This was a woman of earth and sky. All history seemed to pass through her from the indigenous healer to the urban goddess, her voice expressing every conceivable emotion. This was the first time I had shared a concert with her, and although I had admired her recordings, her presence onstage was beyond documentation.

Mercedes is a *grande dame* from Argentina. And after that night, she would always greet me, her arms stretched out as if I were a long-lost daughter come back from the mountains. Several years later, we sang together again in Oakland, California, shortly after the earthquake. I had at first put Mercedes on a pedestal, feeling small and drab next to her plumage. But soon, as happened with Ronnie Gilbert, Alice Walker, Odetta, Charlotte Bunch, Angela Davis, Buffy Sainte-Marie, Pat Ellsberg, Joan Jara, Pat Parker, and Margaret Papandreou, I was able to relax and enjoy the woman behind the brilliance.

I have "grown up" on these women. And now, when young women come up to me, their newborn babies in their arms, and say, "I grew up on your music and now I'm raising my child on it," I am pleased and surprised. Pleased, because I know what "growing up on" means. Surprised, because I forget that I am that wonderfully old.

Lillian Allen, a Jamaican-eastern Canadian, opens a songswap stating that women want to take over the world. Then she introduces Frankie Armstrong. Frankie tries to soften the statement a bit. "I don't know if we need to take over, but we do want to try and . . ." She pauses. "No, I guess you're right, Lillian . . . take over is exactly what we need to do. No sense beating around the bush. The blokes have botched it up good." There is laughter from women and men in the audience that becomes a cheer. This is a sophisticated crowd. They have "come to their senses" and are not defensive. I can remember the first year that the Vancouver Folk Festival began to invite feminists and lesbians to participate. There was tension, some outright battles. Women in the audience shouted down a man who sang a sexist song. Racism was powerfully confronted by Sweet Honey in the Rock. Now the feminist songswaps were among the most popular. A multicultural array of women graced the stage, and what used to frighten now reassures as the crowd gathers to hear these strong women preach/sing. I'm next in the songswap. It is my turn to sing.

"We're Not Alone"

Earth, like a friend who's wounded
Child, you're a fragile promise of tomorrow
You who become a condor in a moment
Will you spread your wings of courage and fly on?

Trees are a story telling
Stars like the burning sun that warms the waters
Wind is a force that cleans our sails of sorrow
Women guide the ship of freedom and sail on

I shall not tire of the road we're walking
Your smile a candle, I shall not tire
I shall not weaken in the face of danger
But draw you close to me, we're not alone

Creatures of courage make a chain that can't be broken
Like my heart can be broken
Links must withstand the strain and pull
That tries to tear our souls apart

Hands like a map I'll follow
Songs are the haunting call that draws me forward
Heart, be the drum that keeps my feet from slowing
Like a cadence that is crying, march on

Force that has turned the flower of the people
Into steel that strikes a fire
Can we use the heat to solder such a chain
And fight on, fight on

I shall not tire of the road we're walking
Your smile a candle, I shall not tire
I shall not weaken in the face of danger
But draw you close to me, we're not alone

Women's music. Thank you, Bobbie Berleffi, for introducing me
to Cris Williamson. Thanks to Maxine Feldman, for recording *Angry
Atthis Bar One* in 1973, produced by Harrison and Tyler, and to all the

women who worked to create, promote, defend, present, distribute, and expand this music of our time. What is *women's music?* It is a song, rising from the footsteps of seven million women who were burned at the stake in the Middle Ages. Or songs that make love; oh, please do listen to the songs that make love. Maybe it is music for those who love or want to learn to love women amid misogyny. It represents our brazenness as well as our tenderness; our brilliance as well as our moments of weakness; our passion as well as our despair; our bravery as well as our fear; our desire to be mothers as well as our choice not to have children; our lesbianism as well as our heterosexuality, bisexuality, or celibacy; but especially our lesbianism, for even if we don't actively live lesbian lives, understanding the desire to make love with a woman is divine approval of making love to ourselves.

What distinguishes women's music from other music? It is the same as that which distinguishes women from men and from each other. Women's music affirms the uniqueness of what women have to say and how we want to say it. *Women's music* was a term that alienated some and healed others. It was bound to happen that way, for that is the nature of feminism. Feminism so completely challenges all that we know, it is not surprising that we cling to the security of the familiar. Whenever new ideas emerge, songs soon follow, and before long the songs are leading.

Society at large may never know much about this creative explosion of feminist music. Major magazines, even *Ms.* for the most part, ignored it. Mainstream newspapers wrote *about* it, but rarely did they herald its historical importance. Nighttime talk shows wouldn't touch it. It was dismissed or "overlooked" by those who were threatened by outspoken and independent women. But women's music liberated thousands of women, as well as men and families, from traditional roles and ideas. This was a movement and a music that, although made fun of and often diminished to a single burning bra, would influence the mainstream's image of women as seen in the issues presented in *Cagney and Lacey, Murphy Brown, Roseanne, The Women of Brewster Place, The Color Purple,* and *Shirley Valentine,* and open the doors for k. d. lang, Tracy Chapman, Phranc, K. T. Oslin, the Indigo Girls, and Melissa Etheridge. This was a music that would be the soundtrack to women falling in love, breaking up, and coping with or enjoying their aloneness. This was music that, because it was dominated by white middle-class women with good intentions and very little experience, would have to face the challenges of racism and class

255

discrimination. Not every woman who sings from a strong, insightful perspective on Top 40 radio today knows that some record executive once told me twenty years ago that I couldn't make it as a pop star because I had "no element of submission" in my voice. And although I believe the young must not always be in a state of gratitude, I find it exciting to know that this is a music that walks in big footsteps: Marian Anderson, who sang on the steps of the Lincoln Memorial when she was refused a concert hall by the Daughters of the American Revolution; Bonnie Raitt, who did not put down her guitar; the unknown trombone player I met in rural Washington State who had been in an all-women's big band during WWII but could not get a job playing her horn after the men came home; "anonymous," the classical composer who would not get her music played or heard if she revealed her gender; Violeta Parra, who walked through the mountains of Chile with instruments once outlawed by the government. No one should have to lay all the bricks.

So we took it a step further, and now we are so pushed out there into the world, we can't even be neatly called "women's music" anymore. We need the radical forum, the cutting edge. There must be artists who are visionaries, adventurers, who look around the corner and see what is next. Instead of being aggravated that we haven't become mainstream enough or thinking we're not needed once the mainstream has what we looked at fifteen years ago, it is simply time for the cutting edge to move on. And we are. We did what we set out to do . . . we moved the world forward . . . and that being a task never completed, we are not finished.

17
SINGING FOR OUR LIVES

BY 1987 I WAS BACK TO HEAVY TOURING—EIGHTY-EIGHT CONCERTS (31 percent of which I did for free); and in 1988, ninety-eight concerts (48 percent of which were for free), but by the end of 1988, J2 and I had paid off all but $80,000 of the debt we had incurred in the expansion. Cynthia Frenz offered us calm, focused skill as our senior staff person at Redwood and unconditional support as our friend. I felt proud of us, the queens of cutting corners, hoping the clutch on the car would last one more year. I doubt anyone but a handful of friends knew what we had just come through. One day when I was feeling blue, J2 brought me a present—a financial breakdown of the money I had contributed or raised for Redwood and for political groups around the world. It came to nearly $10 million! Well, that's why some people thought I was rich. They thought I kept the money! I remembered a woman who wouldn't buy one of my T-shirts, saying she didn't want to support my life-style. She had heard I had a private jet! Right. A one-room apartment, a 1982 Mazda, and a private jet! I threw my head back and laughed.

Many folks commented on how wonderful I looked. People who used to annoy me by telling me my aura had a gray cloud around it were now saying I was surrounded by rainbows full of blue and silver. I felt calm, no longer traveled with my cane, and only rarely used my back brace. I had been fascinated by complexity. Now I felt drawn to simplicity. I had been ignited by trauma. Now I was refueled by peace.

"How did you do it?" they asked again. I made light of it. "Oh, getting older is a wonderful thing." But in truth, getting well was the hardest work I had ever done. As I stood at the 1987 Lesbian and Gay

257

Pride March in Washington, I knew that getting well had also been my best work.

Jesse Jackson, the only presidential candidate invited to speak, was on his way to his next event. I went to say good-bye to him. He asked if I would join the campaign and go on the road with/for him. I didn't know how or when I could fit that in, but I said one of those big yeses. We would worry about the details later. He kissed me and I was amused by the audible sound of ''swoon'' coming from supporters who stood nearby. Jesse Jackson was shaking things up and it felt great to work for a candidate without feeling he was the lesser of two evils.

On this day, October 11, 1987, 600,000 people gathered for the National March on Washington in support of gay and lesbian rights to celebrate, lobby, protest, educate, meet each other, fall in love, refuel, come out, and be counted. The anti-nuke march of 1982 had drawn a million people to New York City, and some of the demonstrations against U.S. involvement in Indochina were huge—700,000 people marching for peace. This was the largest civil rights demonstration in the history of the United States, which by percentages is quite phenomenal given the homophobia in this country. Now, in what some called an apathetic time: 600,000. Arise, you sleeping cynics of the sixties, from your fear that it will never be as good as the good old days. How sad if you value only a four-to-ten-year period of your life! No major magazine would feature this march. And for years to come, it would be conspicuously overlooked when the mainstream referred to the well-attended and historic marches in Washington, D.C. . . . as if it had never happened. Freedom of the press.

The NAMES Project unfolded the quilt; spread out it was the size of two football fields, 2,800 panels lovingly stitched for friends and lovers of people who had died of AIDS. People walked quietly through the garden of remembrances, weeping, recalling, recognizing, and feeling the weight of the catastrophe brought down on our country, on Haiti, on Africa, on the world because of racism, because of the fear of our natural homosexuality, because of research systems that cause scientists to compete rather than work together, because of insurance companies that are in the health-care business for profit, because of drug companies that want to get rich off those who desperately need medicine in order to survive, because of right-wing phony moralists who dare suggest that God has brought this wrath down on gay people but do not suggest chicken pox hits kids because they have sinned, because of frightened and thoughtless parents who would disown their own children before reaching out to them, because the Catholic Church, from the pope in Rome to Cardinal O'Connor in New York City, prefers senseless murder over the discussion of condoms in the classroom. But, most of all, because the president of the most powerful nation of the world, Ronald Reagan, refused to take leadership through one of the most devastating crises ever faced in world health. The crisis of AIDS is about the United States' nonfunctional health-care systems: an absolutely unacceptable condition in the most highly developed technological nation in the world. The largest killer of women in New York City is AIDS. Hundreds of babies are born each month in the United States with AIDS. And as drugs sweep through poor neighborhoods, so does AIDS, passed on through needles and sex without education. Non-Western nations, such as Zaire, are even less equipped to face the crisis of what, in their country, is a heterosexual disease, where 30 percent of the population is HIV positive! The weight of this tragic disease is felt strongly in the arts. Twenty-five percent of the men who have died of AIDS in the United States were in the entertainment industry. Because of the historic and creative impact homosexuality has had on the arts and fashion, AIDS is wiping out a generation of artists. The $400 million spent on AIDS is 1/1000th of the annual defense budget.

The march on Washington was led by people with AIDS, wheeled in by lovers, friends, and caretakers, wrapped in blankets to keep the chill off their fragile bodies. Taped music greeted the first to arrive, Cris Williamson's healing voice singing "Sometimes it takes a rainy day just to let you know . . ." Performers and stage crew stopped their work of preparation for a moment to feel the power of these people before us. My insides screamed, "Reagan, why aren't you here to confess and apologize? You have committed the equivalent of genocide. Weep for your sins, be here with these children of God if they'll have you, hold them without the farcical insult of rubber gloves."

The rally stage was graced with longtime activists and cultural workers who had raised consciousness and money for most of their lives—Romanofsky and Philips, the Washington Sisters, Casselberry and Dupree, Toshie Reagon, Cris Williamson, Tret Fure, Carrie Barton, Robin Tyler, the Gay Men's Chorus, John Bucchino, Sista Boom, Kate Clinton, and many more. There were also straight supporters there, such as Jesse Jackson, Robert Blake, Cesar Chavez, Eleanor Smeal, and Whoopi Goldberg.

Cris and I stood with our arms around each other, silently remembering. She said, "I find if I cry a little bit every day, I can make it." The movement had taught us to wear armor. At first it was armor of steel, but lately it had become softer, even more powerful. I felt with relief our years, our wrinkles, our calluses, our gray hair.

Being "super women of the seventies" had been hard—young warriors doing battle, bleeding, getting up again with spear in hand and little wisdom for backup. Determined to stop the brutal attack of sexism, we took our tender bodies out into the field with a curdling scream. "CHARGE!" Women all over the world felt blood surge through their bodies, and it made us instantly brave. We were not only brave, we tried to be principled. And look at how much we achieved: not simply the flowering of romantic and philosophical debate, but daily pragmatic, useful change instilled in the face of Reaganomics.

And the men who were strong of heart and wide of mind were willing to change but they got confused and then also hurt. They knew they were no longer supposed to defend "their women" and yet where should they stand? Since they had put down their own swords, they felt helpless. We asked them to be soft and allow their weaknesses to show. We found their softness unattractive next to our raging strength. We asked them to be strong so they could withstand our fury. We asked them to go away and then accused them of not being present. And some of them are here still, beautiful in their own internal unraveling.

One cultural warrior after another stopped fighting, with cries of "Sellout" being hurled at them as they walked quietly off the field rather than allow the crowds to see them carried off on stretchers. But some of us were back and all the new, young women on the rise. A new decade before us. "I find if I cry a little bit every day . . ." she said.

I chose a rune out of the velvet bag that held the stones. The runes, from part of my ancestry's ancient Viking tradition, had been a present from my pianist John Bucchino. It was the first day of the new year and I drew the final rune in the cycle of transformation. It said, "180-degree breakthrough." However, if followed by a blank, it could mean death. I decided not to choose a second stone but rather closed my eyes and visualized white light to come and surround the airplane. I called on what I think of as my spirit guides and they arrived so strongly, as if the full council had come to visit, including Jason. Jason I had discovered during a healing meditation back in 1985 when I was trying so hard to get well. He is a long-lost twin who isn't on earth this time around. When I forget how it feels to be unconditionally loved, I call on him. I heard myself pray, "Protect this plane, I am not ready to die." I could feel them smile at me. *Did you hear what you just said, Miss Holly? You who were ready to end it all only a few years ago? Still have things to learn, do you? Breakthrough, 180 degrees.* I looked out the window of the plane and saw the full circle of a rainbow. I had heard that rainbows were circles, not arches, but I had never seen one. There she was, smiling at me in all her glorious splendor. 1988, Happy New Year!

I was told that the organizers couldn't find anyone with national visibility to do the event for the children of Lebanon. Year after year, people had agreed to appear and then called back and declined, apparently having received pressure from some source to cancel. I decided to do the event. It would raise money for a health-care project for the children of Lebanon who suffer as a result of the war. I knew I would be accused of being anti-Semitic, but Arabs are Semites. So, in fact, I would be accused of being anti-Israel. I needed to hold tight to the fact that I oppose Israeli foreign policy just as I oppose United States foreign policy. I needed to remember that I actively respect and defend the rights of Jews, their culture, history, and struggle for liberation. We are taught to hate, fear, and mistrust Arabs. We are taught that Arabs are belly dancers and terrorists. There was some unlearning to be done.

Jewish, black, Arab, and northern European Americans worked to create a unique cross-cultural evening. Lisner Auditorium holds only fifteen hundred people, not a big hall for me. But only about three hundred of my usual D.C. audience showed up and eight hundred Arabs. One of my close friends, a Jew who attends everything I do in D.C., did not know if she would come.

The night before the event I went out to dinner with three Arab women. Hatme told me my pronunciation of her name was very good, which suggested to me that she must go through life with most people not bothering to try to get that warm, rich sound in the backs of their throats.

I apologized for my audience, shaking my head in disappointment. But my new friends threw up their hands and cried, "No! Dear sister, this is pioneering. We are thrilled that you are here, that even three-hundred non-Arabs are coming. Please do not feel bad!" I felt a wave of admiration for my Jewish friends who have for years supported a Palestinian homeland.

Simon Shaheen arrived at our table from the airport. A well-known oudist and violinist, he would play in the concert tomorrow, to be accompanied by a percussionist playing *darabukkah*. Simon and I immediately leaped into discussions of music: "How do you write?" "Do you write the music first or the lyrics?" "At the same time? How is that possible?" "Because I am a singer, my instrument of composition is not separate from my instrument of words. And you, tell me about quarter tones. Do you think I could learn to do that?" "Can you hear them?" "Yes." "Then, of course . . . well, maybe." They all laugh at the blue-eyed girl who wants to learn to sing like an Arab. The waiter brought us a special bottle of wine on the house, offering support for the work we were doing. Although it was past closing time, they didn't rush us.

The next day, I raced to the museum to see the Georgia O'Keeffe exhibit. I liked when she spoke of "laying aside all she had been taught and learning to trust that which she believed to be true."

That afternoon at sound check, I watched Al-Wapan Dabkeh Troupe (a Palestinian dancers group) warm up, defining the boundaries on the stage, unknotting their muscles, which had tied up in the drive down from New York City. Radio personality Casey Kasem emceed the event. He is always so dignified and appropriate. In all the times he has introduced me, he has never once shied away from who I am. I walked out to meet an audience that had been warmed by the bright eyes and costumes of the dancers, and the masterful playing of Simon.

I loved singing to a predominantly new audience. It tingles like a first date. For my encore, I invited Simon and his percussionist to join John and me onstage. We had worked out a surprise backstage at intermission. The oud and *darabukkah* laid down the rhythm and the modal drone. I sang "Mountain Song," changing the melody and the phrasing when necessary so it would fit their improvisation. I heard the words through a different ear as I sang it to Arabs and Jews. "This old mountain raised my many daughters, some died young, but some are still living." In rehearsal we had created only a road map; the rest would be a surprise to us as well as to the audience. At one point, I waved to the Palestinian dancers to join us. My voice soared clear as if I were singing the whole concert from the top of a mountain. The audience rose to meet us and the night was filled with hope. As the dancers left the stage, the song quieted and I heard myself say, "Do not be afraid to try," and I began to sing notes I had heard in my head but had never dared to sing, quarter tones on the Arabic scale. Simon cried out for joy and answered me back on his ancient instrument with a contemporary blues lick. The music had not only stated the purpose of the evening, it had defined the potential.

Are you black like night or red like clay
Gold like sun or brown like earth
Gray like mist or white like moon
My love for you is the reason for my birth

After the concert, Amy Horowitz and I went to the home of our new Arab friends. Simon played and sang, and women rose from the deep purple pillows and danced. When I got home there was a message from my friend who had not known if she would attend. She described how she had felt when the Palestinians started to dance. "I know these dances!" Yes, my friend. Exactly.

"Don't look now," she said, "or you'll draw attention to us, but see that cream-colored Jeep Cherokee with darkened windows? That's the death squad." I waited a moment, then casually turned, feeling my body fill with disbelief, as if someone had said, "Look, there's Big-foot!" But, in fact, there was the cream-colored Jeep Cherokee with darkened windows. They aren't even disguised but flaunt their preoc-cupation with terror. I tried to imagine these men getting up in the morning, kissing wives and children good-bye, and going out to kill people. Do their families know what they do for a living?

That was my first day in El Salvador, April 1988. By the last day I would know people who had been picked up by these killers and released only by public pressure. I would also know the names and stories of some who had been picked up and disappeared into the nightmare of terror behind the darkened windows of cream-colored Jeep Cherokees.

I had been invited on many occasions to come to El Salvador with peace delegations. But I didn't have time, which really meant I didn't have the strength to make the trip. But along came an invitation that had my name on it. The university, two cultural organizations, and the labor organization were cosponsoring the first-ever New Song Festival for Peace, Justice and Sovereignty, Un Canto por la Paz. I was amazed to think they would try such a thing, amid the repression in their country.

Some socially responsible rock stars wanted to put on a peace concert in El Salvador to make a strong statement. But they needed certain assurances—that if they brought a full-scale sound system with them, they would also leave the country with it. They needed guarantees for their physical safety. Those are not unreasonable requests, unless you live in El Salvador. No one's safety is assured. A worker with six children would like his safety secured if he joins a labor union, his children taken care of if he is found dead in a riverbed. An important student leader would have liked his safety guaranteed, but he had been missing for three months when we arrived. A well-known puppeteer would have liked his safety secured, but he was last seen on his way to the National Theater, being pulled into a cream-colored Jeep Cherokee with darkened windows. He had been missing for five years. So it was not possible to offer security to their North American and European friends.

But in spite of the danger, the Salvadorans felt it was time for a New Song Festival, providing an opportunity for artists from the Americas who were willing to come without assurances to gather in solidarity as well as to witness and form a circle of protection for Salvadorans so that they might create a forum for protest. Although not promised safety, we were promised that they, as Salvadoran cultural workers, would put their lives on the line to organize the festival, and that our safety would be a priority. Human Condition from New York, Quinteto Tiempo from Argentina, Amparo Ochoa from Mexico, Adrian Gozuieta with Grupo Experimental from Costa Rica, Grupo Ahora from Venezuela, Thiago de Mello from Brazil via New York, and I with Barbara Higbie from California, all agreed to attend. We joined El Indio, Güinama, and other Salvadoran groups, and although it was a fairly well-kept secret, I knew that the exiled group Cutumay Camones would in fact make a courageous, unexpected appearance onstage. I invited Amy Bank to meet me there and act as translator and personal security.

I called several people to ask them if they would sign a support letter that would help bring attention to the festival. The more people were watching, the safer we would be. I spoke with Haskell Wexler. He expressed his concern and said he wished I wouldn't go. I asked him whether he would go if he were in my shoes. He said, "Of course." We laughed. So often, it does come down to a matter of shoes. But it felt good to know Haskell and so many other friends would have their eye on me and, since I wasn't afraid, I thought maybe it wasn't so bad if someone else was afraid on my behalf.

When I told my mother I was going, she expressed support. Then she called me back a few minutes later and said she was going with me. Our hosts called us "The Holly Near group," or, as they affectionately referred to us individually, "Holy," "Aemy," "Mrs. Ann," and "Bar-bar-rah." The four of us shared a room so that we could start and end the day together. Sometimes we were completely quiet, each lost in her own thoughts. Other times we cried, recalling the horror of what we had seen that day, viewing the pictures of murder and torture displayed at the Human Rights office. One night Barbara read the tarot cards. They were full of messages about authority, conflict over what we felt inside and what we saw outside, confrontation, and, finally, strength and confidence. We tried to experience this journey from many perspectives.

The fourth night we were there, someone in the hotel hired a band to come serenade the American guests. It was two in the morning, the musicians had had too much to drink, and we were concerned about security. We had been told that no one would be coming and going from the hotel once we were all in. But the worst part was that they kept playing "My Way." Barbara eased some of the tension with her dry humor, announcing as she turned over to go back to sleep, "I think it is excessive torture and repression to have to listen to 'My Way' three times!" We would hear the real music of El Salvador the next day at our first concert.

The opening event was called "the inauguration," held in the university auditorium with a thousand students crammed into every corner, sweating and breathing together in the hot, humid afternoon. Statements of welcome to the artists were answered with statements of solidarity from those who had already arrived. (Some were still waiting for visas in airports around the Americas.) Amparo Ochoa whispered in my ear, "They want you and me to sing something together." We laughed, both quite aware that we didn't know anything together. Then I remembered that I had the words to an Isabel Parra song in my bag. I asked Amparo if she knew it. She said she had heard it once. We decided to respect the request and give it a try. And although it was a little rough, the audience loved it, and we vowed to rehearse it so we could sing it together at the festival concert.

We noticed throughout our trip that although the path away from sexism is hard and slow, the Salvadorans seemed to take conscious steps toward the goal. There were often women musicians in the bands, and half the emcees were women leading the crowds of thousands in *consignas*. Huge voices rose out of these young women, who wore dresses and high heels as if they were going to church—voices full of rage and dedication.

The next day, half the musicians headed for Santa Ana to do a concert at the university there. The other groups would go to San Miguel. We arrived at a huge soccer stadium, and while the sound was being set up, Amparo and I practiced "La Llamada Encendida." Of the three verses, she would sing two and I one. Her band plus Barbara would accompany us. Amy suggested that we invite a Salvadoran to do one of the verses. Amparo said, "a Salvadoran woman." Mario, a local musician, went off to find his *compañera* with a strong voice. The rehearsal put us all in the right mood. There had been lots of planning, fund-raising, logistics, talking, waiting—now we were ready for music. Between three and four thousand people joined us. Although sound problems threatened to sabotage the event completely, it all finally came together, and the reason we were there began to soar in circular flight between artist and audience, audience and artist, artists and organizers.

Despite a few hecklers there was no violence and no interruption. I sang "Gypsy," "Harriet Tubman," "Hay Una Mujer Desaparecida," "No More Genocide," "Te Doy Una Canción," and "Gracias a la Vida." After Amparo's set, she invited me and Celia onstage to sing our rehearsed song. It was a great success, and as we loaded the buses and prepared to return to San Salvador, everyone was relieved and happy. It hadn't gone smoothly, but it had gone on, and the spirit of the event was what mattered.

On the ride back, a Venezuelan maraca virtuoso gave Amy and me a priceless maraca lesson. I hadn't understood the nature of the instrument. I will never hear that sound again without thinking of him and the dark road home to San Salvador.

The next day half the groups participated in a concert at the university in San Salvador while the others traveled out of town to San Miguel. I sang at the university for thousands of students who represented some of the strongest activism in the city. The military had taken over and closed the university in the early 1980s, destroying all the supplies, research equipment, and resources. Then the students had taken it back. They got no city funding, but, at great personal sacrifice to all who worked there, from student to teacher to janitor, they had reopened the university. At the end of our concert, the artists were quickly loaded onto buses and whisked away to the hotel. No one lingered at night. The crowd quickly dispersed, leaving only a few paper cups, empty film boxes, and leaflets—newsletters from the FMLN that had been thrown down into the crowd from a tree. A young man stuck a cassette recorder through the window of the bus where I was sitting next to Isaias Mata, an extraordinary painter and art professor. "What do you think of the yanqui imperialists' position on the working class and camposinos?" After "doing media" here for five days I had gotten pretty good at knowing when to answer and when not to respond. Still, I looked to Isaias to confirm my suspicion. He winked and ever-so-slightly shook his head. "I have just come here," I said. "I will know more about that by the time I leave." "That's all?!" demanded the young man with the recorder. I shrugged. "That's all." He gave me a smirk that showed he knew he had been sidestepped and raced off. Isaias squeezed my hand. This country was tricky. I had just finished stating very clearly in music and comments onstage what I thought of "the yanqui imperialists" but still had to outwit a stranger on the move with a tape recorder and a rhetorical question.

We returned to the hotel, but the evening was not yet over. Our friends who had gone to perform in San Miguel were having a rough day and had been on our minds. The university at San Miguel was about a three-and-a-half-hour drive from San Salvador. It was an area of conflict. The musicians were rightfully concerned about their trip, but we had sent them off with our love and best wishes. When they arrived, an advance person stopped them before they reached the stadium where they were to perform. Apparently the army had been there first and had torn up the stage with their bayonets. Many people had decided not to attend, out of fear. But more than five hundred people were waiting in the stands, jeering the army and cheering on the sound man, urging him to keep setting up, demanding the concert.

The organizers decided that for the security of the artists they would send the buses back to San Salvador immediately. If the army was on a rampage they did not want the artists to be on the road after dark. But the artists decided that they needed to drive by the crowd and wave, to let the people know they had tried. Once there, however, the artists couldn't leave. The courage of the people was too great. So the artists decided to perform with or without a stage. Amparo told me later that a soldier had obstructed her way with a rifle and told her to go away. She told him, with her proud, long neck stretched like a grand bird, that she had been invited to this country to sing and that was what she intended to do.

Human Condition went on first. And while they sang, helicopters circled overhead, coming lower and lower, swooping down and then rising up again. Sitting in the open door was a soldier with a machine gun pointing down at them. The helicopters continued to buzz the stadium on through Amparo's set, but meanwhile the rector of the university had called the military high command, the organizers had called all the embassies of the artists' various countries, and people in the States had been notified to call the U.S. ambassador. Who knows what combination of efforts worked, but the helicopters were called off and the concert finished without further disruption. Jo-Lynne, my manager, had first heard that some of the artists had been taken into custody. As she told me later, she cried for three minutes, then launched into emergency action, calling on people in high places. When she listed to me the people who had stepped forward, ready to be a circle of protection for me and my group, I was deeply moved. It made me feel very loved and cared for.

Those of us who waited in San Salvador sighed deeply in relief at the news that our friends in San Miguel were safe. We relaxed into an evening of beer, conversation, and a jam session. We sang old jazz standards, *nueva canción,* and country-and-western tunes. Barbara fiddled a wild version of ''Orange Blossom Special'' and we ended the evening singing six different songs simultaneously, all with the same three chords: ''Blue Moon,'' ''Heart and Soul,'' ''Silhouettes,'' and three similarly mundane Spanish songs. It was a hysterical grand finale, considering the context.

The next day was the real finale, the big concert in the plaza. All the bands would come together to play, and Cutumay Camones would make their courageous appearance. But this was the day when I had to leave early to get back to a previous concert commitment. My heart was breaking that I would miss the concert and the May Day march the following day. I sang the first set before being whisked off to the airport. I had the hardest time saying good-bye to Isaias, and to Amy, who would return to Nicaragua, where she lived. I didn't allow myself to linger. I remember only the force with which lips and cheeks collided, and arms squeezed hard in embraces that would have to last a long time. Mom rode with me to the airport. She was going to stay on with Barbara and Amy and see the weekend through. After I checked in, I watched her go off with the two Salvadoran friends who had driven me. She turned and waved, this strong seventy-three-year-old radical mother of mine. *Damn,* I thought, *I come from a sturdy tree.*

The plane was to leave at five, but it was delayed, again and again. The airport was becoming empty and the day was slipping away into night. I couldn't seem to find out what was happening. It was six P.M. Then eight. Then eight-thirty. I knew there was a landing curfew in Mexico, so after a certain hour, the plane would not take off even if it arrived. No one knew. I had forgotten to get my sweater out of my suitcase before I checked it. The airport was air-conditioned and I was cold. I could have stayed and experienced the whole festival. If the plane didn't come I would miss the concert in St. Louis, too. I was quite sure this plane was canceled. Nine P.M. There were no other flights out, to anywhere. I checked again and again. Here I was in the airport late at night, alone, in San Salvador. I could not ask my hosts to come get me. It would be dangerous for them to make the trip. I didn't want to take a cab back to the city. I didn't trust the cab drivers. Many of them worked for the government, and the long, lonesome road back to the city had government checkpoints as well as rebel activity. Many bodies had been found along the road that led into the city, including the four nuns. I was scared now. I found a phone and called Jo-Lynne. Just the sound of her familiar voice made me cry. I tried to pull it together. I could feel panic rising. There was nothing she could do but be a friend. I promised I would call again if the plane didn't show up. I tried to find coffee. Everything was closed. My mind started to imagine the details of my fear. This was what Salvadorans lived with every day. I had been moved by the courage of these people during my time there. But only now was my understanding elevated to a more realistic level. If it took four hours in an airport to reach this comprehension, then they were four hours well spent. But where the fuck was that airplane! A guard walked by, I sat closer to the other passengers. At a little before ten, the plane landed and took us to Mexico. I slept for a few hours in an airport hotel and then caught a plane to Texas that was delayed because of a flat tire. Finally, I landed in St. Louis after twenty-four hours of travel.

I arrived at the concert site at five-thirty for a seven P.M. show. John was already there and had all the sound and lights in order. I took a shower, did a quick sound check, and the concert began. It was part of a conference on the rights of battered women. In Missouri alone at that time, thirty women were in jail serving sentences of fifty years to life for having defended themselves against violent husbands. The concert was being recorded and would be aired on public radio so that it could be heard by the women in prison. I spoke and sang to them as well as to the audience in the hall. I talked about my trip to El Salvador. I told them about Maria, a woman I had gone to see in a prison in San Salvador. I asked the audience to sign a petition for her release (and she was released, the following week). I sang for the women who had defended themselves. I sang songs about prison, about love, about women, about healing. And I told about the cream-colored Jeep Cherokees with the darkened windows.

Back in San Francisco, poet James Braughton and I shared the honor of being the grand marshals of the Lesbian and Gay Pride March in San Francisco, 1988. We linked arms as we walked in the parade, he with his lover and I with my mother. We were to have ridden in a bright red convertible but it had broken down before the parade even got started, so my mother suggested we not wait around for another car and miss all the fun. The four of us took off on foot enjoying the best parade in town. Look at all these happy people! I remembered my friend Becky, who lived with her lover, Jeanette, who is a therapist. When Becky told her parents she was a lesbian, they suggested she see a therapist. Becky replied, "I *am* seeing a therapist!"

Jesse Jackson's coordinators called to set up my participation in the California campaign. The country was hopping with excitement about Jesse. But racism, even among liberals, was crystal clear. Jesse was the most articulate candidate, was gaining in the polls by leaps and bounds, and still was not considered a serious contender by the Democratic party. I wanted to be counted as one who believed this country deserved black leadership. I hit the campaign trail.

Singing for Our Lives

Jesse could get a crowd going; he could get cynics to feel hope and the lonely to feel loved and the disenfranchised to feel heard. Even the press seemed to have fun. I imagined they were glad to have been assigned to the Jackson campaign and not to Bush or Dukakis. Often my job was to go on just before Jesse and get the audience unified, and on their feet, ready to greet him. I started developing a song that had a rap for the verses and music for the chorus. It allowed me to talk about the issues that were key to the campaign and then get people singing:

". . . We are ready, we are ready for change
And we have walked through fire and rain
To get to this moment"

And when everyone was standing and singing, Jesse would walk onto the stage. It was dramatic and fun. One afternoon I joined Jesse and others for a march in California's central valley. We had come to protest chemicals that were endangering the food, the water, the workers. We had also come to sing together, to support the farmworkers, and promote the renewed boycott of grapes, to mourn the death of yet another child poisoned by chemicals, to be in the world the way we imagined it might be, in a rainbow coalition, a patchwork quilt.

Mom and I walked again down Market Street. This time we marched with the men and women of Redwood Records, carrying our banner and joining thousands in the street who had come to be counted. Women had been too successful and the right wing was raising its head hard and heavy against the new order being embraced by both nuclear and nontraditional families. Equal pay, child care, support of women on welfare, better education and health services, intervention in domestic violence, sex education, safer birth control, lesbian rights, programs to stop rape, criticism of pornography, shutting down the sale of dangerous baby formulas being sold to Third World mothers, opening up drug and alcohol clinics for our children, and expanding low-income housing were among the issues women worked for in the seventies and eighties while Reaganomics pulled the rug viciously out from under our feet. But women were not willing to go away. And their men friends were starting to understand and prefer a world that respected women. So the opposition chose a target; an emotional di-

visive issue is what they needed—abortion was perfect and they began a brutal campaign. Reagan loaded the Supreme Court. Well,
they were not going to have an easy time of it. Millions of people
united around the issue of choice, bringing people into the political
arena who had not been to a demonstration in twenty years or ever.
Gay men who ten years ago would have seen the abortion issue as
having absolutely nothing to do with them walked with women into
the clinics, offering support and defense from the screaming anti-
choice activists. Doctors were stepping forward and taking a strong
pro-choice stand. Movie stars did TV and radio spots. A woman
called out to me once from my audience, "What if our mothers had
had an abortion?" I said, "Some of our mothers did." I thought it
was a highly arrogant question, as if the world could not have gone
on without us. But for the sake of discussion, let me be arrogant.
What if an unsafe illegal abortion had killed my mother? She
wouldn't have been around to have me!

The issue isn't abortion, is it? The issue is that some people want
women to go back to being subservient to men. If one doesn't support
choice, then one supports forced childbearing because women *do* get
pregnant. This is not about the fetus. This is about the woman. Tens
of thousands of women die each year from illegal abortions, so you
see, women have abortions whether they are legal or not. They feel
they have no choice. No woman *wants* an abortion. She wants options.
How can someone be against birth control *and* against abortion? Only
if they are antiwoman and don't give a damn about her life. But if you
threaten the life of the mother, how can that be good for children?
Women must have the right to life.

The Montmartre, a small club in Copenhagen, held about five
hundred people. A tiny staircase wound down to the dressing room in
the belly of the basement. John and I readied ourselves and waited for
Ellen, our friend and Danish road manager, to come say, "It's time."
As I climbed up the stairs, I could hear the excitement. The club was
packed full and the crowd was in the mood even before we began. I
prepared myself to bring them way down so that they would have
somewhere to go as the concert moved forward. They resisted for a
moment and then settled in with a glimmer of tension hovering overhead, but quiet—so quiet I could hear myself breathe. We began to
accelerate with rhythm, sound, humor, passion, rage, romance, grief,

spirit, until there was an explosion and I invited them to restrain themselves no more.

After John and I finished our last number, we made our way to the top of the stairs, waiting in the dark but not going down. We knew there would be an encore. We went back on for a song and retreated several times only to be called out again. I do not know when it happens, but there is a moment when my body and spirit agree to go somewhere I have never gone before. I do not do this every night. And I do not know when, what audience, what current event, what love, will invoke this state. But it had come that night. I returned to the stage. A slow cry came deep from my gut, seduced up and out of me by a power somewhere above the top of my head.

I'm gonna rise like a fire
I'm gonna roar like a mama lion
I'm gonna to rage like a cyclone
And I'm gonna love you

I had never heard this song before. John saw my body start to be drawn into a rhythm. I could hear his left hand start to find it, careful not to define the chords.

You can't just take my dreams away

I lifted one hand and the audience received the message as if it came on the wings of a dove. They began to sing with me.

You can't just take my dreams away
You can't just take my dreams away
You can't just take my dreams away
Oh no

I raised the other hand and offered them a harmony which some grabbed on to, and then I offered them still another. We had three parts now and John had the chords. But the audience was singing too square. I started to move my body to help them feel their own sexuality, to find the pulse of their voices. Yes, now we were getting there.

I started to sing around them. By now they didn't need to be told to hold on. They carried the weight of the song and I was free to elaborate, returning to the fire, the mama lion, and the raging cyclone. I felt a river of sweat running down the small of my back, my thighs were wet, my chest was wet, my brow was wet, my hands were so wet they could hardly hold the mike. My voice grew and grew and then snapped like a gun at the start of a race and John was off, not missing a beat. He turned the piano into thousands of keys, an orchestra of power, and snapped it back to me with the flare of a flamenco dancer. The crowd was cheering, for we did not withhold.

Because we had agreed to come apart, we would always be together.

John and I made our way down the small staircase. I could hardly see for the sweat in my eyes. We sat with each other in the solitude of the dressing room. I pulled off my sweaty jacket and shirt, feeling the cool air dry that soft spot between my breasts, rubbing a rough towel over my skin. I heard John's voice calling me . . . "Holly, Holly . . . listen."

The audience had not stopped. It had been at least five minutes since we came down the stairs. They were in control now and they would not leave. They were singing, "You can't just take my dreams away." John slipped upstairs to hear them and returned to tell me that they were really singing, "You can't just take our Holly away."

I couldn't go back. My performance clothes were lying in a wet heap on the table. I grabbed the white work shirt I'd worn earlier in the day, the sleeves rolled down and the collar pulled up, and I climbed those stairs one more time. We came onto the stage. They felt their power and it felt good. They knew I was amazed and they liked that they could make me feel that way. They started calling out all the songs we didn't do. I was reminded of Judy Garland's Carnegie Hall album, where she says in her wonderful growl, "We'll sing 'em all and stay all night!" But no, we could not do that. Neither did she. What could we do? Something quiet, for we could not go any higher. It was time to come down together. I began to sing a song I had added to my repertoire around the time we first learned of AIDS. It was usually thought of as a fantasy song, but I sing it with its feet very firmly planted on the ground. Quiet, intense, full of all that we were, all that we are, full of Judy. "Over the Rainbow." Good night, Copenhagen. Good night.

Folk festivals, when well conceived, can be a wonderful array of musicians from different cultures and perspectives. A storyteller from

274

the Georgia Sea Islands, a Minnesota boy with songs about the winter fire and the spring tomatoes, a talk/song man come from the picket line to put today's crisis in historical perspective, a cowgirl from the Southwest singing about stampedes of the herd and the heart. I had been having a good time. Then all of a sudden out of nowhere I wanted to scream at them, "There are gay people in every one of your stories. Why don't you ever say so?"

Why was I feeling so upset tonight? I realized I was scared. This is 1988! Can you imagine how huge is the oppression if I, who have been singing and talking about lesbianism and gay rights, I who have been out all over the world for more than a decade, still from time to time am filled with terror? I stood before thousands of people, most of whom lived and worked in heterosexual and nuclear-family circles. So don't mention it. Give yourself a break tonight. I stood before the audience as they sat in the silence, waiting for me to do my next song, but the voices inside were talking to me loud and deep and the faces of the few gay men and lesbians who had ventured into this family scene burned into my eyes. I looked over at John, his tender face looking back at me. I nodded at him to begin.

"Simply Love"
Why does my love make you shift restless in your chair
And leave you in despair
It's simply love, my love for a woman

It's a simple hand on a warm face to say
A glance to see if love is still okay
A glow at dawn when love is still there
Tears and strong arms at the end of the day
And simply love, my love for a woman

It's the laughter as the kids clown
And tease our weary thoughts away
It's looking 'round the table and knowing
Hard work fed us one more day
And simply love, my love for a woman

Why does my love make you shift in your chair
It's the bombs across the border
That should make you tear your hair

And yet it's my love leaves you
Screaming out your nightmare

Perhaps there's something you know you should fear
If my love makes me strong and makes you disappear
It's simply love, my love for a woman

Fred Segal invited me to be his guest at the Dalai Lama's birthday celebration being held in the hills of Malibu, California. As we stood in a graceful column to receive him, the Dalai Lama moved slowly from person to person, genuinely greeting each of us. I was touched by the power of humility, the strength of wisdom, the contagion of joy, and the exquisite beauty of a soul that is dedicated to humanity. This man had been trained from the time he was three to be a peaceful man, to carry on the wisdom of the ages. What if all children were given such an opportunity? Imagine it. We must first imagine it and then perhaps we will find a way to make it true.

I returned to the theater after nearly twenty years to play torch singer, Ann Collier in the *1940s Radio Hour,* directed by my sister Timothy. I had to forget what I had learned about singing in the fifties, sixties, seventies, and eighties . . . my whole life . . . and discover the singing style of the forties. It was exciting work. I sat looking in the dressing room mirror, amused by the red lipstick, forties-style hair rolls, high heels, and the cleavage I'd forgotten I had! World War II. So much death. I was now living in a new age of death . . . and it seemed to be on the minds of so many. It was at that moment I knew my next album would be about life and death. As 1988 turned into 1989, I recorded *Sky Dances,* three friends died of cancer, and one went down on the Pam Am flight.

Joanie, Jo-Lynne, and I decided to give Redwood Records non-profit status. None of us had ever given such a big gift to anyone. It was our life work. But it felt appropriate. Redwood Records became Redwood Cultural Work with a board of directors and a dedicated staff that continues to do the work we have always done but now with the potential to expand that work beyond anything we could have done as a small business. We opened up a membership program so that our fans and supporters could help directly with projects that promote

276

peace, feminism, and understanding through music.[*] RCW preserves, presents, promotes, and distributes ". . . music that rocks the boat."

We celebrated the transition and my fortieth birthday in the summer of 1989, a proud and happy day for me. I watched my partners, my family, the RCW staff, old and new friends, who had come from all over the country, people I had worked with for years and people I would work with for years to come.

See the little girl standing up on Spring Flat in Potter Valley singing to her imaginary world from the top of a mountain? Real people and places had since filled out the song, but I was still the singer.

"Don't Let the Singer Down"

I saw an eagle fly across the sun
The flags came down without a sound
I felt a passion of mixed persuasion
Just then the mountain came tumbling down
I dreamed a rainbow spilled across the night
I want to see it in my time
The harbor opened to ships and saviors
Just then the mountain came tumbling down

I touched a hand that played a thousand drums
A child escaped into the moon
A rage exploded and spread like rumors
Just then the mountain came tumbling down
I saw an eagle fly across the sun
The flags came down without a sound
A soldier kissed me and ran for cover
Just then the mountain came tumbling down

Chorus

If life is like the music
Then be careful you can lose it

---

* The choice I had felt forced to make between global peace work and lesbian feminism in Redwood's early days was no longer an issue. Our politics and our work are holistic and no part of our "selves" is asked to be silenced.

Fire in the Rain...Singer in the Storm

And beware the singer
How the lights come shining
And I'm counting on my timing
Oh the band is playing fine
Tell the cynic to kiss tomorrow
All the moments are melodies
And the songs I have borrowed
They keep coming on back to me
I'm standing on shaky ground
Filling the air with sound
Don't let the singer down

Epilogue: Singer in the Storm

I HAVE LOVED MY FORTIETH YEAR. FROM MY LITTLE STUDIO APART-
ment I can walk to the ocean or ride my bike alongside Venice Beach.
It is here my mind clears, making room for new thoughts. It feels very
romantic to be a writer by the sea.

I toured very little this year, only fifty-some events, which allowed me to reacquaint myself with Los Angeles and the entertainment
industry. I make the gossip columns from time to time for being seen
at gala events ". . . Aside from k.d.'s pipes, what really made our
night was seeing the grand glamour diva herself, Madonna and folk
singer/political activist diva Holly Near in the very same room."

But even as I enjoy a kind of unexpected internal peace, the world
is raging into the new decade . . . earthquakes shaking us to the core,
walls tumbling down, children rising up, and dictators clamping down
. . . humanity at its horrific worst and its brilliant best . . . and I am
simultaneously moved and startled.

I think about twisted language, manipulated morality, and "my
country, right or wrong." What is this democracy we so long for? How
do we bring new meaning to a word that has been so abused? Beware
the nation that embraces freedom in the Eastern Bloc and supports
death squads in El Salvador.

I think about the silencing of opposition, death by invisibility. I
worry about crack. Drugs have been intentionally pumped into our
youth, destroying a whole generation of black children who might have
risen in the footsteps of the influential civil rights movement and taken
power that white people did not and do not want to share. And why is
it that after watching hours and hours of footage on television about the
invasion of Panama, the general population of my country still did not

279

know that many Panamanians are black? When they showed people driving through the streets cheering the U.S. invasion from their cars, how many viewers asked what fraction of Panama's population even own cars?

I think about violence. Whether Rambo or Batman, the theaters are full of violent films that perpetuate isolationism and give the viewer a false sense of power. It is easier to beat up one's neighbor or one's lover than to talk or to face the Pentagon demanding that the money spent on war be used to ease the economic pressures that lead to our despair.

I think about women. In search of equality, women were expected to be more like men rather than men considering the benefits of being more like women.

I think about miners in West Virginia, Indians in Guatemala, whales in the northern seas, Irish kids in Belfast, and farmworkers in Central California.

I think about our friends in the Eastern Bloc, in China, in Miami. I have always felt that many people confuse capitalism with democracy. And while trying to get what "we have," will the new seekers of freedom forget (or having never seen it, innocently overlook) that capitalism has failed at caring for its people, and that what "we have" alongside the very rich is homelessness, a health crisis, illiteracy, violence out of control, and freedom of the press to choose what information and attitudes to impart?

And how do we obtain collective power without it being at someone else's expense? How can we be together on this planet with our glorious differences? How do we take the environment seriously when she speaks to us? In order to be truly human, is it not necessary that we face these questions with our families, with our neighbors, and with the world? How can I coax my naked body in the morning from the warm flannel sheets if I do not ask these questions? How can I write the next song?

The Sandinistas lost the presidency to Violeta Chamorro. Election day was fair and legal, but the ten years leading to it were cruel and all-too-usual punishment, the United States bombing and starving the population into a necessary vote of compromise. The United States would only stop killing them and economically strangling them if UNO won. Nicaraguans did not vote against the revolution. They voted for their survival—the deciding vote included mothers who could not bear to see another child mutilated by the contras, could not stand another

280

year without cooking oil and medicine. I heard the news of Ortega's defeat while sitting in the car in front of my house. I put my head on the steering wheel and wept. Then I heard Ortega speak; his grace, dignity, and understanding moved me so, reminding me that the spirit of the revolution had not been defeated. And Mandela has been released!

The new decade seems to be inviting humanity to put its creative potential to work, to discover alternatives to that which has brought us such disarray . . . not out of guilt or fear but out of curiosity, passion, love, and necessity. Following in the footsteps of political revolution, industrial revolution, and cultural revolution, must there not eventually be a spiritual revolution that is infused with a feminist, pragmatic, scientific, and economic understanding of oppression and nature? Must we not create the solutions we so desperately long for? Is it not a raw and naked time, and if we feel death, is it not time to miss and grieve, shout and cry out, and then move through the wake to the morning light? Is it not time to dance, stretching our muscles to their finest extension?

And what greater work is there than the art of creation? Life is an immense mural that requires each of us to pick up the brush and paint a bold stroke.

And to those who say, "Yes, but don't you lose hope?" I must reply that as inexplicable as it may be, I have come to realize that there is always a fire in the rain . . . and a singer in the storm.

"Singer in the Storm"

A dove flies free from the prison bars
And lights the candles with the stars
And carries news home from afar
She's a singer in the storm, she's a singer in the storm

She does not fear the pouring rains that drench her to the bone
She only fears the consequence of living all alone
She does not mourn the lessons learned
While falling from the sky
She only mourns for those who turn away as they pass by

He who joins with people's voices
He who honors women's choices

281

Epilogue: Singer in the Storm

He who dares to cry, rejoices
With the singer in the storm

She does not fear the raging wind that calls her into a song
She only fears the consequence of a forest dead and gone
She celebrates her lover's touch, it caught her by surprise
Still she mourns for the narrow minds who stare as they pass by

Late in the night she hears the painter scream
And she knows it is not a dream
Again and again recurring themes call for the singer
She who walks the unpaved road
She who picks up half the heavy load
She who knows that the dove is code
For the singer in the storm

The dove flies free from the prison bars
And lights the candles with the stars
And carries news home from afar
Are you the singer in the storm?
The dove flies free
The dove is in me and she lights my way
So I may be the singer in the storm

HOLLY NEAR DISCOGRAPHY

SINGER IN THE STORM
Chameleon Music Group/Redwood Records 1990

SKY DANCES
Redwood Records 1989

DON'T HOLD BACK
Redwood Records 1987

SINGING WITH YOU
    with Ronnie Gilbert
Redwood Records 1986

HARP
    with Arlo Guthrie, Ronnie Gilbert, and Pete Seeger
Redwood Records 1985

SING TO ME THE DREAM
    with Inti-Illimani
Redwood Records 1984

WATCH OUT!
Redwood Records 1984

LIFELINE
    with Ronnie Gilbert
Redwood Records 1984

JOURNEYS
Redwood Records 1983

SPEED OF LIGHT
Redwood Records 1982

FIRE IN THE RAIN
Redwood Records 1981

IMAGINE MY SURPRISE
Redwood Records 1978

YOU CAN KNOW ALL I AM
Redwood Records 1976

A LIVE ALBUM
Redwood Records 1975

HANG IN THERE
Redwood Records 1973

You may find out more about Holly's political work, her albums and tour schedules, from Redwood Cultural Work, P.O. Box 10408, Oakland, California 94610

Index

Index

Index

Index

Index

Index